From
Genesis
to
Genocide

The MIT Press
Cambridge, Massachusetts, and London, England

From
Genesis
to
Genocide

The Meaning of
Human Nature
and the Power
of Behavior Control

Stephan L. Chorover

Second paperback edition, 1983
First paperback edition, 1980
Copyright © 1979 by
The Massachusetts Institute of Technology

This book was set in IBM Composer Theme by To the
Lighthouse Press, printed and bound by Halliday Litho-
graph Corporation, in the United States of America.

Library of Congress Cataloging in Publication Data

Chorover, Stephan L
    From genesis to genocide

    Bibliography: p.
    Includes index.
    1. Social control.   2. Human behavior.   3. Power
(Social sciences)   I. Title. [DNLM: 1. Social control,
Formal.   2. Social control, Informal. HM201 C548f]
HM73.C49   301.15   78-21107
ISBN 0-262-03068-3 (hard)
ISBN 0-262-53039-2 (paper)

To my mother and the memory of my father

From whom came life and love and meaning

Contents

This book first took shape in my mind as little more than a critical survey of contemporary psychotechnology. By that I mean that I was originally intending to review some of the material tools and techniques that have lately become available for measuring and controlling the thoughts and feelings and actions of human beings. There was at the time—indeed there still is—a tendency for writings on the subject to reflect a narrow disciplinary perspective. Hence, there had been books written on the uses of drugs, on behavioral conditioning methods, and on psychosurgery (to name just a few of the many pertinent areas of recent activity). But most of these dealt with matters that were mainly technical, and no one had explored the idea, which seemed to me quite reasonable, that there were certain common denominators to be found beneath the many superficial dissimilarities among the diverse forms of psychotechnology.

My interest in the subject of "behavioral control" had been stimulated around 1970 by the appearance of some evidently serious proposals aimed at the development and deployment of supposedly sophisticated scientific solutions to some of the pressing social problems facing American society. As most readers will remember, there had been a long period of social unrest in the nation during the Indochina war, and in the months and years immediately following the assassinations of Martin Luther King, Jr., and Robert Kennedy, there were riots in many cities and uprisings in a number of the nation's prisons. During that period psychotechnologists were occasionally to be found promoting their own activities as a source of solutions to the problem of violence control. To cite just one noteworthy example, public officials and prison authorities began to receive and look favorably upon proposals to use psychosurgery as a means of "treating" allegedly uncontrollable ghetto residents and prison inmates.

Nor were these mere isolated incidents. At the time I was serving as a member of a scientific review committee that had been organized by the National Institutes of Mental Health of the Public Health Service for the purpose of making recommendations for the support of research in my own field of scientific specialization—neuropsychology. As public apprehension over the prevalence and severity of social violence increased, so did the frequency with which our panel was asked to review various proposals for psychotechnological forms of violence control. It seemed to me at the time (as indeed it still does) that such proposals, although doubtless well intended, were conceptually very muddled and socially very misleading. I found myself vaguely troubled by the idea of attempting to reduce what appeared to be a social problem to the status of a medical one, but I was unable to define my own feelings in more clear-cut, conceptual terms.

In an attempt to clarify my own thoughts on the matter, I began to look somewhat more closely at the arguments that were used to justify the proposals in ostensibly scientific terms. What I repeatedly found was that the scientific foundations were generally nonexistent. As I began to search farther afield in other branches of psychotechnology, it seemed to me that I was encountering a recurrent pattern in which many different kinds of proposals were being couched in essentially equivalent underlying forms. It was then that I began to realize that there was need for an inquiry that would penetrate beneath the superficial conceptual and material details of contemporary behavior control technology, one that would search out the deeper questions of fact and value that make psychotechnology so often and so intensely controversial. Accordingly, I undertook to provide a description of psychotechnology in terms of the broader social context of contemporary American society.

But, after having written the book, I find that it is much broader in its intent and coverage than that. Indeed, what it attempts to provide is a comprehensive conceptual framework for understanding some commonly overlooked or misunderstood aspects of the interplay of science, technology, and society. It attempts to show that in order to understand the controversies that surround so much of psychotechnology today, it is first necessary to recognize and overcome some confused and confusing ideas about the supposedly objective and value-free nature of psychotechnological methods of procedure. As it happens, this entails a broadening of the inquiry to include a search for some causes and consequences of a state of severe conceptual fragmentation that exists in psychological science and technology.

In the spirit of scientific inquiry of which it is intended to be a part, my analysis of psychotechnology consists in large measure of an attempt to demonstrate the existence of regular and lawful connections among things and events that appear at first glance to be separate, distinct, and unrelated. What I have tried to show in broad historical terms is that psychotechnology can be understood as the product of a recurrent social process in which certain classes of ideas and practices systematically interact.

The ideas in question turn out to be, for the most part, ideas about what is commonly called "human nature," that is to say, about what it *means* to be a specifically human being. The practices in question include multifarious methods of procedure (including the methods of modern psychotechnology) with which it is possible to control human behavior. As the subtitle of the volume is intended to suggest, my central contention is that there is, and always has been, a connection between efforts to define the *meaning* of human nature and efforts to exercise the *power* of behavior control. And in order to understand the fundamental character of that connection, it is necessary to understand the character of the broader social context of which these interrelated efforts are a part.

Speaking most generally, what I have tried to do is to show that the interplay of meaning and power is a constant feature of human social existence and that its analysis in any given instance entails the tracing of connections between conceptual and material factors that tend to reflect and reinforce the interests and objectives of relatively powerful individuals and groups. Psychotechnology turns out to be comprehensible only as part of a broader social process in which connections between the meaning of human nature and the power of behavior control alternate and overlap and interpenetrate and combine to determine the texture of the whole. It is a process in which controversies about psychotechnology commonly turn out to be controversies about the efforts of some people to regulate the conduct of other people. Accordingly, in undertaking to write a broad historical account of psychotechnology, it has been necessary for me to focus upon meaning and power as two aspects of a continuous and continuing social struggle between contending social forces. The scale of the work had necessarily to be large in order to show that many seemingly disparate instances are merely variations on a recurrent basic theme and in order to demonstrate that things now going on have been going on since antiquity.

My debts to others are at least as numerous as the authors I have read and as deep as the help I have received from scores of friends and colleagues. The notes at the end of the book acknowledge many of the sources I have consulted and make plain, I hope, that others are exempt from blame for any erroneous uses to which I may have inadvertently put their ideas. This work has been in progress for so long and has benefited so much from the contributions and criticisms of so many that I can here only thank a few whose contributions were particularly important to me at various points along the way. Joseph Hunt, Geri Atkins, and Aase Huggins were part of the creative process from the start. Without their support and encouragement, the entire effort would have been abandoned long ago, and I can hardly begin to distinguish their ideas about psychotechnology from those I would call my own. Charlie Gross, Helen Mahut, Maria-Grazia Marzot, Harold Bronk, Dan and Carol Goodenough, Al and Ele Corkland, Martin and Joan Sokoloff, John and Lori Williams, Steven J. Gould, and Steven Rose read all or part of the manuscript in various stages. I cannot claim to have incorporated all of their criticisms but all of them helped me immeasurably to clarify my ideas. The final editing was done by Joan Rosenstock. Her skill as a weaver of words and ideas helped to reduce a very long manuscript to more manageable and readable proportion.

Over the years, I have been fortunate to have known and worked closely with a large number of exceptionally gifted teachers and students.

Among these none have been more important to my own intellectual development than two who are now departed, Hans-Lukas Teuber and John Asinari.

To write a book is to strain, and yet somehow to strengthen, the bonds of intimacy upon which so much of life depends. My children Nora, Jon, and Katya have understood my need for solitude and have given me much cause to rejoice in their faith that "it" would someday be finished. My wife Beatrice is responsible for many of the ideas that are contained herein. In particular I owe to her the notion that behavior is meaningful only in terms of its context. Her love has been my context and my contentment. Her presence is on every page.

"What, precisely, is behavior control?" ask the editors of a recent series of books on the subject. They answer as follows:

It is simply the manipulation of the environmental conditions to which an organism is exposed so as to bring about a definite behavioral result: to produce new behavior, to maintain or change the organism's tendency to engage in current behavior, or to eliminate past behavior.[1]

I have written this book because the control of human behavior is one of the most important issues in every society and because I believe that this contemporary definition is dangerously misleading. It is at best an uninformative generalization to say that the behavior of organisms can be controlled by the manipulation of environmental conditions, and at worst a way of making behavior control appear scientific and beneficent. What makes such a definition dangerous is its failure to take account of the fact that certain human beings are invariably in control of the manipulations in question, that the manipulations always take place in a social context, and that the aim of the manipulations is often to regulate the conduct of other human beings. It is precisely because the effort to control human behavior necessarily takes place in a social context that it is necessary to regard it as more than "simply" a technical matter of manipulating certain material conditions in order "to bring about a definite behavioral result."

The position taken here is that behavior control needs to be understood as part of the broader field of psychotechnology, which encompasses both the effort to define (or measure) human nature and the effort to control human behavior. Because the form and content of this field vary with different societies and historical circumstances, it is impossible properly to characterize it (let alone to understand it) without taking its contextual relationships into account. Accordingly, I have undertaken in this book to describe psychotechnology in a way that pays particular attention to the social and political goals of its deployment in various contexts and to the moral and ethical values underlying its development in particular directions. The book does not purport to provide an internal account of psychotechnology but focuses, instead, on the relationship between its internal theoretical and practical aspects and the external world of social existence of which it is necessarily a part. The approach that I have taken has been guided throughout by my own desire to understand why efforts to develop and deploy psychotechnological solutions to pressing social problems (such as violence, juvenile delinquency, drug addiction, and crime) have tended to precipitate such vehement (and sometimes violent) partisan disputes.

In the prolonged process of putting my ideas together, I feel that I have learned a great deal and have begun to develop what is for me a new way of thinking about the nature of social problems. Although still far from perfect or complete, the perspective embodied in this book seems to me to provide a simple yet intellectually satisfying way of understanding what makes contemporary psychotechnology so often and so deeply controversial. At its heart is the idea that many superficially dissimilar controversies over psychotechnology are variations on a single fundamental theme. In other words, my thesis is that despite wide variations from time to time and place to place in the form and content of psychotechnology, and despite many obvious differences in the issues around which controversies have swirled, they share a certain common denominator, which has been obscured by the tendency (prevalent in many current discussions) to treat each controversy as if it were an isolated or independent phenomenon.

What are those constancies? My answer is that they comprise a relationship (or rather a network of relationships) between two distinct, but closely interconnected domains of human social existence.

The first domain, which I shall refer to as the domain of meaning, encompasses an almost bewildering array of different conceptual "systems" (including theological, artistic, philosophical and scientific ones) whose most obvious common denominator is their effort to define the world in terms of human existence and purpose. This includes, of course, an interest in describing as precisely as possible, what it means to be a specifically *human* being. It is the conjunction (or, as it has often been, the collision) of such disparate conceptual systems over the meaning of human nature with which this book is mainly concerned.

The second domain, no less important for my thesis than the first, is the domain of power; the domain in which—at any given time or place— there exists a socially organized effort to manage the course of human affairs. Suffice it for the moment to say that this domain encompasses the political behavior of human beings at all levels of social complexity, and that political behavior frequently entails a degree of conflict among contending social forces. Such conflicts commonly turn out to be disputes about the propriety or justifiability of certain kinds of behavior, and efforts to resolve them are frequently marked by struggles among the contending forces to influence the behavior of their adversaries, "to produce new behavior, to maintain or change the . . . tendency to engage in current behavior, or to eliminate past behavior." In other words, my contention is that the exercise of political power often turns out to be intelligible as an exercise in behavior control, and vice versa.

Whether or not such exercises are successful, and irrespective of whether success is measured in terms of mutual compromise or in terms of the ability of one group to bring the behavior of another group under control, all controversies over the propriety or justifiability of behavior, and all socially organized attempts to regulate human conduct, take place at the interface between the domains of meaning and power. Like the "domains" that it joins, this interface is an abstraction, but that does not make it any less real. Indeed, it is my intention to argue that the interplay between meaning and power across this interface not only defines the nature and content of what passes for psychotechnology in any given time, place, or circumstance but also reflects (and helps to reinforce) the broader system of social arrangement of which it is a part. In a society where social policy is ostensibly guided by conventional principles of reason, logic, and justice (which is to say, wherever leadership professes to operate rationally), it might reasonably be expected that systematic efforts to regulate the conduct of individuals or groups will generally correspond to what the leadership conceives to be the essential characteristics of those individuals or groups. In other words, ideas about human nature will influence judgments about the reasonableness of particular social policy objectives and the necessity of specific behavior control programs. But to say that ideas about human nature are likely to have social policy consequences and behavior control implications is only to make an obvious point: what people believe about the essential nature of human beings has a powerful influence upon social expectations. Such beliefs tend to shape the ways in which people in a given social context are treated, and these in turn, significantly influence how they behave.

If ideas about human nature can actually shape social reality, then they obviously deserve to be regarded as powerful instruments of behavior control in their own right. Indeed, it is precisely because of the demonstrably self-fulfilling character of social expectations that I have insisted upon treating definitions of human nature and measurements of human diversity (in addition to the material tools and techniques of behavior control) as a part of psychotechnology.

What determines whether or not a given idea about human nature forms the basis for rationalizing a particular social policy objective or justifies a specific form of behavior control? It is one purpose of my analysis to answer this question by showing that specific relationships between ideas about human nature and programs of behavior control exist in any society. By substantiating the proposition that psychotechnological theories and procedures tend to reflect and reinforce the interests and objectives of dominant social groups, I will show why it is both false and misleading to answer the question with which I began (the definition of behavior control) merely in terms of the available tools and techniques of manipulation. The effort to depict psychotechnology as "simply" a matter of techniques serves to obscure the fact that all socially organized efforts to control human behavior are really efforts by some people to control the behavior of other people. It is also my contention that even the most sophisticated contemporary discussions of behavior control are based upon false and misleading ideas about human nature, versions of which have been fostered since antiquity for the sole purpose of justifying the power of some people to control the behavior of others.

In undertaking to describe a more or less universal process by which ideas about human nature and techniques of behavior control are related to each other and to the organizational interests of powerful social groups, I do not necessarily cast doubt on the moral and ethical legitimacy of this process. I do not mean to suggest, in other words, that behavior control in itself is a bad thing or that there is something inherently sinister or conspiratorial in the existence of a conjunction between efforts to regulate human conduct, to manage public affairs, and to describe human nature. On the contrary, my contention is that such a conjunction is a defining political characteristic of *all* social systems and that it is possible to learn something about the way in which a specific social system functions by analyzing the structure of a few of its distinctive subsystems and by identifying the pattern of their reciprocal relationships. Thus I intend to seek out the general principles governing the interplay between meaning and power as they manifest themselves in varying social contexts.

Let me insist before going further that this is not intended to be a mere academic exercise. In extreme instances questions about behavior control in human society can be (and have been) literally questions of life and death. Imagine, for example, that you are a senior staff member at a large psychiatric hospital located on the outskirts of a major city. The institution is a major teaching center with a long and honorable medical tradition where high-quality clinical training has always been given to students and where patients have generally received the best possible treatments at the hands of skillful and humane experts in neurology and psychiatry.

Imagine, further, that in the company of other people like yourself—staff physicians, research scientists, administrators—a visiting dignitary is being conducted on a tour of inspection. The visitor, who has come from the nation's capital, is a recognized expert in the diagnosis, classification, and treatment of nervous and mental disorders and the author of numerous influential articles on such diverse topics as alcoholism, stress, epilepsy, head injury, and brain inflammation. His administrative credentials are similarly impressive: he is professor of psychiatry at one of the country's principal medical schools and directs a world-renowned clinic. Recently he has been organizing a massive psychotechnology program. A review by panels of experts of the past records and current behavioral status of every mental hospital patient in the country has led to the selection of a large number of patients for inclusion in a special treatment group. This screening process followed a meeting, held about a year earlier, at which a group of top-level psychiatric experts and mental health officials decided that special treatment centers should be built and put into operation at several hospitals throughout the country. Since the one at "your" institution is among the first such installations to have been completed, the visitor has come to observe how the treatment phase of the project is being carried out.

The official tour of inspection has now very nearly reached its conclusion. You and your associates together with the distinguished visitor, observe through a small window as several hospital orderlies escort twenty mental patients into the clean and brightly illuminated treatment area. The patients stand about quietly as the orderlies leave, closing the door behind them. At a signal from one of your colleagues, a member of the hospital staff manipulates a control device. At first the patients seem unaffected; they continue to stand about quietly. Then, quite suddenly, they begin to gasp, grow agitated, stagger, cry out, and totter. Finally, each one drops to the floor. The treatment is over. Environmental manipulation has brought about a definite behavioral result: all twenty of the mental patients are dead.

Although I have presented it in the form of a hypothetical example, this episode actually occurred, as part of a project deliberately aimed at the administrative mass killing of mental patients which was conceived, organized, and carried out in Germany during the past half century. It bore the official designation, "The destruction of lives devoid of value," and was planned in detail at a conference of leading academic psychiatrists and public officials in Berlin during the month of July 1939. One of those present was Dr. Max de Crinis, professor of psychiatry at Berlin University, head of the neuropsychiatric department as the Charité Hospital and a recognized expert on diverse neuropsychiatric subjects. As a member of the board of supervising physicians who were responsible for the project from its inception, Dr. de Crinis paid an official visit early in 1940 to the state mental hospital at Sonnenstein, near Dresden, where, under the circumstances already recounted, he witnessed the killing of at least twenty male mental patients by acute carbon monoxide asphyxiation. Although cited in the proceedings of the Nuremberg War Crimes Tribunal for his participation in the project, Dr. de Crinis never came to trial. During the Soviet encirclement of Berlin in 1945, he committed suicide with a government-supplied capsule of cyanide.

Is it possible to understand what transpired on that day at Sonnenstein? It is at first tempting to say that the episode hardly requires any explanation beyond the fact that it took place in Germany during the era of the Nazi Reich, and was one among many of the bizarre and inexplicable atrocities that took place in Europe during the Nazi period. Such a response defeats understanding rather than enhancing it. Indeed, what continues to demand an explanation is the very fact that the episode at Sonnenstein was not an isolated event. By mid-1940, scenes just like it had become commonplace in mental hospitals all over Germany and, within a few short years, the project that Dr. de Crinis and his professional colleagues had created claimed the lives of an estimated 275,000 psychiatric patients, prisoners, and mentally retarded persons. "The destruction of unworthy life," which was the official overall designation of the Nazi project aimed at the mass extermination of millions of Jews, Slavs, and diverse other groups, followed in time, technique, and justification the precedent set by what purported to be a scientifically objective and morally and ethically neutral exercise in psychotechnology. It is one purpose of this book to trace a connection between the administrative mass killing of mental patients and the subsequent emergence of genocide as an official instrument of Nazi public policy. In effect, my analysis is intended to explain not only what took place at Sonnenstein but also how that episode was connected, on the one hand, to antecedents having nothing explicitly to do with the Nazi movement and, on the other hand, to consequences that not only encompass, but actually go beyond the specific manifestations of Nazi genocide.

At first, the barriers to such an analysis seem overwhelming. The very word "holocaust" seems to invite a retreat from explanation, as from some natural disaster. When confronted with a phenomenon of such monstrous proportions, it is tempting to fall back upon the idea that there are certain historical happenings that the human mind is inherently too weak and too limited ever to comprehend. As Walter Lippmann expressed it many years ago,

... the human mind must take a partial and simplified view of existence. The ocean of experience cannot be poured into the little bottles of our intelligence. The mind is an instrument evolved through the struggle for existence, and the strain of concentrating upon a chain of reasoning is like standing rigidly straight, a very fatiguing posture, which must soon give way to the primordial disposition to crouch or sit down.[2]

This book was written, I confess, from a crouch. But from where I have been sitting and reasoning, I have come to a conclusion quite the opposite of Mr. Lippmann's, namely, that the most formidable barrier to understanding Nazi genocide (and all forms of behavior control, whether or not they are matters of life and death) is not the primordial weakness of the human mind but rather the prevailing strength of certain social preconceptions. Reason, however it has evolved, seeks understanding through the methods of careful observation, analysis, and other forms of intelligent behavior, but even those who set out faithfully to follow reason are likely to be driven or enticed into accepting conclusions about the world they might otherwise reject as irrational. The struggle after meaning by a long line of theorists attests that existence is altogether safer and professional life more secure when one takes the "partial and simplified view of existence" upon which the orderly functioning of certain powerful social institutions depends, institutions that sometimes resort to violence as a means of enforcing their particular view of existence. At such times, thinkers following reason in search of new views occasionally collide with bureaucrats following orders in defense of existing institutions. Collisions between those seeking to construct new meanings and the bureaucratic defenders of power may even be fatal, but even when neither fatal nor violent, their indirect effects may often reasonably be called matters of life and death.

When it comes to understanding a phenomenon such as Nazi genocide, it is easiest to take a "partial and simplified view;" to rest content with having "the little bottles of our intelligence" filled with a jumble of opaque assertions that serve to obscure the part of human existence they are supposed to explain. As a psychologist, I am personally most familiar with the "explanations" of Nazi genocide that take a psychological form. According to such explanations, the "holocaust" occurred because the personalities of the German people as a whole, and particularly of those who participated in, condoned, or had knowledge of Nazi genocide (and perhaps of the victims as well), were deeply and fatally flawed. In other words, the staggering sequence of events in which millions of men, women, and children were systematically persecuted, segregated, incarcerated, manipulated, and killed is supposedly comprehensible in terms of the peculiarly "authoritarian" mass psychology of the German people or as a reflection of the "sadistic" or "masochistic" character structure of their leaders. As I intend to show, however, the effort to explain events of such historic moment in terms of individual dementias or collective derangements is both facile and dangerous. Consider, for example, the explanations based on the allegedly demented or deranged minds of the political leaders who organized and commanded the overall enterprise. Despite its seductive appeal, psychological speculation explains very little, and the effort to invoke Hitler's "unconscious motives" ("his mother was unsuccessfully treated for breast cancer by a Jewish physician when he was a boy") or the psychological instability of his henchmen ("Goering was a drug addict; Goebbels a certifiable paranoid") as a key to understanding mass violence is tantamount to an exercise in political apologetics.

This is not to say that Nazi genocide was devoid of psychological dimensions, but only that attempts to explain genocide in psychological terms are devoid of real explanatory power. Hitler and his henchmen were not a group of psychotic demons who set blind social forces into motion. Furthermore, to the extent that psychohistorical description creates the misleading impression that events in the political and social domains can be "explained" in the narrowly private language of inner psychological determinants, psychohistory itself is an instrument of deception rather than a means of explanation.

A proper understanding of contemporary behavior control cannot be reached without tracing the path that it has followed in the process of becoming what it is today. By the same token, it is necessary to reach an understanding of Nazi genocide before modern exercises in behavior control can be properly understood. But if an understanding of Nazi genocide is a prerequisite for understanding other kinds of behavior control, and if the necessary understanding cannot be found by an analysis of the thoughts and actions of individual participants, what is to be done? My answer is that one must begin with the social context and the antecedent conditions from which genocide emerged as the ultimate instrument of behavior control. It is necessary to follow the sequence of events that led professional psychotechnologists to play a decisive guiding role in fashioning and implementing genocide as the "final solution" to many of Germany's pressing internal problems.

Many lines of converging evidence point to the importance of a few key concepts that took on special significance in the atmosphere of the emerging National Socialist movement. Of particular interest is a family of sociobiological ideas about human inequality and a specific class of political inferences drawn from Darwinism and summed up by such earlier catch phrases as "the struggle for existence" and "the survival of the fittest." Under the force of specific material circumstances—military, political, and economic—these phrases and others like them came to be interpreted at all levels of German society as having the force of universal laws of nature whose implications for public policy were logically obvious, scientifically justifiable, and morally compelling. I will show that the form and content of interpretations of human nature presented by English and American (as well as German) scholars of the time simultaneously reflected and helped to create the monstrous reality of Nazi genocide. Which is to say that Nazi genocide was not an aberrant symptom of national psychosis but a coldly calculated exercise in behavior control that clearly reflected the interplay of meaning and power in a particular place and time.

Considered in these terms, it becomes possible to understand how influential social forces were able to use the symbolic power of allegedly objective sociobiological science to foster, promote, defend, and justify the radical extermination of "biologically inferior" elements of the population; how the systematic preservation of "biologically superior" elements came to be regarded as a vital national necessity; and how the political leaders of a modern industrial society, although deeply divided by political disputes and chronically afflicted with economic troubles, continued to bolster the myths of Aryan supremacy and manifest destiny with biological arguments conducive to the belief that Germany was "naturally" fated to be the world's leading political, military, and economic power. The path was direct, from an allegedly objective brand of scientific discourse about human inequality to a purportedly rational form of moral argument about "lives devoid of value" and thence to the final solution: "the release and destruction of lives devoid of value."

In order to understand this interplay of specific intellectual and material forces, it is necessary to analyze certain ideas about human nature and human diversity and to show how they became powerful instruments of behavior control in German society. The process, seen in historical perspective, not only belies the myth that Nazi genocide arose almost overnight in a society that was largely unprepared to receive it; it also reveals that, on the contrary, the basic sociobiological seeds of genocide were deeply planted in the fertile soil of German political consciousness long before Hitler and his Nazi movement existed.

But my analysis will do more than show that sociobiological ideas like "the struggle for existence" and "lives devoid of value" had been nurtured for some time before they were put to use by the Nazis on behalf of their psychotechnological objectives. Although the links with Nazi genocide are not difficult to trace, sociobiological ideas also have connections with other (and more contemporary) kinds of political partisanship and are thus linked to other kinds of behavior control. That is why it becomes pertinent to identify the source of modern behavior control technology in all its diverse forms, which is a particular set of ideas about human nature (in general) and human inequality (in particular).

The chain of ideas uncovered in the tracing leads deep into the past as well as to the present. In fact, the conceptual roots of modern behavior control (and of the controversies that surround it) lie buried in ancient legends about the creation of the world and myths about the genesis of humanity. Such myths, unchanged in their essence, are still used to define the basic nature of the human beings whose behavior is the subject of control and controversy today. Thus, the terms "genesis" and "genocide," in my title, were not frivolously chosen to provide a superficial play on words. On the contrary, they denote the two basic poles of my inquiry. On the surface, the most obvious thing about these two terms is their disparity. When the distance that separates them has been crossed, it will be clear, I hope, that many superficially dissimilar controversies about behavior control are deeply related to each other and that each one represents—in its own time and place—a particular transformation of a single fundamental and recurrent political paradigm; a paradigm in which conflicts between contending social forces express themselves as a ceaseless and kaleidoscopic interplay between the meaning of human nature and the power of behavior control.

In the last week of May 1543, Nicolaus Copernicus lay on his deathbed at Frauenberg in Poland. He was seventy years old, a famous scholar and a dedicated churchman who had attained honor and renown as a trusted advisor to both the Polish government and the papal court. As he lay dying, friends rushed to his bedside a newly printed copy of his last and greatest work, a book about the structure of the astronomical universe entitled *The Revolutions of the Celestial Orbs*. According to at least one eyewitness account, the old astronomer's first glimpse of the volume was just about his last sight of anything on earth.

What the book contained was truly revolutionary: a theory of the universe that, with elegant simplicity, overthrew the traditionally established doctrines of medieval celestial mechanics and laid the conceptual foundations of modern astronomy. It had been rumored for almost three decades that Copernicus privately entertained doubts about the geocentric theory—traditionally associated with the name of Ptolemy—and officially taught by the schools and churches of his day. According to the Ptolemaic view, which had been invested with tremendous symbolic potency by a long line of Christian theologians, the earth stands still, as fixed as any moral principle, at the very center of a concentric universe, surrounded by successively more distant spheres to which the heavenly bodies are attached. What Copernicus offered as an alternative was the idea that the sun is the center of our planetary system and that it is the actual motion of the earth, as it rotates upon its axis and revolves around the sun, which creates the apparent motions of the relatively stationary sun and stars.

This conceptual rearrangement of the "celestial orbs" brought a new and exciting meaning into astronomy. However, while Copernicus may have believed that his theory contained true statements, and only true statements, about the structure of the astronomical universe, in the light of events during the century and more following the appearance of his book he evidently had good reason to withhold publication. More to the point, he must have understood that the church as an institution had to regard his rejection of the geocentric universe—and the view of man's place in the scheme of things that it implied—as more than an academic exercise.

And, to be sure, the Christian church, which had only recently suffered a profound schism, shortly thereafter began to wage a vehement and sometimes violent battle against the proponents of his theory. My purpose in this chapter is to account for this strenuous opposition and to explain precisely why the advent of new meaning in astronomy was perceived as a threat by the holders of established power in religion. It is not my intention merely to repeat a familiar episode from sixteenth- and seventeenth-century history but rather to use it as a means of illustrating the kind of interplay between meaning and power that continues to characterize the effort to regulate human behavior in society today.

The relatively recent explosion of techniques for managing and manipulating human behavior has not introduced anything profoundly new into the psychotechnological arena. Undoubtedly, the power to control behavior has lately been augmented by technical developments in many fields (including behavioral conditioning, psychopharmacology, psychometrics, psychosurgery, and others, but my argument will be to show the most powerfully effective and commonly employed behavior control devices continue to be what they have always been throughout recorded history, namely, the ideas that human beings entertain about the universe and their place in it. More precisely, I intend to show that of all the ideas by which human behavior can be shaped, by far the most important and most persuasive (if not always the most credible) are the ones that purport to define what it means to be a human being.

If any single example epitomized the confrontation between astronomers and theologians over the structure of the universe, it was the trial of Galileo. For years, this man, whose observations with his newly invented telescope served to confirm many of the predictions of Copernicus' theory, and who had openly declared himself to be an adherent of the heliocentric view, had been commanded "in the name of his Holiness the Pope and the whole congregation of The Holy Office to relinquish altogether the opinion that the sun is the center of the world and immovable, and that the earth moves."[1] Finally, after extended negotiations and repeated delays, during which he never quite accepted or rejected the admonishment not to "hold, teach or defend (the theory) in any way whatsoever, verbally or in writing," Galileo was summoned in 1633 to Rome, where under humiliating circumstances, he was compelled by the power of the Holy Inquisition to utter this public recantation: "I, Galileo, being in my seventieth year, being a prisoner and on my knees and before your eminences, having before me The Holy Gospel which I touch with my hands, adjure, curse, and detest the error and the heresy of the movement of the earth."[2]

Now, it is hardly necessary to say that something important and theologically sensitive caused the Inquisition to condemn as heretical an old astronomer's opinion of the movement of the earth. What was it?

The most obvious answer is that the church felt compelled to combat the Copernican conception because it was irreconcilable with the literal interpretation of certain biblical texts. Protestant theologians were especially inclined to take this view. John Calvin, for example, flatly denounced the heliocentric theory as contradictory to the sacred truths of Scripture. "Who," he demanded to know, "will venture to place the authority of Copernicus above that of the Holy Spirit?" Martin Luther likewise threw his considerable theological authority behind the view that in astronomy as elsewhere, the divinely appointed way of arriving at the

Genesis: Human Nature as a Social Weapon

truth was by literally interpreting the sacred texts. Like Calvin, he emphasized that the differences were irreconcilable and had this to say about Copernicus:

People gave ear to an upstart astrologer who strove to show that the earth revolves, not the heavens or the firmament, the sun and the moon. Whoever wishes to appear clever must devise some new system which, of all systems is of course the very best. This fool wishes to reverse the entire science of astronomy; but sacred Scripture tells us that Joshua commanded the sun to stand still, and not the earth.[3]

The question still unanswered is *why* the theological authorities were so committed to opposing the propagation of this particular astronomical idea. The answer will not be found in its technical contradiction of scriptural statements about the structure of the universe or in the motives of individuals but in a consideration of the interplay between the meaning of particular ideas and the power of particular organizations. A rejection of Copernican theory more fundamental than Luther's is suggested by what one of the foremost Catholic theologians of the day had to say about the Copernican theory: "This pretended discovery," he complained, "vitiates the whole Christian plan of salvation."[4] The theologian in this case was the Lord Cardinal Robert Bellarmine, an Inquisitor of great learning who had established his formidable reputation partly on the basis of a detailed theological argument that justified the burning of young heretics on the grounds that the longer they lived, the more damnation they were bound to acquire.

Cardinal Bellarmine was plainly convinced that Copernican astronomy posed a mortal danger to the organizational interests of the church, and when an Inquisitor raised the specter of heresy, it was because he perceived a threat, even if it was not the one he explicitly attacked. What, then, was the *real* nature of this danger? Why did Renaissance Christianity, in all of its disparate sects, unite in regarding the conceptual rearrangement of the astronomical universe as so inimical to its doctrines?

By a habit of thought that is at least as old as the *Book of Genesis*, ideas about the structure of the astronomical universe have been closely linked to ideas about the ultimate destiny of the human species. Long before the advent of Copernicus, it had become an article of faith among Christians to believe not only that the earth stands still at the center of the universe but also that it occupies that particular location by virtue of divine decree, according to which its main purpose was to serve as the stage upon which the great drama of human salvation was to be played out. As Father Melchior Inchofer, a Jesuit scholar, put it in 1634, "The opinion of the earth's motion is of all heresies the most abominable, the most pernicious, the most scandalous; the immovability of the earth is thrice sacred; argument against the immortality of the soul, the existence of God and the incarnation, should be tolerated sooner than an argument to prove that the earth moves."[5] What was it that made the idea that the earth moves with a double motion more than "just another heresy"? Why was it impossible for the theologians of Copernicus's day to take the more prudent (and well-traveled) course of attempting to reconcile it with scriptural truths? Copernican astronomy came under such vehement attack because it undermined the doctrine of original sin, an idea about human nature basic to the church's existence as an institution. It was this idea of inherent human sinfulness upon which, as Cardinal Bellarmine put it, the "whole Christian plan for salvation" was predicated.

The idea of original sin is not made explicit in *The Book of Genesis*, but it is there that we must begin in order to understand its origin and role in the context of Renaissance Christianity. Like the creation myths of many human groups, *The Book of Genesis* attributes the existence of the world and its contents to the art of an Almighty Creator, of whom human beings are supposedly an imperfect image. As Andrew D. White has pointed out, "down to a period almost within living memory, it was held, virtually 'always, everywhere, and by all' that the universe as we now see it, was created literally and directly by the voice or hands of The Almighty, or by both—out of nothing—in an instant or in six days or both—about four thousand years before the Christian era—and for the convenience of the dwellers upon the earth, which was at the base and foundation of the whole structure."[6] Visions of this time-honored conception are to be found represented in many forms, during the period prior to the advent of the heliocentric theory, but perhaps the crowning example remains the tremendous frescoes that Michelangelo painted on the vaulted ceilings of the Sistine Chapel over a four-year period ending in 1512. There, as if floating in the infinite expanse of heaven, God—in human form—is seen sweeping across the abyss, completing the work of creation in accordance with the description in *The Book of Genesis*, whose culminating moment comes when God reaches out to touch the hand of a rather languid Adam. Then, having "created man in his own image . . . The Lord God took the man and put him into the Garden of Eden." Thus in the Judaeo-Christian tradition the structure of the universe and the genesis of human beings are linked in both the manner and form of their creation. But that is not the whole story. At a still further point, Michelangelo depicted the additional event which allegedly made salvation necessary: the familiar biblical story of Adam's "fall," although it is of course, not on the fall itself but upon its meaning that subsequent lines of scholars and theologians have been unable to agree. Some interpreters maintained that Adam and Eve literally ate "of the tree of knowledge of good and evil," but more global interpretations predominated in which the fall came to symbolize every possible kind of transgression. As Milton said, "What sin can be named which was not included in this one act?"

Although the Scriptures are imprecise about the exact nature of Adam's fall and the process by which the flaw, so grievous and fatal in its effects, came to be present in a being who had been created in the image of God, the story of the fall was gradually transformed by a long line of Christian theologians into the doctrine of original sin which eventually assumed the status of a primal cosmic fact. The Puritan proverb, "In Adam's fall sinned we all," succinctly states the opinion that gradually came to occupy the pivotal position among the doctrines of organized Christianity: first, that the fall signified sin—and not merely suffering, as the original texts imply— and second, that Adam's sin has been inherited by all of his descendents and thus reproduced as an essential characteristic of all human nature. Without this doctrine, human beings would have no need of salvation, and no need for membership in a church that purported to provide a plan for attaining it. In short, the idea of original sin was inseparably linked to the destiny of organized Christianity, and any assault (however indirect) upon the meaning of this doctrine was bound to be regarded by theological authorities as an attempt to subvert the power of the church itself.

It is pertinent to note that nowhere in the surviving utterances of Jesus of Nazareth is there anything to suggest that he believed in the doctrine of original sin, or that the movement he founded was committed by him to the task of overcoming it. But whatever the character of Christianity in its beginnings, as it moved toward theological supremacy during the ensuing centuries, many of its doctrines were modified by the force of changing circumstances, and the behavior of its leaders came to be increasingly shaped by the need to preserve and strengthen the political power of an established organization.

Like most hierarchically organized societies (including most nations and most parties), the Christian churches officially endorsed the idea that their own hierarchical structure reflected what Aristotle called a "justice of proportional worth." To promote their own survival, hierarchs reward the conformity of thought and action of their subordinates and punish deviance or dissent from organizationally required beliefs and behavior. Thus, they are inclined to put their power behind meanings mainly on the basis of their correspondence to organizational interests and not necessarily on the basis of their correspondence to facts. The tendency to blur the distinction between questions of truth and falsity and questions of doctrinal conformity is thus consistent with hierarchical power arrangements as a whole. And to the extent that hierarchs tend to put the survival of their organizations ahead of everything else, they are paradoxically transformed into prisoners of the partial (and sometimes false) meanings upon which their power depends.

From all of this, it follows that one way to understand the conflicts that arose within Christendom between thinkers like Galileo, who were mainly concerned with new ideas and hierarchs like Cardinal Bellarmine, who were mainly concerned with promoting the survival of established organizations is to make a careful distinction between two kinds of questions; for questions about the truth or falsity of ideas are different from questions about the relations between the meaning of ideas and the power of organizations. Questions of the first kind arise, for example, in science, and elsewhere within the domain of meaning, and the effort to answer such questions usually focuses upon the search for reliable methods for determining whether or not a given assertion corresponds to what is actually the case. Questions of the second kind arise, however, at interfaces between the domains of meaning and power. To the extent that these two domains do not coincide, the effort to answer such questions can (and does) lead to conflict between them. The point may be illustrated by returning to the example of original sin.

Historically the doctrine of original sin was a fundamental article of Christian faith and, as such, was supposed to be a standard object of belief "always, everywhere and by all" within Christendom. Belief in this doctrine was the basis of the need for salvation upon which the various sacraments of the church were predicated. Original sin and the destiny of organized Christianity were strongly linked by a chain of reasoning in which the existence, prosperity, and survival of the church depended upon the idea that man was sinful by nature. Thus, we can reasonably ask whether the doctrine of original sin was promulgated mainly for its meaning (as a reflection of the individual Christian's need for salvation) or for its power (as a reflection of the church's need for allegiance). A question remains within the domain of meaning only insofar as it is devoid of organizational implications; on the other hand, it was (and always has been) in the organizational interests of church hierarchs to assert that human sinfulness is a natural, profound, and inescapable fact.

Although the dichotomy is somewhat strained, it may be clarified by considering an episode in which the church, having reached the zenith of its power, was confronted with a controversy that came close to threatening its basic reason for existence. The episode in question also concerned the doctrine of original sin, and one of its principal protagonists was St. Augustine. Indeed, it was Augustine himself who first gave the doctrine of original sin its full rigor, when he said that "God, the Author of all natures but not of their defects created man good, but man, corrupt by choice and condemned by justice, has produced a progeny that is both corrupt and condemned."[7]

In saying that Adam had been created good but had become "corrupt by choice," Augustine apparently meant that in the Garden of Eden, Adam and Eve had dwelt in a state of perfect freedom, which included the freedom to choose. Augustine contended that because Adam chose the path leading to a fall from grace, human beings (as his progeny) were innately, essentially, and irretrievably devoid of free will and had lost the ability to control their own destiny. "The whole mass of mankind," wrote Augustine, "is cankered at the roots" and has not the slightest prospect of saving itself. Thus, because of original sin, no one could be assured of safety and grace in this world and because people possessed no free will, neither righteousness nor virtuous behavior could be depended upon as a basis for redemption and eventual salvation in the next. With this dubious pair of assertions enlarged into a standard Christian doctrine, the only apparent recourse for the faithful was for them to submit themselves to control by God's appointees; to follow the church hierarchs and to pray that they would turn out to be among the "fixed number of saints" with which God (according to Augustine) would fill his City. In short, Augustine introduced, in unified form, two essential articles of doctrine: innate depravity and the negation of free will. A challenge to Augustine's denial of free will soon developed, and charges and countercharges of heresy issued from both sides. The principals in the dispute were numerous, but Augustine's most persistent and perhaps his most incisive critic was a monk named Pelagius. Over a period lasting several years, the problem of free will was argued between them. Both Augustine and Pelagius were keenly aware of the sloth and license that characterized the Roman Empire during its decline. To the former, the prevalence of predatory, immoral, and unethical behavior tended to support the doctrine of original sin, and he readily interpreted it as a natural and inevitable reflection of flawed human nature. To the latter, however, it seemed that the true causes of contemporary depravity had to be sought elsewhere. Pelagius believed that Augustine's denial of free will only served to justify and reinforce the predatory and licentious behavior of people and that his insistence upon the innate impotence of human nature was an unconscionable attempt to evade social responsibility.

Although the central focus of Pelagius' attack upon Augustinian doctrine was the question of free will, his writings betray a deeper and more genuinely psychological interest in the fundamental analysis of complex human behavior, which he divided into three elements: *posse* (ability), *velle* (will), and *esse* (existence). *Posse*, Pelagius wrote, is the only aspect of behavior that is properly ascribed to human nature *as such;* the other two (will and existence) are aspects of behavior for which human beings are properly to be held accountable.

Everything good and everything evil, in respect of which we are either worthy of praise or of blame is *done by us,* not *born with us.* We are not born in our full development, but with a capacity (*posse*) for good and evil; we are begotten as well without virtue as without vice, and before the activity of our own personal will there is nothing in man but what God has stored in him.[8]

On all of these points, Pelagius seems to me to be both clear and correct. The idea that there is nothing in human nature but the capacity for behavior upon which human will and existence depend yields various additional inferences, but the most pertinent of these is the idea that human beings have a capacity to make meaningful choices in matters of belief and behavior.

Obviously, by asserting the possibility of individual responsibility, Pelagian doctrine threatened the survival of a church predicated upon the need for institutionally authorized redemption. Conditions prevailing throughout the Roman Empire at this time meant that those accused of fomenting schism were liable to have rigorous penalties inflicted upon them. Thus the power of the church to punish was a potent factor in controlling the behavior and beliefs of its members.

For his own part, Augustine never doubted that Pelagian doctrine was a threat. As a bishop, he was an administrator as well as a theoretician. One may suppose, therefore, that he had more than the problem of reconciling divergent doctrines in mind when he asserted that Pelagius's ideas "rendered the Cross of Christ of none effect." As Gibbon noted, Augustine's most conspicuous virtue was "an ardent zeal against heretics of every denomination," and in his responses to Pelagius, which took the form of scores of letters, treatises, and sermons, Augustine laid bare the dire organizational implications of Pelagianism. The conclusion, if not foregone, was at least predictable: Pelagius was officially condemned as a heretic, his doctrines were outlawed; the possessions of his followers were confiscated, and they were banished.

It has been more than fifteen hundred years since the time of Augustine and Pelagius. Throughout this period, sides have continued to be taken and skirmish after skirmish has been fought across the lines of free will and predestination which divided them. In the ebb and flow of the ensuing controversies, certain terminological and procedural refinements have occurred, but Augustinian concepts continue to prosper today in many forms of sociobiological determinism, and these continue to be opposed by more contemporary versions of Pelagian thought.

The vehemence with which the church of Augustine's day responded to the Pelagian heresy foreshadowed and helps to explain the vehemence of its response to Copernican astronomy. Although the persecution of Galileo remains the classic case study of the response of entrenched theological power to the advent of heretical astronomical meaning, the tragic story of Giordano Bruno, another Renaissance thinker, epitomizes even better the life and death struggle the church was prepared to wage in defense of a doctrine it saw as fundamental to its existence as an institution.

Although Bruno was not a professional astronomer, or even a scientist, he had read enough about the heliocentric theory to become persuaded by its elegance and simplicity. Furthermore, he was perhaps the first person to glimpse one of its more startling implications, an insight that was to cost him his life. What Bruno realized is that the heliocentric theory, by explaining the apparent motions of the stars in terms of the revolutions and rotations of the earth, destroyed the only logical grounds for believing that the stars were located on a single plane that was everywhere equidistant from the earth. If the stars do not rotate around the earth, he reasoned, there is nothing to prevent one from thinking that they may be broadly scattered throughout infinite space. In that event, he conjectured, perhaps every star is really a sun, and perhaps there are other solar systems in the universe, which might (like our own) be inhabited. Indeed, he went on to proclaim his opinion that this view was not only logically plausible but also theologically reasonable, since if the creator was infinitely powerful, he argued, "any finite world would have been unworthy."

All Bruno had done was to draw a plausible inference from the heliocentric theory and describe the kind of universe it seemed to imply. As a matter of fact, his ideas bear a striking resemblance to the ones that almost all astronomers presently entertain. Yet, in daring to imagine the possibility of other inhabited worlds, Bruno had opened the door to two questions more theologically fearful than any that Copernicus himself had raised. If the earth is but one among many inhabited worlds, what is to become of the idea (upon which all of Christian theology is built) that the one God who created everything in the universe out of nothing is a god whose image is a *human* being? For having made such questions askable, Bruno was arrested and charged with "pantheism." He was relentlessly commanded to abjure his heresies, but he steadfastly refused to recant. After several years, during which he languished in the dungeons of the Inquisition, he was tied to a stake and burned as a heretic.

It should be noted that while officially authorized exercises in behavior control, like this one, are sometimes exercises in cruelty, they are always more than that. In this case, the exercise not only succeeded in eliminating Bruno's heretical behavior but also served as an object lesson which other real or potential heretics were likely to heed. Thus, the power of behavior control, when aimed at a particular target, is likely to affect the behavior of other parties as well, perhaps even to have this aim as its main objective. It is likely, in other words, to have effects much more far-reaching than the ones envisaged by narrow technical definitions of behavior control as "simply" a way "to produce new behavior, to maintain or change the . . . tendency to engage in current behavior, or to eliminate past behavior."

In stressing, as I have up until now, the influence of organized social power upon the shape of behavior control efforts and the course of intellectual life, I do not mean to suggest that all organizations are bad because they promote and defend certain interests or that all leaders are evil because they stand at the head of organizations. Nor do I mean to imply that all independent thought is necessarily virtuous or that all systematic efforts to regulate human conduct are wicked. On the contrary, because human life, for as long as anything is known about it, has always been social and therefore organized, human conduct has always been subject to social control. The proposition to consider, therefore, is not whether human behavior is socially controlled but rather whether the behavioral goals and methods of control are justifiable in any given case. The occasional strife between meaning and power is only the overt manifestation of the interplay that invariably characterizes the effort to regulate human conduct in human society.

In spite of church opposition, with the development of the scientific method, in the sixteenth and seventeenth centuries an important change began to take place in the grounds that people were willing to accept as a basis for beliefs about the world and its contents. A comparable intellectual upheaval occurred in the ancient Greek world, beginning around the sixth century B.C. Of particular moment in the present connection is not the fact that the ancient Greeks invented something closely resembling the modern scientific method, but the fact that they established the foundations of modern political theory. In the process, they created a mode of political discourse based upon a form of mythology still honored among political theorists of almost every persuasion.

According to the paradigm the Greeks established, a vision of an essential human nature provides the ultimate frame of reference for all political theory. For example, they held that the degree of social justice existing in a given society can be inferred by determining the degree of correspondence between actually prevailing conditions and those that would ideally prevail if there were complete conformity to the "natural" inclinations of human beings. In the course of these efforts, they discovered, or invented, the idea of using myths about human nature as standards for judging the correspondence of social structure to fundamental human characteristics.

But before exploring the mythology of human nature, I should make it clear that I am using the term *mythology* to refer to more than merely a collection of ancient notions of doubtful factual authenticity. More to the point, I ascribe to it the dictionary meaning of "an unproved collective belief that is accepted uncritically and is used to justify a social institution." The latter portion of this definition is central to my thesis, since my aim is to show that (1) the uncritical acceptance of certain mythological beliefs about human nature is required to make certain proposed social structures based upon them (such as utopias) appear reasonable, and (2) where social structures already exist, dominant groups will propagate whichever myths about human nature justify those structures as "natural." Illustrations from the works of Plato and Aristotle will be presented in support of these propositions. It is important to note that the Athenian political structure encouraged, and even demanded, the participation of philosophers in public affairs.

Plato was foremost among the ancient philosophers who used myths about human nature to justify political structures, thereby establishing the symbolic potency of theories in which the power of the state reflects, in just proportion, the essential meaning of human nature. His *Republic* is the most famous of utopian treatises and is written in the form of dialogues among scholars engaged in an extended political debate. At issue are the principles and goals of the ideal society and the proper means of bringing about its establishment. The book's central character, Plato's fabled and beloved teacher, Socrates, during his own life appears to have expressed, in his beliefs and behavior, the noble image of the philosopher as a "lover of wisdom," yet he had been condemned to death by the Athenian authorities for allegedly subverting the national theology and corrupting the country's youth. For these and other reasons Plato was contemptuous of the political organization of the Athenian city-state and had undertaken in *The Republic* to devise an alternative to the oligarchy built upon chattel slavery to which his contemporaries had given the name democracy.

It is to Socrates that Plato assigns the task of designing an "ideal commonwealth" to replace Athenian society—an "ideal commonwealth" that turns out to be itself a socially stratified society in which each citizen has a rightful rank and place. From the vantage point of the present, the republic devised by Plato may best be described as a meritocracy. There were to be three distinct social classes; the guardians (or rulers), the auxiliaries (or soldiers), and the common people (including artisans, shepherds, and so forth). According to Plato's plan, all power and meaning was to derive from the guardians; they alone were to be responsible for making the rules by which public and private conduct was regulated and for forming the laws governing the internal and external affairs of the republic.

Now, Plato's creation of a socially stratified society was constrained not only by logical principles but also by the paradigm of correspondence with essential human nature. In other words, his concept of human nature had to be such as to justify his claim that the intended social hierarchy was natural, inevitable, and just.

The participants in the lively dialogues of *The Republic*, which probably accurately reflect the prevailing mode and content of contemporary political discourse, are effectively drawn by Plato as "lovers of wisdom," wholly and unflinchingly committed to truth. Yet, around the middle of

Book Two, Socrates suddenly and inexplicably draws back from an expected rejection of falsehoods and uncharacteristically begins, instead, to defend dishonesty as a useful, indeed a necessary, instrument of public policy. He asserts frankly that the rulers of the ideal commonwealth may properly resort to lying when it suits their political purposes. The lie, he says, "is in certain cases useful," such as when dealing with enemies, or in tales of mythology—"because we do not know the truth about ancient times, we make falsehood as much like truth as we can, and so turn it to account."

Given that this justification of official lying does not follow compellingly from the arguments which precede it, why does Plato cause Socrates to utter these words? The answer is simply that they lay the groundwork for a later passage, surely the most amazing in this entire work.

In the course of a dialogue with a philosopher named Glaucon, Socrates touches, at first very tentatively, upon the absence of any real or obvious basis for assigning citizens to positions in the social hierarchy. Socrates concludes with obvious discomfort that there is *no way in truth* to justify the partitioning of the public into the three proposed classes, and unwilling to abandon the meritocratic ideal, he decides that the best way to proceed is to invent a myth: a politically useful falsehood—and we now understand the earlier discussion of "useful lies." Having defended deception, Plato now fashions one of the boldest lies in the history of political thought in the passage containing the well-known "myth of the metals":

Socrates:
How then may we devise one of those needful falsehoods of which we lately spoke—just one royal lie which may deceive the (present) rulers, if that be possible, and at any rate the rest of the city?

Glaucon:
What sort of a lie?

Socrates:
Nothing new: only an old Phoenician tale of what has often occurred before now in other places (as the poets say, and have made the world believe) though not in our time, and I do not know whether such an event could ever happen again, or could now even be made probable if it did.

Glaucon:
How your words seem to hesitate on your lips!

Socrates:
You will not wonder at my hesitations when you have heard.

Glaucon:
Speak, and fear not.

Socrates:
Well then, I will speak, although I really know not how to look you in the face, or in what words to utter the audacious fiction, which I propose to communicate gradually, first to the rulers, then to the soldiers, and lastly to the people. They are to be told that their youth was a dream, and the education and training which they received from us, an appearance only;

in reality during all that time they were being formed and fed in the womb of the earth where they themselves ... were manufactured; when they were completed, the earth, their mother sent them up; and so, their country being their mother and also their nurse, they are bound to advise for her good, and to defend her against attacks. ...

Glaucon:
You had good reason to be ashamed of the lie which you were going to tell.

Socrates:
True, but there is more coming; I have only told you half. "Citizens," we shall say to them in our tale, "you are brothers, yet God has framed you differently. Some of you have the power of command, and in the composition of these he has mingled gold, wherefore they also have the greatest honour; others he has made of silver to be auxiliaries; others again who are to be husbandmen and craftsmen he has composed of brass and iron; and the species will generally be preserved in the children. But as all are of the same original stock, a golden parent will sometimes have a silver son, or a silver parent a golden son. And God proclaims as a first principle to the rulers, that above all else, there is nothing which they should so anxiously guard ... as ... the purity of the race. They should observe what elements mingle in their offspring; for if the son of a golden or silver parent has an admixture of brass and iron, then nature orders a transposition of ranks. ... For an oracle says that when a man of brass or iron guards the State, it will be destroyed." Such is the tale; is there any possibility of making our citizens believe it?

Glaucon:
Not in the present generation ... but their sons may be made to believe in the tale, and their sons' sons, and posterity after them.[9]

What precisely, is Plato's "needful falsehood" or "royal lie"? It is first of all intended to justify social stratification in such a way that it appears to be dictated by human nature, rather than by the arbitrary power of a ruling class. The first half of the lie concludes with the implication that the ideal state must be defined as an extension of the innate characteristics of its citizens. In other words, the ideal mode of social organization, the innate determinants of human nature, and the actual conditions of social existence are asserted by Plato to be three different aspects of the same thing.

It follows that to justify social stratification Plato must make the case that it corresponds to innate and "natural" human inequality. And in order to do this he is literally forced to lie. In summary, a particular set of ideas about human nature was simply invented in an effort to justify social conditions that obviously could not be justified in and of themselves. In this instance, the conditions in question were hierarchical ones, marked by a form of social stratification which literally put some people in a position to control the behavior of others.

But the problem of justifying hierarchical social structures has not disappeared with the ensuing ages; disparities in power and social status have remained with us, and some people still have the power to control others.

And it is still the case that the actual pattern of prevailing disparities is not in any obvious or independent sense ideal. Inequalities among people in the area of behavior control (who controls whom) are particularly difficult to justify in their own terms, and I will show that falsehoods about innate human inequality continue to be advanced, as they were by Plato, in order to make what *is* appear to be what *must be*. Further, I will argue that the basic texture of human nature mythology remains everywhere and always the same and that Plato's myth of the metals may be considered a prototype for today's myths, the main difference being that rather than attributing human differences to the work of God, modern theorists of human nature rely on something resembling science to buttress their arguments. Since science in the present age is treated with much more respect than the Greeks treated their gods, its corruption for political ends is therefore less defensible.

The question of human nature mythology aside, all of us know that no two people in the world are exactly alike. Human beings vary tremendously among themselves and are "framed" in an array of shapes, sizes, skin colors, temperaments, constitutions, and so forth. They exhibit an enormous range of traits, talents, moods, preferences, beliefs, languages, thoughts, and actions. It matters little for present purposes whether those differences are wholly or in part attributable to innate factors. What is at stake here is Plato's contention that innately determined differences comprise a hierarchy of social value. In other words, Plato's big lie was not that diversity exists or that it is innately determined but that it is inherently definable according to a scale of social value. That is, he established a conjunction between his proposed social value scale of political inequality and the fact of human diversity by calling the latter a God-given or "natural" value hierarchy, using the analogy of more or less precious metals from which people were forged. Thus he proposed stratification according to value as the ideal form of social organization.

"Natural ordering" is not always used prescriptively, as in Plato's design of a utopia; it is frequently used descriptively, to explain or justify existing social inequalities. But in both cases, the meaning of the argument is the same and can best be understood as an excuse or apology for inequalities in wealth, social status, and other amenities of power.

Plato's successors, time and again, have attempted to map the biological fact of human diversity onto the social fact of human inequality, and to excuse the latter fact in terms of the former. To do this, they have had to argue first that biological diversity includes inherent differences in value (or "mettle") and second that these differences correspond to a natural social value differential. In other words, disparities in wealth, power, and status, far from being the hallmarks of an unjust society, are the just and natural expression of biological ordering. According to innate "fitness" or merit, society bestows on each of its members appropriate positions and rewards.

Whether the scale of merit has been devised in terms of metals or I.Q. points, its use throughout history has been to justify the concentration of social, political, and economic power in the hands of relatively privileged minorities. Whether the arguments have been theological, philosophical, or "scientific," the aim has been consistent: to justify as inevitable the concentration of social, political, and economic power in the hands of those who are alleged to be the inherently deserving.

A second example drawn from ancient Greece will illustrate another version of the human nature argument, this one not in defense of a proposed utopia but in defense of prevailing social conditions. Aristotle, in his *Politics,* followed Plato's lead in stressing the importance of the state. His particular goal was to trace the development of Athenian social structure from simple "natural" elements; in particular, from the basic social unit of the family and its yet more fundamental relationships. The latter were seen as three separate power dichotomies: husbands and wives, parents and children, and masters and slaves. Aristotle argued that all levels of society reflected these basic and natural relationships of power and subordination.

Now, it might be imagined that, as a philosopher, he could have rested content with pointing out that disparities in social power prevailed at all levels of Athenian society and that these were reflected in the structure of the Athenian family as well. Alternatively, he might have tried to make a critical analysis of the intellectual and material bases of the prevailing relationships between dominant and subordinate persons. But Aristotle chose a third alternative. Taking the actual state of affairs as given, he went on to "explain" that the existing dispositions of power were natural, inevitable, and just. More specifically, he asserted that the power of husbands and fathers over their wives and children reflected "justice of proportional worth" and that inferiors should love and obey superiors more than superiors should love and obey them. A good and proper marriage, he concluded, is one in which "the man rules in accordance with his worth," although he may turn over to his wife the management of housework, the raising of children, and other "matters that befit a woman." Like a long line of theorists after him, Aristotle appears to have been disinclined toward a critical examination of the basic power relationships upon which the orderly functioning of the state depends. Accordingly, he argued that social life at all levels consists both rightfully and naturally in power relationships. How flimsy a foundation he erected to support his argument may be seen in his defense of chattel slavery.

It is pertinent to point out that by the fourth century B.C., there was already a certain amount of skepticism about the legitimacy of slave owning within the Athenian democracy. In part this was due to the impossibility of drawing decisive distinctions between masters and slaves on the basis of any obvious physical criteria. Indeed, since most of the slaves were themselves Greeks who had been captured in the course of military expeditions against neighboring city-states, they were otherwise wholly undistinguishable from free citizens, and because of this both skepticism and confusion had arisen. The source of the confusion, as described by Aristotle, was that "the Athenian people is not better clothed than the slave or alien, nor in personal appearance is there any superiority." Suppose, he conjectured, that it were legal for a slave to be beaten by a citizen. Were that the case, might it not frequently happen that an Athenian would be mistaken for a slave and receive a beating?

Although some of his contemporaries were inclined to argue that the absence of distinctive differences between masters and slaves implied a defect in the system of slavery, Aristotle pursued another course. He contended that there are human beings who are slaves by nature, resembling other people in outward appearance but nonetheless destined from birth for subjection just as surely as their masters are destined from birth to rule over them. Tame animals, he asserted, are better off when controlled by their keepers, and by the same token certain human beings are better off when their behavior is under the control of their natural superiors. "He is then by nature formed a slave," concluded Aristotle, "who is fitted to become the chattel of another person, *and on that account is so.*"

That, incredible as it may seem, is the sum and substance of Aristotle's defense of slavery. The problem is not that he has misstated the facts, but that he has presented no argument at all. More specifically, the "argument" consists solely in the assertion that whoever happens to *be* a slave (or a master, for that matter) was intended by nature to be one. What is missing, of course, is the test of nature's "intention," which would be required to dignify the statement as a verifiable proposition.

To conclude only that Aristotle's defense of slavery was implausible even in the context of his own culture, however, is to miss an important point; namely, that the defense was presented by a leading philosopher in a society that conferred great respect upon him and others of his profession. Aristotle occupied a position that needs to be reckoned with, and his professional standing probably helped him to get away with making nonsensical assertions about the biological basis of social organization, assertions that in all likelihood would have been treated with scorn if they had been made by someone of lesser stature. The traditional presumption that biological characteristics of the human species determine the nature of social institutions means that those who have the power to define human nature command a most powerful instrument of social control. If one wanted to epitomize the relationship between theories of human nature and systems of political control, it would be difficult to imagine a more pointed example than that of Thomas Hobbes and his famous political treatise *Leviathan,* which was published in 1651. •

As a student at Magdalen Hall, the principal locus of Puritan theology at Oxford, Hobbes had absorbed a good measure of Calvinism, with its remorseless emphasis on human wickedness. As an adult, amid the turbulence and civil strife surrounding the struggle over Stuart absolutism in England, and in the aftermath of the events recounted at the start of this chapter, Hobbes became obsessed with the idea of creating—in a rigorously logical and explicitly scientific fashion—the outlines of a political system capable of controlling what he perceived as the growing confusion and lawlessness of the times.

Because the essential depravity of human nature was the touchstone of his notion that an absolutist civil power was necessary to maintain order, and because he was intent on constructing his argument with postulates that were self-evident, Hobbes began his book with a section entitled "On Man." Its purpose was to establish innate depravity and "a perpetual and restless desire of power after power" as the root causes of human social conflict. From this it was nonetheless supposed to follow that human beings could be persuaded to submit themselves to the authority of a "common power" capable of keeping "them all in awe" and thus preventing what would otherwise and inevitably remain as "war . . . of every man against every man."[10]

The point that deserves emphasis, in light of what was said previously about Augustine and Calvin, is that ideas about innate depravity need not be framed in theological language. It is only necessary that they be put persuasively in order to serve as an excuse for behavior control arrangements that might otherwise be plainly inexcusable. For example, in his well-known utopian novel, *Walden Two,* the contemporary behaviorist psychologist B. F. Skinner attempts to justify his own prescription for an engineered society on the grounds that "each of us . . . is engaged in a pitched battle with the rest of mankind. . . . Each of us has interests which conflict with the interests of everybody else. That's our original sin, and it can't be helped. . . ."[11]

My purpose so far has been to trace the history of some perennial notions about human nature and to show how intimately they have been related to programs of social control. This intimate relationship remains a feature of contemporary political life; more specifically, myths about essential human inequality and depravity continue to play a crucial role in what passes for objective scholarship on questions of human nature and behavior control today.

Plato concocted his myth of the metals as a useful means of justifying social stratification. This chapter and the next are concerned with its contemporary counterpart: a myth about IQ (or "mental mettle") that purports to assign value to individuals not only more precisely than Plato could but in a completely honest and "scientific" way.

That contemporary society is socially stratified is not a matter open to serious dispute. Controversy begins only with the question of what social, economic, and political stratification means. According to some observers, the prevalence of large disparities in status, wealth, and power among various segments of contemporary American society represents social discrimination and the preservation of privilege on a massive scale. According to others, the hierarchical stratification apparent in many spheres of contemporary existence reflects primarily the fact that rather special mental abilities are required in order to attain preeminence in modern society, and those abilities are more limited among the general population. In other words, the contention on this side of the question is that what may look like a socially discriminatory maldistribution of wealth, power, and status is really nothing of the kind. Instead, it is merely a reflection of nature's unequal distribution of mental abilities.

It may seem unjust, and bleeding hearts may deplore it, but the hard truth is (according to this view) that social stratification is an inevitable fact of life in any just society, because in a just society, people tend to rise or fall on their own merits and thus generally end up at the particular level in the social hierarchy to which their native abilities are most nearly suited. It may not be an ideal state of affairs, say the proponents of this opinion, but it is a state of affairs in which people tend to get the treatment they inherently deserve; moreover, it is the only state of affairs in which the amenities of privilege and the facts of behavioral science go hand in hand.

Behavioral scientists have developed ways of measuring something they call the "intelligence quotient" (or IQ) and measurements of IQ (or its equivalents) tend to correlate positively with wealth, power, status, and other measures of social success. The fact of the matter is that the relatively poor, powerless, and socially subordinate inhabitants of depressed inner city and rural areas tend, as a class, to have relatively low IQ test scores, while the relatively rich, powerful, and socially dominant inhabitants of cities, suburbs, and the surrounding countryside tend, as a class, to have relatively higher scores.

But what do these facts mean? They mean, according to a prevalent interpretation that, roughly speaking, the members of the first group are where they are in the social hierarchy because they are relatively stupid, and they are relatively stupid mainly because they were born that way. By the same token, members of the second group are where they are in the social hierarchy because they are relatively smart, also mainly because they were born that way. If this interpretation of the facts is correct, that is something we will all have to accept. For my own part, I propose to argue that it is neither more nor less than Plato's myth of the metals parading in the guise of science, under the aegis of modern psychotechnological scholarship.

We live today in a socially stratified society that has produced an extraordinary array of mental measurement technology. Millions of IQ, scholastic aptitude, and achievement tests are administered every year in the United States alone. Most of the test takers are children between five and fifteen years of age. The design, development, printing, distribution, administration, scoring, and interpretation of results are all parts of a massive, multimillion-dollar mental measurements industry whose main product has had a profound impact upon the course of many millions of lives.[1] The nature and scope of that impact may be inferred from the tenor of a dispute that has arisen in recent years over the fact (itself never a matter of doubt) that black children tend on the whole to perform more poorly than white children on standard IQ tests. The dispute started, or rather was reopened, in 1969, amid a more wide-ranging national controversy over the future of Head Start and other so-called compensatory education programs. The first shot was fired by an educational psychologist, Arthur Jensen. The title of his long and detailed article in the prestigious *Harvard Educational Review* posed the question, "How much can we boost IQ and scholastic achievement?" Jensen's own answer was, in effect, "Not much." His article began with the statement that "compensatory education has been tried and it apparently has failed. . . ." Why? The rest of his article claimed to provide the answer, which was, in essence as follows:

1. Scholastic achievement (success in school) depends upon mental ability (commonly called "intelligence").
2. Intelligence is a complex trait and is difficult to define but it can be measured independently by performance on IQ tests.
3. IQ test scores correlate strongly with scholastic success, family income, parents' occupational status, and other sociocultural indices.
4. Differences in IQ scores (whether between individuals or groups) are mainly attributable to genetic factors.
5. Because the differences in mental ability responsible for the differences in IQ test performance and scholastic achievement are attributable to genetic factors, efforts to "boost" them have been (and must forever be) largely unsuccessful.

As we have already seen, ideas about the innate determinants of human diversity are very old, and the effort to justify social inequalities by invoking the existence of a natural human hierarchy has an ancient, if not an honorable, history. At issue here, however, is the claim, made by Jensen and others, that behavioral scientists have finally succeeded in removing the discussion of "mental mettle" from the realm of philosophical speculation and placed it, for perhaps the first time in human history, upon a firm scientific foundation.

The foundation consists of many studies, which Jensen reviews in detail, that were conducted in the United States and elsewhere during the past several decades. From the point of view of Jensen's thesis, the most important among them are studies purporting to demonstrate that the ability to do well on IQ tests (and, of course, in school) is genetically determined. Thus, at the very heart of Jensen's thesis—and of its more popular counterparts—is the crucial contention that IQ test scores measure innate intelligence ("native or natural brightness," so to say).

There are at least two distinct questions to consider in this connection. The first is whether what IQ tests measure is or is not innate in the sense of being genetically determined, and the second is whether IQ tests measure intelligence in the usual sense of the term.

An adequate answer to these questions must place them in the context of their intellectual antecedents, which will also serve to dispel the notion (which many mental testers have helped to foster) that the scientific details and technical intricacies of IQ testing are extremely difficult—perhaps impossible—for the ordinary person ever properly to understand. To be sure, mental testers ("psychometricians," as they generally prefer to be called) use plenty of jargon and are not always understandable, but that is not necessarily anyone's problem but their own.

The origins of the present controversy are traceable to the work of a Victorian Englishman, Sir Francis Galton, who published a book about the inheritance of mental ability just one hundred years before the appearance of Arthur Jensen's article. Galton had undertaken to show that intelligence is transmitted as a biological trait from parents to their children. His book, *Hereditary Genius,* claimed to demonstrate scientifically what everyone in Victorian England already knew, namely, that eminent Victorians tended to be the offspring of eminent parents. Galton's detailed biographical and genealogical data on the family trees of distinguished men, tabulated and analyzed in timely statistical fashion, showed that renowned English judges, statesmen, churchmen, politicians, essayists, and scientists were generally the descendents of other judges, statesmen, and churchmen of comparable renown. Here, argued Galton, was incontrovertible proof that intellectual talent was mainly hereditary.

Genetics, considered as a modern science, is centrally concerned with heredity; of how like beget like. The field of human genetics, not yet established in Galton's time, deals largely with the problem of human diversity; that is, of "individual differences" in biology. Many years after Galton's book was written, Mendel's work on genetic inheritance was rediscovered, initiating a biological revolution that culminated in the discovery of DNA (deoxyribonucleic acid) as the basic genetic material. But if we ask ourselves what is wrong with Galton's "proof," it turns out to be largely irrelevant that it predated an understanding of genetic principles.

The basic flaw in Galton's thesis was the preconceived view that social eminence was *prima faciae* evidence of high mental capacity. The presupposition that reputation, success, and social standing are correlated positively with intelligence not only yields an absurdly circular definition of mental capacity in which intelligence equals eminence and eminence equals intelligence, it reflects a bias in favor of the prevailing social order. In other words, it guarantees in advance that persons of low social standing will inevitably be defined as having lower intelligence.

There was a second, lesser flaw in Galton's thesis. Galton presumed that a trait that "runs in families" must have been inherited genetically. But by defining intelligence in the way he did, Galton made it impossible to determine whether variations in eminence (or intelligence) were due to genetic or social transmission. It is obvious that the children of eminent parents in Victorian society tended to inherit their wealth and social status, and that they did so in a way that was bound to be inextricable from the effects of genetic transmission.

But Galton was not interested only in proving the obvious fact that eminence in Victorian society tended to run in families. His real goal was to show that eminent persons owed their rank in society to mental characteristics inherited genetically from their eminent parents, and to achieve it he proceeded to establish a psychological laboratory for the scientific measurement of intellectual differences in human beings.[2]

Since the question will recur throughout the ensuing discussion, it is pertinent to pause for a moment and ask, What is measurement?

In science, as elsewhere in life, the term *measurement* refers to the assignment of numbers to objects or events according to certain formal rules. The principle and practice—indeed the very possibility—of measurement depends upon the idea that a degree of correspondence exists between the properties of numbers and the properties of objects or events to which they may be assigned. The measurement and ordering of phenomena is basically a process of comparison which has meaning only with reference to something other than itself. And where moral and ethical values influence the description and definition of the phenomena to be measured, as is the case with human characteristics, the measurement or scaling of those characteristics, no matter how precisely carried out, will be influenced as well. After all, the power to measure is merely an extension of the power to define. The point is worth pondering because throughout its history the measurement of human diversity has been linked to claims of human superiority and inferiority and has thereby been used to justify prevailing patterns of behavior control.

As far as I can determine, the first aspect of human diversity to be used as a basis for measurements explicitly intended to show the intellectual and behavioral superiority of some human groups over others was the facial angle, a measurement based upon the shape of the head that corresponds roughly to the slope of the forehead in profile (see figure). The term and the concept to which it refers were introduced by an eighteenth-century Dutch anatomist and art historian named Peter Camper. In a treatise on *Beauty as Exhibited in Ancient Paintings and Engravings,* Camper noted that ancient Greek sculptors had incorporated into their statues the idea that variations in the form and cast of the skull betokened underlying differences in intelligence. Camper credited Aristotle with having first recognized a connection between the shape of the forehead and intellectual ability and cited facial angles exceeding one hundred degrees as common in artistic depictions of the gods of Greek mythology. By contrast, he argued, statues of ordinary people and slaves were made with progressively smaller facial angles. "The idea of stupidity," he wrote, "is associated even by the vulgar, with the elongation of the snout...," and he urged the artists of his own day to improve the realism of their portraits by using the facial angle as a guide. He believed that he had established a universal standard of physical beauty and mental perfection, and in his later writings he turned his attention to comparisons of the facial angles of different racial groups. He reported his findings in a *Treatise on the Natural Differences of Features in Persons of Various Countries and Ages:*

The two extremities...of the [human] facial line are from 70 to 100 degrees, from the negro to the Crecian [i.e., Ancient Greek] antique; make it under 70, and you describe an orang or an ape; lessen it still more, and you have the head of a dog.[3]

Whether or not facial angle measurements may serve as an aid to realistic portraiture, Camper's assertions regarding the correlation between beauty and intelligence illustrate the influence of social preconceptions on aesthetic ideals and the effect of both on attitudes toward human diversity. While he had succeeded in expressing an aspect of human diversity in numbers ordered on a scale, the fact that the scale of measurement had been devised in accordance with prevailing aesthetic and social standards was easy to forget. And it was quickly forgotten by many scholars who were eager for a "real science" of mental comparison. The nineteenth-century spawned several such "sciences," which tended to focus either on the head and its contents (the brain) as indicators of mental traits and behavior or on different mental and behavioral characteristics in their own right.

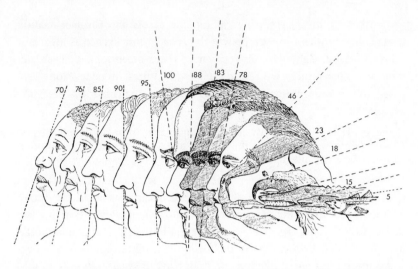

Facial angles as represented in nineteenth-century texts. After John J. Jeffries, *Natural History of the Human Races* (1869) and Ransom Dexter, "The Facial Angles," *Popular Science Monthly*, November 1874, pp. 587–592.

Galton's interests were of the latter kind. He was a statistician of high repute who believed that measurement is the mark of a mature science. His preoccupation with mental measurement (later called "psychometrics") led him to set up a system of lettered grades which was, in effect, the first "intelligence scale." He also devised the first "intelligence test," consisting of items intended to measure memory, sensory acuity, motor quickness, and other aspects of behavior. Galton's avowed objective was to test large numbers of people from all social classes and to prove that their performance correlated with their position along his scale of social eminence. Unfortunately for him, the results were not as he had hoped. After many years of effort, he reluctantly concluded that there was no positive correlation between test performance and social standing. In other words, the Victorian elites did not, on the average, perform better than members of the lower classes on his tests.

Under the circumstances, it might reasonably be expected that Galton would have questioned his assumptions, but like many of his Victorian contemporaries, Galton was so deeply wedded to the social perspectives of his own class that he was unable to do so. In fact, in *Hereditary Genius* he extended his conclusions well beyond the limits of social class, using the alleged equivalence between intelligence and eminence to make invidious comparisons between the mental capacities of different races, historical epochs, sexes, and cultures. "The average intellectual standard of the negro race," he said, "is some two grades below our own," and Athenian society was declared to be as far above Victorian civilization as the latter was above that of the Negro. Even in looking across the Channel, Galton judged that nowhere in Europe was the level of intelligence as high as it was in England. Galton was also convinced that women were intellectually inferior to men, and in this regard, as in many others, his conclusions were based on preconceptions that were readily confirmed by everyday experience:

If the sensitivity of women were superior to that of men, the self-interest of merchants would lead to their being always employed; but as the reverse is the case, the opposite supposition is likely to be the true one.[4]

Were the theorists who developed the IQ test, as we know it today equally guilty of allowing certain social preconceptions about the nature of intelligence to influence supposedly scientific measurements of intellectual capacity? If so, they were more successful than Galton at incorporating their biases, because the results of modern IQ testing tend to reflect and reinforce the social divisions prevailing in our society. In spite of this, many contemporary mental testers have attempted to defend themselves against accusations of social bias by insisting that their work is totally objective. When pressed further, they often invoke "academic freedom" and maintain that it is a scholar's right and responsibility to pursue and publish the truth without fear or favor, that it is neither sensible nor morally justifiable to protest against unpalatable facts or to close one's eyes to truth for fear of unpleasant consequences. Such arguments are obviously appealing, and I have heard them made in a most appealing way. For this reason, I intend to meet them on their own ground, and it is with the question of "objectivity" in mind that I propose to examine the foundations upon which the unpalatable truths of the mental testing movement are based.

After the middle of the nineteenth century, industrialization in America and western Europe forced a growing demand for universal public schooling as the means whereby children could be taught the skills and values that national progress required. Horace Mann argued for the common school as the "balance wheel of the social machinery," but as the pace of industrialization quickened, the schools were called upon more and more frequently to provide a better and more modern "product." The task of educational institutions was to identify and develop the needed skills and to shape social attitudes in such a way that children would fit into their proper occupational niche within the evolving industrial state.

It was in this industrially oriented educational climate that the French minister of education commissioned Alfred Binet, director of the psychology laboratory at the Sorbonne, to develop a testing procedure capable of identifying students in need of special schooling. The task, as defined, was essentially a technical one, and Binet approached it in a straightforward, practical fashion. He amassed hundreds of test items (questions), most of them based upon material from the school curriculum, and covering a broad range of difficulty. His basic idea was to design a test that could be given to children of varying ages and on which children at a given age or grade level would do either well or poorly, depending upon whether they were already doing either well or poorly in school. Preliminary versions of the test were administered to small groups of children whose scores were compared with their teachers' ratings of classroom performance. In the process, items were deleted or added in order to bring about the closest possible correspondence between test performance and educational age norms. In its final form, Binet's test provided an index of scholastic performance based upon the prevailing standard of scholastic success. In other words, scores on his test generally correlated with the ratings assigned by teachers in French classrooms of the day.

By using teacher's judgments of classroom performance as the standard by which his test was validated, Binet established a practical basis for its use as a predictor of success in the school system. Because his aim had been to identify children who were likely to require special schooling, he did not require a theory or definition of intelligence. Moreover, he did not make a distinction between acquired and congenital feeblemindedness and did not argue that poor performance on his test was a sign of innate mental inferiority. On the contrary, he issued a stern rebuke to those of his contemporaries who contended that intelligence is a fixed quantity which cannot be augmented:

The familiar proverb which says: "When one is stupid, it's for a long time" seems to be taken literally, without criticism, by some schoolmasters . . . who disinterest themselves in students who lack intelligence; they have for them neither sympathy nor even respect, [and] their intemperance of language makes them say before these children such things as: "This is a child who will never accomplish anything . . . he is poorly gifted. . . ." Never! What a large word![5]

Binet's reaction against such "brutal pessimism" was spelled out in a chapter on "The Training of Intelligence." It began with the words, "After the illness, the remedy . . . ," and it prescribed therapeutic courses in "mental orthopedics" for children with low test scores. Nevertheless, the fact is that Binet had (1) constructed a test that was based upon success in school and (2) called it an "intelligence" test, although he understood that a child's failure in the classroom to show the capacity for reasoning and understanding by which intelligence is usually defined did not imply that the child lacked the ability to do so.

Binet's choice of teacher ratings as the standard basis of comparison for his test was something of an advance over Galton's use of social standing as an index of native intelligence. It is obvious, however, that if success in school depends upon factors other than innate mental ability, a child's innate mental ability cannot be inferred accurately from the score obtained on an IQ test. The question is basic, because, unlike Binet, modern testers like Jensen frequently claim that IQ scores do reflect innate mental ability, although all widely used IQ tests since Binet's have been based—in one way or another—on criteria of social, scholastic, occupational, or economic success. Thus conclusions about intelligence drawn from test scores require us to assume an equivalence between success and mental ability.

How seriously has the American mental testing movement considered the possibility that this assumption is mistaken? The answer to this question is clear when one looks at what actually happened when Binet's test was brought to the United States. The importers of the IQ test (1) immediately and uncritically accepted Binet's use of success as the standard to which IQ test scores were referred and (2) instantly and unequivocally rejected his opinion about the flexible nature of intelligence, in favor of the view that IQ was a direct measure of innate mental capacity.

The result of this dual action was even more startling than the speed with which it was taken, for it meant that the pioneers of the American mental testing movement had suddenly put themselves in the position of claiming that they had a test capable of measuring mental capacity directly. This claim, although the grounds for it remained obscure, was to become the central dogma of the mental testing movement. And dogma is what it was: "We must assume," declared a leading member of the movement, "that we are measuring native or inborn intelligence."[6] This assumption had social consequences far more serious than any Binet might have imagined possible when he spoke of "brutal pessimism."

The first detailed adaptation of the IQ test (the Stanford-Binet test) was published in America in 1916 by Lewis M. Terman, a professor of psychology at Stanford University. Its publication coincided with a quickening of the movement toward modernization of the educational system in accordance with the economic needs of industry.

It is seldom said so forthrightly nowadays, but the idea that schools exist mainly to serve the leading economic interests of society was advanced unflinchingly by many professional educators during the so-called progressive era. Leading educational administrators and theorists commonly alluded to schools as factories involved in the mass production of students. Ellwood P. Cubberly, Professor Terman's colleague at Stanford and for sixteen years dean of the school of education there, was speaking for many professional educators when he wrote,

Our schools are . . . factories in which the raw products are to be shaped and fashioned into products. . . . The specifications for manufacturing come from the demands of twentieth-century civilization, and it is the business of the school to build its pupils according to the specifications laid down. This demands good tools, specialized machinery, continuous measurement of production. . . .[7]

It would be a mistake to see mere analogy in this. The central problem facing the industrial and political leaders of the United States in the decade before World War I was to control, in an orderly and efficient way, the growth of rapidly expanding mass production industries. This task required the kind of human quality control implied by Cubberly's remarks, and it is not surprising to discover that those who directed the public education system worked closely with established economic and political institutions toward an optimal balance of interests.

To achieve this end, the mental testers applied their tests of "native or inborn intelligence" to large numbers of children as a means of helping the school system "to build its pupils according to the specifications laid down." Robert M. Yerkes, a leading mental tester at Harvard, pointed out that ". . . the psychologist may be of great value in getting the subject into the most suitable place in society."[8]

However, men like Cubberly and Yerkes saw themselves not as agents of the industrial establishment but as benefactors of society as a whole. The image they projected was that of dedicated scholars, cultivating a new profession of education and a new science of mental testing while at the same time pursuing the overall national interest. They shared a view of themselves as experts in the identification and development of natural talent and a vision of the prevailing social order as a meritocracy in which each person would have a rightful rank and place. They saw further that, in the physical sciences, the process of classifying, ordering, and measuring phenomena had meant an increase in the power to predict and control natural events. And they were sure that the same process would lead to a comparable advance in the power to predict and control the behavior of human beings.

It was thus with great faith in the power of science, and with a firm commitment to a particular social cause, that many educators and psychologists undertook to play their appointed roles in the emerging progressive era. In the process they became deeply involved in the overall problems of the nation: industrialization, immigration, urbanization, and mobilization for war. At the same time, these problems were also being addressed by various bureaucratic agencies representing established labor, corporate, and political interests and committed to forging an alliance on behalf of industrial efficiency and social stability. This alliance sponsored research on scientific management techniques—techniques of human assessment and quality control.

The formation of private foundations and civic organizations led to pressure for the reorganization of public institutions and for an increase in administrative effectiveness at all levels. In the fields of education and mental testing, many of the organizations providing moral and financial support were corporate foundations, whose influence was a significant factor in shaping public policies from early in the twentieth century. By 1913, however, growing public hostility toward the partisan involvement of large amounts of corporate money in national affairs led a concerned Congress to direct the Industrial Relations Commission to investigate foundations' impact on public policy. After a year of inquiry, the findings of the commission did little to calm the controversy. The majority concluded that "the domination of men in whose hands the final control of a large part of American industry rests is not limited to their employees, but is being rapidly extended to control the education and social service of the nation."[9] The commission did not claim that such domination and control were necessarily a menace to the public. But they pointed out that the policy objectives of corporate foundations, whether or not they served the public interest, were unlikely to challenge the interests of their sponsoring corporations. Corporate wealth and the support of influential foundations were not solely responsible for the rise of the American mental testing movement. On the contrary, public acceptance was also required. And it needs to be emphasized that the American mental testing movement emerged in an America where, notwithstanding the familiar slogans about human equality, there was a deep concern with blood and breeding. This concern helped to create the climate conducive to discussions about innate mental inequality.

The spectre of "hereditary degeneracy" ("bad blood" and "bad breeding") was in the background long before Binet's test was invented and longer still before IQ scores were given an innate or genetic interpretation. Although there was as yet no science of genetics and no tenable theory of how human behavior was acquired and transmitted from generation to generation, the notion was widely entertained that dependency, mental defectiveness, criminality, and social deviance more generally were due to inborn and inheritable "dysgenic" taints.

Galton's inquiry into "hereditary genius" led him to view "the incompetent, the ailing, and the desponding" as a threat to the well-being of society because of their habit of producing large numbers of impoverished, sick, and miserable children. The upper classes, he argued, should be encouraged to have more children, whereas the lower classes should be induced, if possible, or compelled, if necessary, to have fewer. It was on behalf of this central idea of racial improvement—of increasing the relative number of "healthier, wealthier, and wiser" offspring—that Galton sought to rally people of his own kind. To this idea and this effort, Galton gave the name *eugenics* in 1883; it was destined to prove a rallying point for many forms of behavior control during the twentieth century. Under the banner of eugenics, many scientists and social reformers argued for the enactment of laws that would prevent "degenerates" from having offspring. Thus, as early as 1898, a eugenic sterilization bill, introduced in the Michigan Legislature, provided for the castration of all inmates of the Michigan Home for the Feeble-Minded and Epileptic and of all persons convicted for a felony for the third time.[10]

"Deviance," that is, behavior deemed to be socially disturbing, disruptive, or dangerous, and "disability," a condition deemed to be a handicap for the affected individual, are almost invariably linked in proposals to do something about dysgenics. Thus, proposals aimed at controlling behavior that seems to threaten the interests of powerful groups may be cloaked in the language of humanitarian betterment. In the same year that the Michigan bill was filed, a report appeared describing an effort plainly intended to control deviant behavior by treating it like disease. It described the "therapeutic castration" of twenty-six male children in Massachusetts. Of these, twenty-four were operated on because of "persistent epilepsy and masturbation," one for "epilepsy with imbecility," and one for "masturbation with weakness of mind."

Like the mental testing movement, the eugenics movement was fueled, in large measure, by funds obtained from corporate foundations. In 1904, the Carnegie Institution of Washington—endowed by Andrew Carnegie, the steel manufacturer—financed the establishment of a biological experiment station at Cold Spring Harbor, New York. The station's director was Charles Benedict Davenport, a zoologist whose earlier scientific interests in animal breeding had begun to wane and who, having studied Galton, was converted to an interest in eugenics. He encouraged other scientists to develop methods of identifying individuals who carried "defective germ plasm" and sought to persuade other foundations to fund the work. Davenport was particularly interested in securing passage of legislation for eugenic control and devoted much effort to the dissemination of information on that subject.

A year later, in 1905, the Pennsylvania State Legislature passed *An Act for the Prevention of Idiocy* which contained a sterilization clause. It was vetoed by Governor Pennypacker, who said,

These feeble-minded and imbecile children have been entrusted to the institutions by their parents or guardians for the purpose of training and instruction. It is proposed [by this bill] to experiment upon them; not for their instruction, but in order to help society in the future . . . without their consent, which they cannot give. . . . This bill assumes that they cannot be . . . instructed and trained. . . . [However, their] mental condition is due to causes . . . entirely beyond our knowledge.[11]

But the barriers against eugenics control laws crumbled rapidly thereafter.

Two years later, a eugenic sterilization act was passed and signed into law in the state of Indiana. Its preamble stated flatly, "Whereas, heredity plays a most important part in the transmission of crime, idiocy and imbecility. ..." That language, with minor variations, was repeated in similar laws passed in quick succession in fifteen states. At the urging of eugenicists, other traits were added to the list of those in which heredity purportedly played "a most important part." A New Jersey law of 1911 added "feeble-mindedness, epilepsy, criminal tendencies, and other defects." The Iowa law enacted the same year provided for the "unsexing of criminals, idiots, etc." The unsexing provision was modified two years later to read "prevention of procreation" and the "etcetera" was spelled out to include "criminals, rapists, idiots, feeble-minded, imbeciles, lunatics, drunkards, drug fiends, epileptics, syphilitics, moral and sexual perverts, and diseased and degenerate persons." In short, between 1907 and 1928, twenty-one states enacted eugenic sterilization laws aimed at controlling the reproductive behavior of socially deviant individuals. Some of these laws were never enforced, but many were, and most of them are still on the books in one form or another. It has been estimated that about 8,500 sterilizations were performed under the provisions of these laws prior to 1929.[12]

By 1910, the eugenics movement began to devote itself in an organized way to rationalizing and documenting the policies it had helped to promote. For example, with funds donated by Mrs. E. H. Harriman (widow of the railroad magnate), Davenport set up the Eugenics Record Office and brought together scientists from various fields to study, report upon, and make recommendations about public policies regarding their common objective. The office was aided by "expert advisory committees" on such subjects as "The Inheritance of Mental Traits," "Heredity of the Feeble-Minded," and "Sterilization."

Under the auspices of one of the expert committees, a subcommittee was formed "to study and report on the best practical means of cutting off the defective germ plasm in the American population." The chairman, Harry H. Laughlin, and other members of the committee "inquired and found" that approximately 10 percent of the population carried "bad seed." More precisely, they asserted the existence of an inherent conjunction between low intelligence and immorality. This conjunction, it was argued, characterized the "feeble-minded, insane, criminalistic (including the delinquent and the wayward), epileptic, inebriate, diseased, blind, deaf, deformed and dependent (including orphans, ne'er-do-wells, the homeless, tramps and paupers)." Making the claim (already officially established in the preambles to laws in many states) that the root cause of social deviance was bad breeding and that "society must look upon germ-plasm as belonging to society and not solely to the individual who carries it," Laughlin's committee concluded that eugenic sterilization was "the best practical means of cutting off the defective germ plasm in the American population."[13] There was, at the time, no science of quantitative human genetics, no tenable theory of how behavioral characteristics might be inherited, and no data on IQ test performance among the country's general population. But, in America, the notion that dependency, disease, poverty, degeneracy, deformity, deviance, and other social problems were biologically determined by bad blood and bad breeding was an idea whose time had come.

Thus, the United States became the first nation in modern times to enact and enforce laws providing for eugenic sterilization in the name of "purifying the race."

The belief that the poor, the nonwhite, and other disadvantaged groups were genetically inferior had enormous social consequences. An illustrative episode was "the great pellagra cover-up," which Allan Chase has recently brought to light.[14] Pellagra, a disease of malnutrition that produces rough, red skin eruptions and eventual physical and mental debility, was endemic throughout many regions of the rural south during the nineteenth century, particularly among the very poor. In 1912, a national Pellagra Commission was organized to search for the cause and cure of the disease; a prominent member of the commission was C. B. Davenport, director of the Eugenics Record Office. Davenport was firmly convinced that pellagra was a hereditary disease, on grounds that it had been clearly established that pellagra was exclusively a disease of the poor and was especially common in institutions containing the deviant and socially dependent poor, like insane asylums, prisons, and orphanages. (The fact that the professional staffs of these institutions never contracted the disease indicated that it was not infectious.) In addition, among whites the disease occurred most often among the group derisively labeled "poor white trash," a group reputed to be especially lazy, shiftless, and ignorant and one that had been for some time a subject of concern to Davenport and other eugenicists, who considered them a subrace of "chronic pauper stock" doomed by their defective genetic endowment and "bad blood" to perpetual poverty, degeneracy, and disease. Davenport, who was likewise convinced that most forms of insanity, feeblemindedness, deviance, and low social status were due to defective germ plasm, did not believe that pellagra was inherited in the sense that eye color is genetically transmitted but maintained that it depended upon "certain constitutional, inheritable traits of the affected individual." In spite of the fact that as early as 1914 a Public Health Service epidemiologist, Joseph Goldberger, had discovered the true cause of pellagra and published his results to the acclaim of the medical world, the final report of the Pellagra Commission, issued in 1917, described pellagra as a heredity disease that infected people of inferior breeding stock. For the next two decades, the commission report was generally accepted as definitive, while scientists and policymakers alike despaired of the prospect of a cure. By 1929 pellagra was responsible for at least six thousand deaths annually and was not finally conquered until the depression, when impoverishment of many previously self-sufficient people led the government to establish relief programs, and in 1943 to require the enrichment of white bread with vitamins and minerals. Faced with the claim on the one hand that pellagra was caused mainly by poverty and on the other that it was a genetically determined disease that could not be eradicated by social or economic reforms, those who had the power to decide matters of public policy found it easier to believe the theory that demanded neither higher wages nor better living conditions for the poor.

It can hardly be called coincidental that the pioneers of IQ testing first made their impact felt in connection with the specter of "hereditary feeble-mindedness" and it alleged causal involvement in crime, poverty, moral degeneracy, and industrial inefficiency. This was a specter that the eugenics movement both exploited and helped to create. Consider, for example, the view of Henry Goddard, an early user of Binet's test at the Training School for Feeble-Minded Children at Vineland, New Jersey, and an outspoken eugenics advocate: ". . . we have discovered that pauperism and crime are increasing at an enormous rate, and we are led to pause and ask, "Why?" Even a superficial investigation shows us that a large percentage of these troubles come from the feeble-minded."[15]

The image of a perpetual underclass—mentally deficient, impoverished, and criminally inclined—doomed to make trouble by virtue of their inherent defects, is an image that dies hard in a society such as ours. In 1971, almost sixty years later, Professor Richard Herrnstein of Harvard took up Goddard's theme anew in the *Atlantic Monthly:*

. . . the tendency to be unemployed may run in the genes of a family about as certainly as bad teeth. . . . As the wealth and complexity of human society grow, there will be precipitated out of the mass of humanity a low capacity (intellectual and otherwise) residue that may be unable to master the common occupations, cannot compete for success and achievement, and are most likely to be born to parents who have similarly failed. . . . The troubles . . . have already caught the attention of alert social scientists . . . (who have described) the increasingly chronic lower class in America's central cities.[16]

According to Goddard and other early mental testers, the IQ test could and should be used to identify the mentally deficient at an early age, so that timely intervention could bring their socially deviant propensities under control. Thus, the work of the pioneer psychometricians must be understood as part of a larger movement that believed society could solve its problems only if an effective means were first found to eliminate certain classes of mentally defective and socially undesirable individuals. What the mental testers contributed to this mode of problem solving was "scientific evidence" that these two groups were for all intents and purposes the same.

When the first fully Americanized version of the IQ test was published by Terman in 1916, its promise as an instrument of behavior control was made explicit:

... all feeble-minded are at least potential criminals. That every feeble-minded woman is a potential prostitute would hardly be disputed by anyone. Moral judgement, like business judgement social judgement or any other kind of higher thought process, is a function of intelligence.

... in the near future intelligence tests will bring tens of thousands of these high-grade defectives under the surveillance and protection of society. This will ultimately result in curtailing the reproduction of feeblemindedness and in the elimination of an enormous amount of crime, pauperism, and industrial inefficiency. It is hardly necessary to emphasize that the high-grade cases, of the type now so frequently overlooked, are precisely the ones whose guardianship is most important for the State to assume.[17]

Writing a year later about "The Menace of Feeblemindedness," Terman criticized socially inspired efforts to aid the feebleminded. Such efforts, he argued, were doubtless well-intended, but they only served to make things worse by fostering "the survival of individuals who would otherwise not be able to live and reproduce." The feebleminded continue to multiply, he stated, but "if we would preserve our state for a class of people worthy to possess it, we must prevent, as far as possible, the propagation of mental degenerates . . . curtailing the increasing spawn of degeneracy."[18]

Terman's state (California) led the nation in eugenic sterilizations. Approximately 6,200 sterilizations were performed under a law that was passed and enforced with the vigorous support of the Human Betterment Foundation, which counted Terman as one of its leading members. Terman was also responsible for injecting race into the IQ debate. He claimed that mental deficiency

is very common among Spanish-Indian and Mexican families of the Southwest and also among negroes. Their dullness seems to be racial or at least inherent in the family stocks from which they come. . . . [T]he whole question of racial differences in mental traits will have to be taken up anew and by experimental methods. The writer predicts that when this is done there will be discovered enormously significant racial differences in general intelligence, differences which cannot be wiped out by any scheme of mental culture.

He recommended that

children of this group should be segregated in special classes. . . . They cannot master abstractions, but they can often be made efficient workers. . . . There is no possibility at present of convincing society that they should not be allowed to reproduce, although from a eugenic point of view they constitute a grave problem because of their unusually prolific breeding.[19]

The rise of the eugenics and mental testing movements coincided with an acceleration in the rate of European immigration into the United States and was accompanied by a growing and quite widespread preoccupation with social conformity. Consequently, while the emphasis on "degenerates" was not always a matter of racism, it was invariably an attempt to define and to enforce certain norms whose violation would mark deviant individuals for special treatment.

Eugenic sterilization of those defined as degenerate is not a dead issue in the United States.[20] The authority of the state to dictate sterilization for eugenic purposes was affirmed in a famous Supreme Court case (*Buck v. Bell*) when Justice Holmes declared that "the principle that sustains compulsory vaccination is broad enough to cover the cutting of the Fallopian tubes ... three generations of imbeciles are enough." It would be an exaggeration, however, to say that the eugenic sterilization laws that were enacted during the first quarter of this century had a profound impact upon target populations in the United States. In contrast to the laws enacted several decades later in Germany, the American laws were only fitfully enforced. An indication of what might have happened, however, may be gleaned from a projected "segregation and sterilization program" drafted in 1914 at the First National Conference on Race Betterment. Based upon an assumption that 10 percent of the total population was made up of "defective and antisocial varieties," which it was desirable to eliminate, calculations were presented to show that the incidence could be reduced to 5.77 percent by 1955, provided that a total of approximately 5.76 million sterilizations were performed during that forty-year period.[21]

It would also be an exaggeration to say that the opinions of psychologists on questions of intelligence and morality produced a fundamental change in American public policy. On the contrary, the pronouncements made by the mental testers were wholly consonant with the prevailing concern with economic efficiency and orderly public administration. Which is simply to say that the bulk of psychological scholarship during this period reflected and reinforced the social and economic elitism of those who supported and benefited from it. As Edward Thorndike, chairman of the psychology department at Columbia University, stated,

It is the great good fortune of mankind that there is a substantial positive correlation between intelligence and morality, including good will toward one's fellows. Consequently our superiors in ability are on the average our benefactors, and it is often safer to trust our interests to them than to ourselves. No group of men can be expected to act one hundred per cent in the interest of mankind, but this group of the ablest men will come nearest to the ideal.[22]

A twist of logic could join democracy and elitism in an uneasy alliance:

The disturbing fear is that the masses—the seventy million or even the eighty-six million—will take matters into their own hands. The fact is, matters are already in their hands and have been since the adoption of the

Constitution. But it is equally true that the (masses) are in the hands of the . . . four million. Provided always that the four million apply their very superior intelligence to the practical problem of social welfare and efficiency.[23]

The attempts to link intelligence and moral fitness led Henry Goddard, the author of this passage, from his work with the Binet Scale to a study of the so-called inheritance of immorality. In a book entitled *The Kallikak Family*, he traced the descendants of one Martin Kallikak, who was said to have sired both good and bad branches of his family tree. The good side descended from his marriage to a chaste and worthy Quaker woman, while the bad branch began with his dalliance with an allegedly feebleminded tavern-girl who bore a bastard son known as "Old Horror," whose progeny consisted of hundreds of "social pests . . . paupers, criminals, prostitutes and drunkards." Although the geneology itself is dubious, as late as 1955, at least one widely used general psychology textbook projected the Kallikak story as evidence of the connection between mental inferiority and moral degeneracy by way of genetics. The book in question was written by Henry E. Garrett, Thorndike's successor at Columbia and a former president of the American Psychological Association. Lest the student miss his point, Garrett included a vivid drawing in which Old Horror and his progeny were pictured with horns, while the good members of the other side of the family were portrayed in chaste Puritan garb.[24]

A decade later, in the midst of the civil rights movement in the United States, Professor Garrett produced a series of pamphlets delineating what he believed to be the inevitable degenerative consequences of racial integration in the United States. In one of these pamphlets, entitled *Breeding Down*, he attempted to justify race segregation on the grounds of black mental inferiority:

You can no more mix the two races and maintain the standards of White Civilization than you can add 80 (the average IQ of Negroes) and 100 (the average IQ of Whites), divide by two and get 100. What you would get would be a race of 90's, and it is that 10 per cent differential that spells the difference between a spire and a mud hut; 10 per cent—or less—is the margin of civilization's "profit"; it is the difference between a cultured society and savagery. Therefore, it follows, if miscegenation would be bad for White people, it would be bad for Negroes as well. For, if leadership is destroyed, all is destroyed.[25]

Garrett claimed—as Galton had done almost a century earlier—that black people are some 200,000 years behind whites in cultural evolution and cannot "measure up" to prevailing American standards of intellectual achievement. Desegregation must be opposed, said Garrett, because it may lead to intermarriage, and intermarriage is bound to destroy the white "genetic lead." "Breeding down" is bad biology, he argued, and the state should prevent it. Although the idea of "purity" in human genetics is

IQ: Mental Measurement for Social Control

scientifically meaningless, it is not without a social meaning to those who entertain the myth that the diversity of human beings can be reduced to differences in value according to an arbitrary scale of intellectual capacity.

"Education is to man what manure is to the pea," wrote a young English geneticist in 1907, and the idea that genetic endowment forecloses social possibilities continues to figure prominently in contemporary arguments about race mixing in American public schools. During the 1960s 500,000 copies of Henry Garrett's pamphlets on the evils of miscegenation were distributed free of charge to American teachers by opponents of integrated education. In 1975, in the midst of the growing school-busing controversy, an advertisement in the *Boston Globe* announced the publication of a book by Dr. Garrett entitled *IQ and Racial Differences* which consisted of a warmed-over version of his earlier ideas about innate black inferiority. The advertisement encouraged the reader to buy the book for "sufficient ammunition to answer and demolish . . . arguments for school integration point by point."

Today, assertions about the alleged inherent mental inferiority of particular human groups are aimed mainly at black people, and IQ test results figure prominently in contemporary public debates about public school integration. They are also invoked from time to time in connection with other social problems, including what is sometimes referred to as "the welfare mess." And it is a fact that poor people (of whom a large proportion in this society are nonwhite) tend to perform poorly on IQ tests. According to some psychometricians, this is properly interpreted as a sign of the mental inferiority that is at the root of their poverty. This conclusion may lead, in turn, to proposals aimed at "weeding out"individuals with low test scores by eugenic means. Thus, a few years ago, Professor William Shockley advanced a proposal based on the idea that people at the bottom of the socioeconomic hierarchy are innately predestined to be poor by virtue of their biology.

Shockley's solution to the problem of dysgenics was not far removed from the programs of earlier eugenics advocates. In an address to the American Psychological Association, he proposed that a voluntary sterilization program be set up for welfare recipients. Under his plan, the government would pay a bonus of $1,000 for every IQ point below 100 to welfare clients willing to submit to sterilization. By this, he argued, the incentive would be greatest for those individuals who had the lowest scores, and he predicted, as a consequence, that the dysgenic problem of low IQ and the social problem of huge welfare rolls would be solved within a generation.[26]

Are there any grounds at all for believing that IQ tests measure innate intelligence? Up to this point, I have tried to show that if IQ test scores correlate with anything, it is with various measures of scholastic, social, and economic success, although "success" is no better as a standard for judging intelligence than Galton's criterion of "eminence." From the 1950s until quite recently, it seemed that better evidence regarding the genetic basis of IQ had been obtained from research on the distribution of IQ scores within families carried out by a British psychometrician, the late Sir Cyril Burt. Burt was convinced (as Galton had been) that intellectual excellence is a genetically transmitted trait and that the commonest cause of poor scholastic performance was "inborn inferiority of general intelligence." Burt's opinions on such matters were fundamental in shaping British educational practices from the late 1920s until the time of his death in 1971, as in his endorsement of a policy—already in effect—of sexually segregating mentally subnormal persons so that they would not reproduce and his influence on the passage of the English General Education Act (1944), which established a "triple-track" school system into which children were channeled on the basis of test performance. Since only one track (the grammar school) gave access to higher education, Burt's theory that intelligence is fixed and innate effectively served to exclude large numbers of English school children from middle class occupations.

Between 1955 and 1966 Burt published three papers on the close correspondence between the IQ test scores of twins which had a heavy influence on the work of Professor Jensen in the United States and have often been cited as models in demonstrating that differences in intelligence are largely inherited. In these papers, Burt reported a statistical measure (correlation coefficient) of the degree to which the IQ test scores of identical twins resembled each other. The nature of this particular statistic is that it varies from minus one (a completely negative correlation, indicating that within a pair of scores, the two IQ's are invariably very different from one another), through zero (which would mean *no* systematic relationship) to plus one (a completely positive correlation, indicating that two scores of any given pair are identical). The following table illustrates Burt's findings.

Table 1
Professor Burt's correlation coefficients showing alleged degree of similarity in performance on his "group test" of intelligence by monozygotic ("identical") twins reared either apart or together

| Year of Report | Data for Monozygotic Twins | | | | |
| | Reared Apart | | Reared Together | |
	No. of Pairs	Correl.	No. of Pairs	Correl.
1955	21	.771	83	.944
1958	42	.771	NA	.944
1966	53	.771	95	.944

Source: Adapted from Leon Kamin, "Heredity, Intelligence, Politics, and Psychology: 1," in N. J. Block and G. Dworkin, eds., *The IQ Controversy* (New York: Pantheon, 1976), table 5, p. 246.

The data in this table were first drawn together by Professor Leon Kamin of Princeton University while writing a book entitled *The Science and Politics of IQ.* In addition to detecting a number of puzzling inconsistencies in Burt's data, Kamin discovered the astonishing consistency of results illustrated here, in which identical pairs of correlation coefficients, accurate to three decimal places, are reported from six different analyses, no one of which had the same number of subjects. This is a statistical impossibility, and Professor Kamin has found no fewer than twenty similar instances in Burt's work of correlations remaining miraculously constant while the number of individuals in the sample changed. As Kamin remarks, "The numbers left behind by Professor Burt are simply not worthy of serious scientific attention."[27]

Upon learning of Kamin's reanalysis of the data upon which his own conclusions about the inheritance of intelligence were based, Professor Jensen apparently agreed that "there is no way out of this morass, except possibly to examine Burt's raw data." Jensen attempted to do so and reported that "alas, nothing remained of Burt's possessions . . . unfortunately, the original data are lost, and all that remains are the results of the statistical analyses. . . ."[28]

Until very recently, it appeared as if an explanation of Burt's remarkably consistent and extremely influential findings would never be found. There is now good reason to think that Burt's results are mythical, invented by him solely to deceive others into accepting his belief in inherited IQ, and uncritically accepted by his colleagues because of his eminence as a psychologist and psychometrician. This astounding conclusion emerges from a remarkable job of investigative reporting by Dr. Oliver Gillie, medical correspondent for the London *Sunday Times,* whose discovery that two of Burt's later collaborators were probably fictitious seemed to confirm previous doubts about the validity of his research.[29]

Binet, it will be recalled, invented his intelligence test without defining intelligence; teachers' judgments of students' mental ability were used as a standard for validating the test. Such judgments are notoriously unreliable and are now in disrepute among psychometricians. Yet psychometricians continue to "validate" their tests against results obtained on other, earlier IQ tests. Terman's Stanford-Binet, for example, is currently the most influential test for this use. As I have noted, it is basically a translation and adaptation of Binet's test, and, as such, *its* original validating standard was the judgments of teachers, with their attendant shortcomings. Thus, the IQ tests currently in use are part of a vicious circle because they were developed in the absence of an independent definition of intelligence. As one psychometrician (a former teacher of Professor Jensen's) candidly remarks,

It is often believed that intelligence tests are developed and constructed according to a rationale deriving from some scientific theory. . . . In actual fact . . . intelligence tests are not based on any very sound scientific principles, and there is not a great deal of agreement among experts regarding the nature of intelligence. . . . Because the intelligence tests, originally constructed in the early years of this century did such a good job when applied to various practical problems, psychologists interested in the subject tended to become technologists eager to exploit and improve these tools, rather than scientists eager to carry out the requisite fundamental research, most of which still remains to be done. Society, of course, always interested in the immediate application of technological advances and disinterested [sic] in pure research, must bear its share of the responsibility for this unfortunate state of affairs.[30]

There was a great debate about the meaning of IQ in the 1920s. Edwin G. Boring of Harvard tried to resolve the problem of defining intelligence with a Humpty-Dumptyesque stipulation that became known as "Boring's dictum": "Intelligence as a measurable capacity must *at the start* be defined as the capacity to do well in an intelligence test. *Intelligence is what the tests test.*"[31] Indeed, Humpty-Dumpty's whimsical kind of discourse was used by Arthur Jensen to defend psychometrics against the charge that it was arrogating to itself the power to define the meaning of intelligence. People who think that, said Professor Jensen, are not using the term intelligence properly.

The notion is sometimes expressed that psychologists have misaimed with their intelligence tests. Although the tests may predict scholastic performance, it is said, they do not *really* measure intelligence—as if somehow the "real thing" has eluded measurement and perhaps always will. But this is a misconception. We *can* measure intelligence. As the late Professor Edwin C. Boring pointed out, intelligence, by definition, is what intelligence tests measure. The trouble comes only when we attribute more to "intelligence" and to our measurements of it than do the psychologists who use the concept in its proper sense.[32]

To understand what Boring and Jensen are saying when they say that "intelligence is what IQ tests measure," consider the following example: Every automobile contains an instrument called a fuel gauge; its purpose is to measure the amount of fuel in the tank. Now, if one were to follow Boring's dictum, one might say, "Fuel as a measurable substance must *at the start* be defined as a substance capable of causing the fuel gauge to register." If that stipulation sounds satisfactory, and if no further definition is required concerning what fuel really is, let me suggest that the next time the fuel gauge on your car reads empty, you find a water hose and fill your tank from it. The car will thereafter take you about as far as Boring's dictum does, and it will do so with what he would have to call a full tank of fuel.

It is not uncommon to find psychometricians simultaneously creating and deploring public misconceptions about what intelligence tests actually test. But if intelligence has any real meaning, it is of more than casual interest to ask if the test is measuring what it is supposed to be measuring. Whereas psychometricians may insist that there is a special or proper way to understand their definitions, the actual fact is that they define intelligence in the same way that everyone else does. They use the terms *intelligence* and *IQ* as synonyms for *brightness, smartness, cleverness, mental ability,* and so forth. And they do so in ways clearly calculated to transfer to IQ test scores the conceptual, evaluative, emotional, and subjective connotations that are normally evoked when someone is called "smart" or "stupid."

The psychometricians are trying to have their cake and eat it too. They deplore public misconceptions, but they simultaneously foster and exploit the idea that a person's IQ is a measure of how bright that person is in the ordinary sense. Whatever the reason for this, it frequently induces them to engage in scholastic exercises in deception. Arthur Jensen, for example, tells his readers that "the term 'intelligence,' as used by psychologists, is itself of fairly recent origin. Having been introduced as a technical term in psychology near the turn of the century, *it has since filtered down into common parlance. . . .*"[33] On this point (but not on this point alone) psychometric expertise consists in putting the cart before the horse. The word *intelligence* had a long history in "common parlance" long before psychologists and psychometricians took control of its definition. The *Oxford English Dictionary* takes almost an entire page to show that *intelligent* and *intelligence* have been used continuously since the late fourteenth century to mean precisely what people commonly mean by those terms today.

Conflicts about the meaning of a word, about whose use of a word is proper, seem like nitpicking because they often act to screen off the real issue, which is one of power. That is why it is necessary to examine very closely the way in which contemporary psychometricians formulate and enforce definitions of intelligence.

Whether or not the definition of intelligence is a conventional matter and whether or not the measurement of intelligence is a matter of stipulation, the ultimate justification for developing, discussing, and using intelligence tests is the claim that an IQ score is synonymous with intelligence in the ordinary sense. In the absence of an independent theory and definition of intelligence, there are only two ways to evaluate the real nature of IQ tests.

The first is obviously to evaluate the method of test construction itself. Terman and his colleagues maintained from the start that the IQ was a measure of native intelligence. But a striking sex difference was found on the first version of the Stanford-Binet intelligence test, published by Terman in 1916: females at all age levels outscored males of the same ages by an average of 2 to 4 percent. Now, if one accepts the claim that IQ scores reflect native intelligence, there is (one might think—no way of escaping the obvious conclusion that girls must be, on the average, and however slightly, more intelligent that boys of equal chronological age. One might think that Terman and his colleagues, having discovered that females were somewhat brighter than males, were obliged to let it go at that. Not so, for women were not supposed to be more intelligent than men. Indeed at that time they did not even have the right to vote.

Consequently, Terman and his colleagues decided to save society from an embarrassing fact. In reviewing the test, they found that there were certain items on which females consistently tended to excel, so they simply "revised" the test by (1) deleting a number of those items and (2) adding a number of items of the kind on which males tended to do better than females. In other words, the test was "cooked" in order to bring its results into conformity with the testers' preconceptions. Thus was it established as a fact that males and females of equal are are, on the average, *equal* in IQ. It was—and is—a genuinely *manufactured* result.

The point deserves emphasis that different human groups (black versus white, native-born versus foreign-born, urban versus rural, as well as male versus female) *do* tend to perform differently on different kinds of test items. As the foregoing example suggests, it is a fairly simple matter to manipulate a test in order to produce almost any desired result. Since test makers can and do manipulate their tests in order to make the results conform with prevailing social and scholastic standards, it is pertinent to wonder whether Terman would have revised his test if—by a more "fortunate" choice of original items—males had tended to outscore females.

The second possible way of determining the real nature of what IQ tests measure is to look at the kinds of items the tests contain. Lest there by any remaining doubt that the Stanford-Binet test was constructed to contain items that would discriminate in favor of the values, attitudes, and information possessed by middle and upper-class whites, let us consider some of the items that the test includes. On the 1960 revision (the latest version of the test), a six-year old child is shown the following pictures and asked which is prettier:

From L. M. Terman and M. Merrill, *Stanford-Binet Intelligence Scale*, 3rd ed. (Boston: Houghton-Mifflin, 1960).

It is obvious that certain children or children from certain ethnic and racial groups may choose the incorrect answer. More poignant, the child who perceives the expected answer and gives it is submitting to what may be an alien concept of "pretty." Nor are these the only kinds of items that discriminate against minority groups and have formed the basis for policies like immigration restriction and educational tracking.

It is not difficult to design and construct a test that will tap information, modes of reasoning, knowledge, and cognitive skills that are differentially available to people with different sociocultural backgrounds, and to do so in a way that clearly favors individuals of a given race, ethnic group, or social class. To cite an example, Robert L. Williams, a professor of psychology at Washington University in St. Louis, developed a test that favors black Americans, which he called the Black Intelligence Test of Cultural Homogeneity (BITCH). Since it requires knowledge of a kind that is widely shared within the black community but not elsewhere, it discriminates strongly against nonblacks. Items from a recent revision of the test (the S.O.B. test, as Williams calls it) include:

the bump (is):
a) a condition caused by a forceful blow
b) a suit
c) a car
d) a dance

running a game (means):
a) writing a bad check
b) looking at something
c) directing a contest
d) getting what one wants from another person or thing

In the Alice-in-Wonderland world of psychometrics intuitively reasonable and commonsense conceptions of intelligence have been systematically rejected in favor of definitions that reflect prevailing patterns of social success. This has led in turn to the development of an effort to create so-called "culture-free" or "culture-fair" IQ tests. What this amounts to, in essence, is an attempt to devise tests composed of items that possess no detectable bias in favor of any identifiable human group. Thus, if one were to look at such a test one would fail to find any explicitly "offensive" or "loaded" items of the kind that I have lately been discussing. But what does this mean? So long as the fundamental and inescapable requirement is for an IQ test to be able to predict scholastic and social success, the development of all "new" tests (of any kind) will be constrained by the requirement that they must yield results consistent with prevailing patterns of success and hence comparable to those obtained with previously standardized IQ tests. Thus the *results* of IQ testing will continue to reflect the determinants of academic success and failure which have always been the standards upon which the "validity" of IQ tests have been based.

I do not claim to know what intelligence is. If pressed to suggest a working definition I would say that it most surely is not a unitary thing that can be reduced to a single number or adequately expressed in terms of a relative position along a one-dimensional scale. A primary fact of intelligence—and of human behavior generally—is its diversity. If by intelligence is meant that set of qualities enabling people to perceive, learn, remember, reason, and solve problems—in short, to organize their life experiences into a coherent and integrated whole—then it surely follows that people of different cultural backgrounds (and different individuals from similar backgrounds) manifest their intelligence in different ways. But having said that, it becomes clear that something other than scientific objectivity is involved in attempts to assign a numerical value to mental abilities according to a one-dimensional "intelligence scale."

Intellectual diversity is an undeniable fact of human life. Its interpretation, however, is rarely unequivocal. From its inception to the present, the mental testing movement has done little to illuminate the important psychological questions of how people think and of what intelligence has to do with what people think about. Because concepts like *mind, mentality,* and *intelligence* are complex and poorly understood, it is more than a matter of scientific interest when mental testers attribute superiority or inferiority to individuals or groups on the basis of their performance on IQ tests.

I have tried to show that it is really beside the point whether a child's IQ is determined by genetic factors or not and that the more basic questions that need to be considered are concerned with prevailing attitudes toward the fact of human diversity. When powerful segments of a society distrust and fear diversity, the task of behavior control technology becomes one of keeping all sorts of people in their "proper" place. The next chapter will examine the coalescence of two fields of psychotechnology, psychometrics and eugenics, as they were brought to bear on the regulation of large-scale European immigration to the American continent, especially in the early twentieth century.

Over a period of about one hundred years, from 1830 to 1930, millions of Europeans made the long and arduous journey to America, mostly to the United States. Historians generally divide this century-long era into two periods: the "old" (1830–1882) and the "new" (1882–1930). The history of both periods is filled with tales of unbearable hardship and poverty; of deceit and entrapment by unscrupulous shipping merchants and boarding-house agents; of ordeals suffered while crossing the ocean in cramped and vermin-infested vessels; and of exploitation in urban slums and sweatshops. It is also filled with stories of heroism and enthusiasm; of success and riches; of efforts to preserve traditional cultural values in the face of priva-tion. What is less often told is the role of sociobiological theories in justify-ing discrimination and prejudice against those who made up the majority of immigrants during the latter half of the great immigration period.

During the "old" period, the importation or immigration of aliens into the United States was essentially uncontrolled. Before 1880, approxi-mately ten million Europeans had arrived, chiefly from northern and western Europe. In that period, the United States was a largely agricul-tural and rural nation; the decline in immigration from Ireland, Germany and Scandinavia and the rise of immigration from eastern and southern Europe coincided with its transformation into a commercial and industrial power. More specifically, large numbers of Slavs, Jews, Italians, Poles, Russians, and other eastern Europeans began to arrive in the United States at precisely the time when organized labor, manufacturer's associations, corporate philanthropies, and various civic organizations were beginning to call, in unison, for greater uniformity, progress, and efficiency in the realms of social, cultural and economic affairs. Thus, at a moment when socially established interests committed to large-scale industrial develop-ment required a pool of relatively standardized workers (and consumers), the new immigrants were arriving from the less industrialized regions of Europe. Although some of them were equipped with industrial skills, the vast majority were not. Before 1882, concern over the deplorable condi-tions of steerage accommodations on transatlantic sailing ships led to the enactment of some state and federal regulations aimed at protecting the health and welfare of arriving aliens. But as the economic character of the country and the ethnic composition of the immigrants began to change, the tenor of legislation shifted away from efforts to regulate the policies of shipowners and toward efforts to control the character of their human cargoes.

The effort to restrict what came to be called, somewhat ominously, the great "tide" or "flood" of immigrants, first became the subject of federal legislation in 1875. The law passed in that year placed no numerical quotas on ethnic or national groups, but it did establish the precedent of excluding from immigration certain classes of people who were deemed to be "undesirable" aliens. Included in this category by the 1875 law were "coolies, convicts and prostitutes." Additional groups were added gradually over the years: "lunatics and idiots" in 1882, "epileptics and insane persons" in 1903; and "imbeciles and feeble-minded persons" in 1907.

As the restrictive tenor of the immigration laws became more firmly established, procedures were set up to permit the examination of arriving immigrants in order to identify and exclude those who did not meet the legally stipulated criteria. But once the new period of immigration had begun, it became apparent to those who were already in a position to make the force of their opinions felt that the traditional "open door" policy (even with the addition of a few restrictions) no longer served their interests.

Under existing federal statutes, prior to World War I, the only legally authorized criteria for exclusion were of the kind already mentioned. Yet as early as 1892, at the principal port of entry in New York harbor, the U.S. Immigration and Public Health Services had combined their efforts to produce a means of excluding and deporting a wide variety of allegedly undesirable types. The nature and intent of the screening process, or line inspection as it was called, may be inferred from the following passages in an official U.S. Public Health Service report published in 1917.

The alien after passing the scrutiny of the first medical officer passes on to the end of the line, where he is quickly inspected again by the second examiner. This examiner is known in service parlance as the "eye man." He stands at the end of the line with his back to the window and faces the approaching alien. This position affords good light, which is so essential for eye examinations. The approaching alien is scrutinized by the eye man immediately in front of whom he comes to a standstill. The officer will frequently ask a question or two so as to ascertain the condition of the immigrant's mentality. He may pick up a symptom, mental or physical, that has been overlooked by the first examiner.[1]

Immigrants who could afford the purchase of cabin-class accommodations for the transatlantic passage were not subjected to this procedure, but since the vast majority of immigrants were forced by their economic circumstances to travel in steerage, the line inspection was an exercise in social discrimination on a massive scale.

The prospective immigrant was scrutinized by the inspectors immediately after disembarking, and while, with the advent of steamships, it was possible by 1911 to cross the Atlantic Ocean in slightly less than two weeks, this did not mean that steerage conditions were drastically improved over the old wind-powered vessels. It merely meant that the immigrants who were packed into steerage were forced to endure almost unbearable living conditions for a much shorter period of time. In 1910, a commission set up by the United States Immigration Service sent an investigator to Europe with orders to return in steerage disguised as an alien immigrant.

During those twelve days in the steerage I lived in a disorder and in surroundings that offended every sense. Only the fresh breeze from the sea overcame the sickening odors. The vile language of the [crew] men, the screams of the women defending themselves, the crying of children, wretched because of their surroundings, and practically every sound that reached the ear, irritated beyond endurance. There was no sight before which the eye did not prefer to close. Everything was dirty, sticky, and disagreeable to the touch. Every impression was offensive. Worse than this was the general air of immorality. For fifteen hours each day I witnessed all around me this improper, indecent and forced mingling of men and women who were total strangers and often did not understand one word of the same language. People can not live in such surroundings and not be influenced.[2]

These were precisely the people in whose appearance and behavior the line inspectors were looking for evidence of abnormal influences.

The alien's manner of entering the line, his conversation, style of dress, any peculiarity or unusual incident in regard to him are all observed. Knowledge of racial characteristics in physique, costume and behavior are important in this primary sifting process.

Every effort is made to detect signs and symptoms of mental disease and defect. Any suggestion, no matter how trivial, that would point to abnormal mentality is sufficient cause to defer the immigrant for a thorough examination.

The following signs and symptoms occurring in immigrants at the line inspection might suggest an active or maniacal psychosis: Striking peculiarities in dress, talkativeness, witticism, facetiousness detailing, apparent shrewdness, keenness, excitement, impatience in word or manner, impudence, unruliness, flightiness, nervousness, restlessness, egotism, smiling, facial expression of mirth, laughing, eroticism, boisterous conduct, meddling with the affairs of others, and uncommon activity.

Psychoses of a depressive nature would be indicated by: Slow speech, low voice, trembling articulation, sad [facial appearance], tearful eyes, perplexity, difficulty in thinking, delayed responses, psycho motor retardation.

Alcoholism, [syphilis] and organic dementias may exhibit the following signs: Surliness, apprehensiveness, untidyness, intoxication, apparent intoxication, confusion, aimlessness, dullness, stupidity, expressionless face, tremulousness, tremor and twitching of facial muscles, [unsteady gait], stuttering and tremulous speech, great amount of calmness, jovial air, self-confident smile, talkativeness, fabrications, grandioseness, sullenness, fussiness, excessive friendliness, defective memory, misstatement of age, disorientation, difficulty in computation, pupil [eye] symptoms, and other physical signs.

Various kinds of dementia, mental deficiency or epilepsy would by suggested by: Stigmata of degeneration, facial scars, acne-form rashes, stupidity, confusion, inattention, lack of comprehension, facial expression of earnestness or preoccupation, inability to add simple digits, general untidiness, forgetfulness, verbigeration [verbosity; meaningless chatter], neologisms, talking to one's self, incoherent talk, impulsive or stereotyped actions, constrained bearing, suspicious attitude, refusing to be examined, objecting to have eyelids turned, nonresponse to questions, evidences of negativism, silly laughing, hallucinating, awkward manner, biting nails, unnatural actions, mannerisms, and other eccentricities.[3]

Did the inspecting officers ever doubt their ability to distinguish mental and behavioral abnormalities in people who were so very different from themselves and whose language they did not understand? Evidently not, for as the report goes on to assert: "Experience enables the inspecting officer to tell at a glance the race of an alien," although an alien whose race is wrongly identified may be stopped and questioned on the grounds that he is behaving abnormally. Once the error has been cleared up, however, "the peculiar attitude of the alien in question is no longer peculiar; it is readily accounted for by racial consideration." Thus, when the appearance and behavior of an alien coincided with the inspecting officer's racial stereotype of the group to which he or she belonged, "the officer passes him on as a mentally normal person." It was only a further short step to the assertion (made in the report) that "almost every race has its own type of reaction during the line inspection," which set the stage for admitting or excluding aliens purely on the basis of their conformity or nonconformity with prevailing racial stereotypes. Thus, "if an Englishman reacts to questions in the manner of an Irishman, his lack of mental balance would be suspected. . . . If the Italian responded to questions as the Russian Finn responds, the former would in all probability be suffering with a depressive psychosis."

If, in the course of the line inspection, an examining officer suspected an alien of harboring "eccentricities" or other offensive disorders, he made a chalk mark on that person's clothing, and he was held, pending further examination, for possible deportation. However, even for the fortunate immigrant who managed to get by the first inspector and the "eye man" without receiving a chalk mark, the official scrutiny was not yet over. Although he had successfully survived the medical part of the weeding out process, he had to show he was free of any social taint through a further examination by an immigration officer, who determined whether he was "an anarchist, bigamist, pauper, criminal or otherwise unfit."

The line inspection at Ellis Island showed in microcosm a process that in the United States culminated in the restrictive immigration policies of the 1920s. In order to understand the events, it is necessary to trace the transformation in ideas about human nature and human diversity which, starting in the eighteenth century, required "scientific evidence" to demonstrate the inherent intellectual, moral, and biological inferiority of particular human groups and to thereby explain, condone, and justify their social subordination. While the new prestige of science meant that arguments were supposed to issue from carefully verified facts, the power to give names and to enforce definitions remained the power of a minority and, as such, remained a useful instrument of behavior control. Variations in the facial angle, which the Dutch anatomist Peter Camper had used as a guide to portraiture and an index of mental ability, were taken up in the name of racial science around the end of the eighteenth century by a well-known physician and surgeon named Charles White. White was a member of the prestigious Royal Society of England and had established his scientific reputation with a book on childbirth and midwifery. By his account, a desire "to investigate the truth" had inspired him to undertake a scientific study of what theologians had traditionally called the Great Chain of Being.[4]

The Great Chain of Being was the biological component within the hierarchical world view of medieval Christianity. In the eighteenth century it was a common tenet that God had created all living beings in a single stroke, had formed them "after their kind" with a firm immutability, and had endowed them with precisely the degree of "intelligence and active powers" appropriate to their rank in the overall scheme of things. It was White's intention to prove, on the basis of science, and without resort to theology, that the world of living things was hierarchically organized in exactly this way. While "The Book of Revelation," he wrote, "cannot be read as a handbook of Natural History," comparative anatomy makes it possible to bring sacred Scripture into consonance with natural facts.

As long as Scripture and Greek philosophy guided human thinking about human nature, the problem of accommodating belief was essentially a matter of speculation. But as natural science developed and the place of human beings in the hierarchy of living things became clear, new forms of accommodation had to be devised. It was plainly impossible to doubt that human beings differed among themselves. Thus, if all creation was one vast hierarchy linking humanity to the animals, and if human beings differed among themselves, would it not appear to follow that different individuals or classes of individuals were naturally intended to occupy different ranks or stations in the hierarchy? To White, the answer seemed inescapable. Furthermore, he reasoned, if human beings are natural creatures, an analysis of their physiognomic, anatomical, and behavioral traits ought to provide the evidence needed to determine who ranked where.

Accordingly, when he came in his text to consider the question of human diversity, White said that he had decided to devote his attention "chiefly to the extremes: . . . to the European [and] to the African who seems to approach nearer to the brute creation than any other of the human species." "If I could prove," he went on, "a specific distinction betwixt these two, the intermediate gradations would be more easily allowed." Thus, in a manner reminiscent of Aristotle's defense of slavery, White started out by assuming as a basis for his argument what the argument was intended to prove.

The key to White's system of gradation was its roots in aesthetics and its reliance upon the facial angle, which he took to be a direct index of mental capacity. White owed the use of this measurement to Dr. John Hunter, a prominent English surgeon who had been influenced by Camper and who had a collection of animal and human skulls displayed around the borders of a pool in his private museum. On a visit to Hunter's museum, White had noticed that skulls identified as belonging to an African, an American Indian, an Asiatic, and a European had increasingly larger facial angles. Thus, without any apparent knowledge of the aesthetic criteria by which Camper had arrived at his sequence, and without any resort to ancient authority or "vulgar" opinion, White proceeded to match facial angle data with comparative statements about the behavior and mental capacity of different human groups. One of his sources for such comparisons was Thomas Jefferson, whose views on the inherent inferiority of Africans were well known at the time.

Measurements of facial angle were not White's sole interest, however. He reported, and later measurements would subsequently confirm, that Africans have coarser and larger-caliber hair than Europeans. The fact that the caliber of hair taken from African apes was closer in diameter to that of blacks than of whites led White to the familiar conclusion that blacks were "closer to the apes." What this is intended to mean, of course, is that blacks are, on the average, "behind" or "below" whites in terms of their biological, intellectual, and moral development.

It is worth noting, in connection with this argument, that it is not necessary to employ explicitly perjorative stereotypes as a means of formulating questions about superior and inferior classes of human beings. All that is required is a system of measurement and an uncritical acceptance of the concept of biological hierarchy. The choice of what to measure can be more crucial than the results of the measurements themselves, a factor that is often neglected in evaluating the meaning of measurements. Although the entire notion of "closer to the apes" is scientifically meaningless, let us assume, for purposes of illustration, that a scientist wished to make measurements of Europeans, Africans, and various apes and that hair was one factor (or variable) chosen for comparison. Let us assume, further, that the chimpanzee and the gorilla were the great apes chosen for the purpose of making the comparison to humans. Now, by the criterion of hair caliber, and in accordance with the meaning of closeness or similarity, it is stating neither more nor less than the facts to say that "blacks are closer to the apes." But suppose the scientist had chosen the location or amount of body hair as the dimension to be measured. As it turns out, Africans usually have bodies only sparsely covered with hair, while many Europeans have extremely hairy bodies. Thus by this measure and by virtue of the same criteria, Europeans are clearly "closer to the apes."

This is not an isolated example of the kind of bias that is characteristically involved in the choice of things to be measured. The measurements themselves may be as "objective" as you please and may have greater or lesser precision, but they often tell us less about the question being asked than about the preconceptions of the investigator. Thus the familiar stereotype of the "apelike African" tells us more about the psychological effect of prejudice upon perception than it does about the biological foundations of human diversity.

White himself categorically denied any animosity toward blacks and explicitly rejected the use of his findings to defend the slave trade. In his view, he had put absolutely nothing in his book that might "be construed so as to give the smallest countenance to the pernicious practice of enslaving mankind." Nevertheless, it is pertinent to note that physicians like White continued to play a leading role in the articulation of the theme of innate black inferiority. Unlike White, many American physicians made free use of it as a justification for slavery and became adept at identifying the behavioral and biological attributes of blacks as signs of derangement, disorder, and disease.

In 1850, for example, Dr. Samuel A. Cartwright, a respected physician who had practiced medicine for many years in and around New Orleans, was appointed by the Louisiana Medical Association to head a committee to investigate and report upon "the diseases and physical peculiarities of the negro race."At the convention of the association in March of the following year, Cartwright delivered his report, which subsequently appeared as a lead article in the *New Orleans Medical and Surgical Journal.*[5] It begins by claiming that the biological and medical status of blacks "has not been made the subject of much scientific investigation, and is almost entirely unnoticed in medical books and schools." Cartwright proposed to remedy this lack with an ingenious psychobiological theory in which the "defective . . . atmospherization of the blood, conjoined with a deficiency of cerebral matter in the cranium," was put forward as "the true cause of that debasement of mind, which has rendered the people of Africa unable to take care of themselves."

During the first half of the nineteenth century, medicine in general was much concerned with ideas about "good blood" and "bad blood," and according to a widely prevalent theory of disease many pathological conditions were due to imperfect purification of the blood caused by inadequate functioning of the lungs. Both physical and mental vigor were thought to depend upon proper "vitalization" of the blood, a condition, according to Cartwright, that blacks could achieve only under forced physical labor, since otherwise they would indulge their natural penchant for idleness: "It is the red, vital blood, sent to the brain, that liberates their mind when under the white man's control; and it is the want of . . . red, vital blood, that chains their mind to ignorance and barbarism, when in freedom." Thus, by a remarkable transformation, freedom and human dignity for blacks was asserted to be inconsistent with the laws of brain physiology, whereas slavery was shown to unchain the mind from ignorance, superstition, and barbarism. Attacking the "false dogma" of the abolitionists that "all mankind possess the same mental, physiological and anatomical organization," Cartwright concluded by claiming to have demonstrated

. . . that there is a radical, internal, or physical difference between the two races, so great in kind as to make what is wholesome and beneficial for the white man . . . not only unsuitable to the negro race, but actually poisonous to its happiness.

By taking a positive, rather than a merely palliative, view of slavery, Cartwright had no need to shrink from pointing out its economic benefits, since "the three million bales of cotton made by negro labor, afford a cheap clothing for the civilized world. The laboring classes of all mankind, having less to pay for clothing, have more money to spend in educating their children, and in intellectual, moral and religious progress."

Cartwright's theories about the physiological basis of black inferiority had no immediate application, but when several decades later "the laboring classes of all mankind" began to pour into the United States, theories of this kind became the basis for procedures designed to exclude "undesirables." The nineteenth century came to a close in a climate of public opinion in which knowledge of biological diversity was expected to inform rational efforts to solve social problems, and in which subordinate human groups were increasingly subjected to the kinds of measurements that would make them easier to manage and control. At the same time, the growth in the diversity of arriving immigrants led to a rising clamor for some form of immigrant "quality control" on the part of many well-entrenched economic interests.

Although many of the demands for "quality control" called upon the Public Health and Immigration services to tighten their procedures for detecting mentally unbalanced aliens, the focus upon economic expansion stimulated an effort to make sure that arriving immigrants were intelligent enough to follow written and spoken orders.

By this time, the IQ test had been introduced into the United States, along with the claim that it provided a direct assessment of innate intelligence. The Public Health Service was under mounting pressure to tighten its procedures for excluding "undesirable" aliens, and in 1912 it invited Henry Goddard to Ellis Island to administer the Binet test and other mental tests to arriving immigrants. Goddard was happy to lend his expert services to the nation, and after administering his tests to "the great mass of average immigrants" he reported that 83 percent of the Jews, 80 percent of the Hungarians, 79 percent of the Italians, and 87 percent of the Russians seeking entry into the United States were "feebleminded."[6]

These findings, in the guise of "scientific facts," were sure to produce grave concern in the minds of thoughtful citizens, especially in a time when there was already strong public apprehension over the menace of feeblemindedness. Amid growing antipathy toward "the new and exotic ethnic breeds," Goddard was able to report proudly that "the number of aliens deported because of febble-mindedness ... increased approximately 350 percent in 1913 and 570 percent in 1914." This increase was owing, he said, "to the untiring efforts [on the part of Public Health Service Inspectors] inspired by the belief that mental tests could be used for the detection of feeble-minded aliens."[7]

This innovation received predictably enthusiastic support from foundation-sponsored eugenics organizations, such as the Eugenics Research Association, but the year was 1917, and there were larger historical forces at work. In February, the United States broke off diplomatic relations with Germany, and on April 6 it entered the First World War. The immigration issue receded as the mental testers turned their attention to the problem of wartime mobilization and the mass mental testing of military draftees. Their efforts in screening recruits did not have a great influence upon the placement of men, and surely did not significantly affect the outcome of the war. However, more than 1.7 million men were given mental tests for purposes of classification, and the results were widely publicized after the war. When the enormous amount of IQ test data generated by the classification process was statistically analyzed in terms of racial, ethnic, and national background, profound inferences for public policy were drawn in the areas of assimilation and immigration.

The president of the American Psychological Association (APA) when the United States entered the war was Robert M. Yerkes, professor of psychology at Harvard University. An early proponent of mental testing as a means of fitting people into their "proper place" in society Professor Yerkes had developed his own version of the Binet test. His views on the heritability of IQ were similar to those of Terman and Goddard, and his convictions about the biological determinism of mental traits had led to an active enlistment in the cause of eugenics. Yerkes had earlier been a member of the Committee on Eugenics of the National Commission on Prisons, and in the year that he served as president of the APA he also assumed the chairmanship of the Committee on the Inheritance of Mental Traits of the Eugenics Research Association.

The task of providing mental assessments that would aid in the assignment of draftees to suitable military jobs was planned by a committee of psychologists which included Terman, Goddard, and Yerkes. Under their guidance, two group intelligence tests were rapidly devised which could be easily administered to large numbers of men in a single session. The first, or *Alpha*, test involved written instructions, while the second, called *Beta*, intended for illiterate and non-English-speaking draftees, had instructions in pantomime. However, both *Alpha* and *Beta* were composed of items based on the stock educational materials of early twentieth-century American schooling: the euphemisms, homilies, and morals of *Poor Richard's Almanac*, Noah Webster's *Speller*, and *McGuffey's Readers*.[8] At a time when a large proportion of the draftees were either uneducated or born in a foreign country, such test items represented social discrimination of massive dimensions. Small wonder, therefore, that when the results were analyzed in detail after the war they showed a decisive bias in favor of native, English-speaking, white Americans.

The results of the Army tests were published in 1921, by the National Academy of Sciences under the editorship of Colonel Yerkes. The chapter entitled "Relation of Intelligence Ratings to Nativity" ranked draftees' "intelligence ratings," expressed in letter grades from A to E, according to countries of origin. For those who received a rating of D, for example, the percentage of draftees of English origin was lowest and of Polish highest. The results implied that immigrants from foreign countries could be ranked in descending order of intelligence, and they were interpreted accordingly. Table 2 illustrates how the data were presented in a textbook published in 1941.

Colonel Yerkes did not hesitate to draw the obvious conclusion that "in general, the Scandinavian and English speaking countries stand high on the list, while the Slavic and Latin countries are low...,"[9] and publication of the test results added to the postwar clamor for a more restrictive immigration policy. In 1917, Congress had taken a first step toward bringing immigration policy into line with modern mental science by adding "persons of constitutional psychopathic inferiority" to the list of those to be excluded. In 1921, when Yerkes's report appeared, a numerical restriction on immigration became law. It was the first such action ever taken by the American government; it was neither the last nor the most lasting.

Certain segments of the business community in the postwar period favored a "sliding-door" immigration policy which would regulate the availability of foreign labor in accordance with fluctuating market needs. This was the position taken by the National Association of Manufacturers and various chambers of commerce, which at the time were primarily devoted to the interests of small manufacturing and commercial enterprises. Most larger manufacturers and labor organizations favored a more restrictive policy. The National Civic Federation, for example, which numbered both Andrew Carnegie, the steelmaker, and Samuel Gompers, the labor leader, among its members, was committed to protecting the pre-

Table 2
National-racial differences in intelligence

Country of Birth	Number of Men	Mean Intelligence Score*
England	411	14.87
Scotland	146	14.34
Holland	140	14.32
Germany	308	13.88
Denmark	325	13.69
Canada	972	13.66
Sweden	691	13.30
Norway	611	12.98
Belgium	129	12.79
Ireland	658	12.32
Austria	301	12.27
Turkey	423	12.02
Greece	572	11.90
Russia	2,340	11.34
Italy	4,009	11.01
Poland	382	10.74

*Numbers represent combined-scale scores made up of various measures. The maximum possible score was 25.
Source: H. E. Garrett, *Great Experiments in Psychology*, rev. ed. (New York: Appleton-Century-Crofts, 1941), p. 50.

vailing structure of wealth and power. The leaders of major corporations and labor unions felt that their mutual interests would best be served by social policies that eliminated competition while serving "as a counterpoise to the threat of working class revolution."[10] Not surprisingly, corporate philanthropies were inclined to adopt the same view of foreign labor. As Edward A. Filene, a Boston merchant, pioneer in modern business management, and founder of the Cooperative League, the predecessor to the Twentieth Century Fund, pointed out,

Employers do not need an increased labor supply, since increased use of labor-saving machinery and elimination of waste in production and distribution will for many years reduce costs more rapidly than wages increase, and so prevent undue domination of labor.[11]

The force of the foundations, fueled by corporate wealth, was only part of the power that was brought to bear against the tide of immigration. It cannot be called a conspiracy, but there was at least a broad consensus in many quarters, to which President Coolidge was giving voice when he proclaimed that "America must be kept American." In the 1920s America was the land of the "red scare," the Ku Klux Klan, the Sacco and Vanzetti case, the Palmer Raids, and the Scopes Trial. The open door, which had offered the chance of a new life to millions of immigrants, was closing, as Congress began to fashion a new immigration law, and the mental testing movement finally came into its own.

During the early twenties, the immigration issue provided a rallying point of the kind that brings occasional encouragement to those who entertain conspiracy theories of history; a coming together—in this case—of scholars and politicans mutually committed to a single goal: the amelioration of social problems and the advancement of national destiny by means of scientific analysis and enlightened legislation. The nature of the new alliance is illustrated by the appointment in 1920 of the biologist Harry Laughlin, long-time secretary of the Eugenics Research Association and editor of *Eugenical News*, as "expert eugenics agent" of the House Committee on Immigration and Naturalization of the U.S. Congress, followed in 1923 by the election of the Immigration Committee's chairman, Albert Johnson, to the chairmanship of the Eugenics Research Association. Implicit in this congenial reciprocity was the desire (shared by many leading scientists and politicians) to achieve an efficient and expedient resolution of immigration issues, a resolution that was to be reached (or at least made to seem as if it had been reached) in accord with the best available scientific evidence, and without regard for partisan political considerations.

The scientists and politicans were ostensibly drawn together by their shared belief in scientific and social progress, and by their common desire to see scientific expertise inform legislative decision making on questions of grave moment to the future of the nation. But below the surface—and by unspoken agreement never mentioned in official discourse—lay a shared vision of the kind of immigration policy that was most desirable for the future of the state.

The substance of this vision was selective exclusion based upon the eugenic ideal of "racial purification." Had not the army intelligence test results shown that immigrants from northern and western Europe were mentally superior to those from southern and eastern regions? Was it not a fact that approximately 70 percent of the total postwar immigration came from nations whose inhabitants were tainted with inferior germ plasm?

To the advocates of racial purification, an impediment to decisive legislative action was the politically sensitive nature of the subject. Neither the populists nor the urban ethnic populations were easily managed, and the threat of serious civil strife loomed. What was needed was a means of defusing the issue, of removing serious discussion of the immigration question from the charged atmosphere of the political arena and placing it on the firm foundation of ostensibly objective scientific inquiry.[12] Having a scientist serve as an expert adviser to Congress while a congressman served as chairman of the eugenics society set the stage for one of the solutions that was finally arrived at: the initiation of federal support of relevant scientific research.

The National Research Council established, within its Division of

Anthropology and Psychology, a committee on Scientific Problems of Human Migration. The chairman of the committee was Robert Yerkes. The recipient of the committee's first research grant was Carl Brigham, then an assistant professor of psychology at Princeton University. In 1923, Brigham had published a book called *A Study of American Intelligence* in which he reanalyzed the Army test results on immigrant intelligence. It included a foreword by Yerkes, praising Brigham for having "rendered a notable service" to the moral and economic well-being of the nation by presenting "not theories or opinions, but facts." As Leon Kamin points out in his incisive critique of the early mental testing movement, Brigham's book was something of a landmark, and "though it has disappeared from contemporary reference lists, it can be argued that few works in the history of psychology have had so significant an impact."[3]

Brigham's analysis of the Army test data began with the fact that the performance of American Negro draftees was significantly poorer than that of whites. It further showed that 46 percent of Polish, 42 percent of Italian, and 39 percent of Russian immigrant draftees scored at or below the Negro average. As Goddard had done earlier, Brigham drew from the data some dire implications for immigration policy. However, he had first to deal with what he called a "very remarkable fact," namely, that when the scores of immigrants from all countries were categorized according to the number of years of residence in America before being tested, the average IQ was found to increase in proportion to the duration of residence. Indeed, immigrants who had lived in the United States twenty or more years prior to being drafted had scores that were, on the average equal to those of native-born Americans, while those who had spent fewer than five years in this country either had very low scores or were measured as feebleminded. One would think that the correlation between residency time and IQ pointed to a cultural bias in the tests that favored people who had grown up amid American customs and language. That, however, was not Brigham's conclusion.

Brigham understood that if increases in IQ scores were actually the result of increased duration of residency in the United States, the testers would have to abandon their basic claim that IQ was an index of intelligence. He faced the dilemma in a most ingenious way, by "explaining" the effect of residency while preserving the central dogma that IQ was an index of innate intelligence. "We are forced to . . . accept the hypothesis," he wrote, that there was "a general deterioration in the class of immigrants . . . who came to this country in each succeeding five year period since 1902." Here is Brigham's explanation—"the race hypothesis." As Kamin describes it, Brigham

. . . proceeded to estimate "the proportion of Nordic, Alpine and Mediterranean blood in each of the European countries" and to calculate the numbers of immigrants arriving from each country during each time period. These combined operations produced a sequential picture of the blood composition of the immigrant stream over time. There was thereby unearthed a remarkable parallelism: as the proportion of Nordic blood had decreased, and the proportions of Alpine and Mediterranean blood increased, the intelligence of the immigrants was deduced to have decreased.[14]

In this way, Brigham was able to conclude that "our test results indicate a genuine intellectual superiority of the Nordic group." Based on this conclusion he issued some stern eugenic admonitions, such as that "we must face a possibility of racial admixture here that is definitely worse than that faced by any European country today, for we are incorporating the negro into our racial stock, while all of Europe is comparatively free from this taint. . . . ." Nevertheless,

The steps that should be taken to preserve or increase our present intellectual capacity must of course be dictated by science and not by political expediency. Immigration should not only be restrictive but highly selective. And the revision of the immigration and naturalization laws will only afford a slight relief from our present difficulty. The really important steps are those looking toward the prevention of the continued propagation of defective strains in the present population. If all immigration were stopped now, the decline of American intelligence would still be inevitable. This is the problem which must be met, and our manner of meeting it will determine the future course of our national life.[15]

Brigham's warnings about the "decline of American intelligence" by placing the popular horror of "racial taint" on an ostensibly objective scientific basis, won him not only public prestige as a defender of restrictive immigration laws but also the approbation of his professional colleagues. He found a particularly fertile ground for his sociobiological ideas in the field of higher education. As secretary of the College Entrance Examination Board, he developed the Scholastic Aptitude Test, which is still used to screen students for admission to college, and in the late twenties he was elected secretary of the American Psychological Association.[16]

At the time that Brigham's book was published, approximately 70 percent of the total immigration into the United States came from Alpine and Mediterranean regions. When Congress began work in 1923 on what was to become the Johnson-Lodge Immigration Act of 1924, the findings of the IQ testers emerged as a crucial source of support for the selective exclusion of aliens from certain countries.

The House Committee on Immigration, under the chairmanship of Congressman Johnson, began its deliberations in an atmosphere of some urgency. On January 24, 1923, it was told by one witness that "we have been overrun with a horde of the unfit." That witness was Dr. Arthur Sweeney, who went on to say in his prepared text on "Mental Tests for Immigrants":

The fact that the immigrants are illiterate or unable to understand the English language is not an obstacle. . . . "Beta" . . . is entirely objective. . . We . . . strenuously object to immigration from Italy . . . Russia . . . Poland . . . Greece . . . Turkey. The Slavic and Latin countries show a marked contrast in intelligence with the western and northern European group . . . we shall degenerate to the level of the Slav and Latin races. . . .[17]

Francis Kinnicutt, testifying on behalf of the Immigration Restriction League before the Senate Committee on Immigration, February 20, 1923, introduced a note of anti-Semitism into the record. He argued not only that the immigrants from southern and eastern Europe were "of a very low degree of intelligence" but also that "a large proportion of this immigration . . . consists . . . of the Hebrew elements . . . engaged in the garment-making industry." That these people were of low intelligence was only part of the problem, according to Kinnicutt; he observed that they were more generally a threat to society because "some of their labor unions are among the most radical in the whole country."[18]

There was disagreement among the mental testers about the alleged intellectual inferiority of Jews. Lewis Terman apparently excluded them from the class of "degenerate" immigrants. Addressing the National Education Association at Oakland, California, in July 1923, as president of the American Psychological Association, Terman said his research, which had been supported by the Commonwealth Fund, had shown that "the racial stocks most prolific of gifted children are those from northern and western Europe, and the Jewish. The less prolific are the Mediterranean races, the Mexicans and the Negroes."[19] Professor Brigham was not so sure that Jews were properly numbered among the gifted:

We have no separate intelligence distributions for the Jews. . . . Our army sample of immigrants from Russia is at least one half Jewish. . . . Our figures, then, would rather tend to disprove the popular belief that the Jew is intelligent. . . . He has the head, form, stature, and color of his Slavic neighbors. He is an Alpine Slav.[20]

The "scientific" partitioning of immigrants was, from the beginning, a smokescreen to obscure deeper attitudes of social prejudice. The testimony of the chairman of the Allied Patriotic Societies of New York before Congressman Johnson's Committee on Immigration and Naturalization in January 1924 shows how profoundly useful the findings of the mental testers were to those who most wanted to keep America American:

. . . the bulk of the "newer" immigration is made up of Italians, Hebrews, and Slavs. During the war, . . . intelligence tests made by our army . . . threw considerable light on the mental qualities of the "newer" (immigrants). . . . The results . . . have been analyzed . . . particularly in the work of Prof. Carl Brigham of Princeton. . . . Professor Brigham figures out, moreover, that as many as 2,000,000 persons have been admitted . . . whose intelligence was nearer the intelligence of the average negro . . . than to the average intelligence of the American white.[21]

A few days later Congressman Johnson received and placed into the records of his committee's deliberations a report prepared by the Committee on Selective Immigration of the Eugenics Committee of the United States of America. The principal signatory of the report was Madison Grant, who in 1916 had published *The Passing of the Great Race*, a treatise on Nordic superiority. He was also a founder of the Galton Society, a group set up in 1918, as *Eugenical News* had reported, by some self-selected "students of man," and whose charter provided for the election of up to twenty-five "native Americans who are anthropologically, socially and politically sound," as Grant described them in a letter.[22] It is hardly surprising, therefore, that the report prepared by Grant's "committee on selective immigration" mirrored the eugenical perspective of the Galton Society's namesake and stressed the importance of the mental testers' findings, pointing out that "the questions . . . were selected with a view to measuring innate ability. . . . Had mental tests been in operation [previously] . . . over 6,000,000 aliens now living in this country . . . would never have been admitted. . . ."[23]

Among those who served on Grant's committee were Edward L. Thorndike, professor of psychology at Columbia University, and the most influential shaper of American elementary school education during the first half of this century, and Harry Laughlin, the peripatetic "expert eugenics agent." On March 8, 1924, as Representative Johnson's committee was nearing the end of its extended series of hearings, Dr. Laughlin was invited to present a lecture in which he summarized his researches on the "natural qualities of immigrants." There are, he stated, some inherent qualities that are naturally desirable, which those of "American stock especially prized." These include truth loving, inventiveness, industriousness, common sense, artistic sense, love of beauty, responsibility, social instinct, and the natural sense of a square deal. "Of course," he added, "all of these elements are of a biological order."

Although Laughlin was unable to provide scientific measurements of these qualities, he was pleased to advise the committee that measurements of "naked natural intelligence" had been documented with precision. In this connection, Professor Brigham's charts of immigrant intelligence and the statistical tables provided by the National Academy of Sciences were introduced to show that the country had among its foreign-born white population more than six million men with a mental age below 9.5 years (an IQ below 70). These foreigners, supposedly mentally and morally as well as economically inferior, were "untrainable socially or economically." Their "cost of supervision," said Laughlin, was "greater than value of labor." They were "slow in adaptability; supervision needed," and the country would obviously be much better off if others like them were excluded.[24]

The Johnson-Lodge Immigration Act of 1924 which grew out of the congressional hearings reflected the input of the mental testing and eugenics movements and accorded with the broader spirit of "Americanism" prevailing in the nation at that time. Previously, in 1921, a law had been enacted on a temporary basis embodying the principle of "national origin quotas," under which the number of aliens admitted yearly from a given country was limited to 3 percent of the number of immigrants from that country already residing in the United States, as determined by the census of 1910. The Johnson-Lodge Act established national origin quotas as a permanent aspect of immigration policy and reduced the quota to 2 percent. But even more important, its quotas were based on the census figures for 1890. The use of the 1890 census (rather than 1920 data) had only one purpose, acknowledged by the bill's supporters: the "new immigration" had begun after 1890, and the law was designed to exclude the "biologically inferior" people of southeastern Europe.

The Johnson-Lodge Immigration Law was intended to promote the racial purification process and to make the country safe from what Yerkes had called "the menace of race deterioration." Less than a decade later, when these Slavic, Alpine, Mediterranean, and Semitic "undesirables" became the prime targets of the Third Reich's eugenic policies, great numbers of them sought to escape incarceration or extermination by fleeing to the United States. They were denied admission to this country on the grounds that their national quotas were filled. The mental testers thus indirectly helped to seal the fate of millions who were the victims of Nazi genocide.

What moral can we draw from this melancholy history? The great immigration debate is over, and the victims of Nazi genocide are dead. There are today few mental testers who believe in the innate mental inferiority of Russians, Poles, Jews, Italians, and other ethnic groups of European origin, but there are many who still subscribe to the myth of mental mettle and at least a few who think that the systematic extermination of certain classes of people is an acceptable solution to "the problem of dysgenics." In other words, there are still domestic problems of a kind resembling the immigration problem. And there are still theorists (including mental testers and eugenicists) who claim that contemporary social problems have a biological source in the innate mental inferiority of the lower classes of our society.

Many ostensibly scientific versions of biological determinism have been thoroughly debunked. In the case of IQ, the evidence for high genetic heritability and for differences between various human groups has even been intentionally "cooked," faked, or otherwise grossly biased. Yet contentions that human behavior is biologically determined continue to receive wide currency and a respectable hearing. Is that because of the primordial weakness of the human mind, or because of the established power of social organizations?

5   **Genocide:
The Apotheosis of
Behavior Control**

Rudolph Virchow (1821–1902) was the type of physician who made German scientific medicine respected and renowned throughout the world during the last half of the nineteenth century. Although he was best known as the founder of cellular pathology, he contributed widely to many branches of medicine and helped to place modern medical practice on a firm scientific footing. He was also active in political affairs, and as a leader of the liberal Progressive party, he served in the Prussian legislature and later in the Reichstag.

The task of medicine, for Virchow, was to specify the obstacles which stand in the way of the normal fulfillment of the life processes and bring about their elimination. He placed great faith in the power of medical science as a source of solutions to social problems. Like many of his profession, he felt that physicians who were armed with scientific principles and techniques capable of treating the suffering of individuals were obliged to apply their knowledge and skills to the life of the community as a whole. As shaped by Virchow and other like-minded reformers, late nineteenth- and early twentieth-century German medicine was devoted to the ideal of socially responsible health care and to transforming this ideal into a national reality. Toward that end, various reforms were instituted in medical education, health-care delivery, and the application of medical concepts and methods to broad social problem areas. It is the last of these topics that mainly concerns me here, but a few words must be said about the other two.

From about 1870 until the outbreak of the First World War, the German system of medical education commanded worldwide admiration. Its preeminence was freely admitted in the United States, for example, and many aspiring physicians traveled from America to study there. They returned with glowing reports of dedicated teachers, stimulating instruction, and an innovative spirit of scientific progress. The generally high quality of German medical education was due, in part, to a system of uniform standards that were set and monitored by the government. The Reich Ministry of the Interior, for example, controlled various aspects of the curriculum of instruction that was followed in each of the country's twenty-four medical faculties.

However, the establishment of high educational standards was only one aspect of government involvement in German medical schools. The state also controlled faculty employment and in this way was able to restrict the numbers of socialists, Jews, and other politically or ethnically "undesirable" elements who were allowed to work as physicians and medical-school teachers. State control of elementary school education and university entrance examinations constituted another mechanism for restricting the admission of students to medical schools. The criteria actually employed for this purpose tended to exclude virtually all medical-school applicants who were not from the more prosperous and "reliable" classes of the population.[1]

The rapid transformation of Germany from an essentially agrarian society to a modern industrial state after political unification in 1870 had by the 1880s led to some of the same social problems facing other economically advanced nations. Germany's political leader, Bismarck, took the lead in securing passage of social legislation. He did so not out of sympathy for the plight of the German masses but rather because he considered a paternalistic system of social controls to be the most effective way of discouraging social unrest among the working classes. One such piece of legislation, enacted by the Reichstag in 1883, was a Sickness Insurance Law intended to extend the availability of medical service and make the delivery of health care more efficient. While liberal reformers like Virchow had sought this socialization of medicine out of a desire to improve the quality of life in German society, the more reactionary elements among the German ruling classes generally rejected reforms in favor of a policy of brutal suppression. Bismarck's solution was to create the appearance of reform while insuring that the levers of social control remained in the hands of the elite. As one writer put it, he was "trying to take the wind out of the sails of the Socialist propaganda and weaning away the masses from their rebel leaders to their fatherly ruler and protector."[2]

The idea that it might profit German employers to protect the health of their employees was not new. As early as 1813, the armaments firm of Alfred Krupp had set up a system of sickness insurance. The law of 1883, rather than bringing health insurance under direct government control, left already established private insurance companies as the sole agents for managing the health care plan. As the pace of industrialization quickened, and the rolls of the medical insurance programs swelled, the quality of health care declined, and many physicians were alarmed to find the prestige and power of their profession declining as well. Bismarck's original plan for placating the proletariat had forced the majority of the populace to become dependent upon private insurance companies. The physicians, too, having been reduced to mere employees of these companies, became more and more "proletarianized." Well before World War I, discontent with the medical insurance program was already widespread among physicians, and in 1922 when a severe economic crisis developed, many doctors, already disillusioned with their social role, were alarmed to find themselves in dire financial straits.

Thus, by the end of the Weimar period, the German medical profession was deeply alienated from the Social Democratic regime and its policies. Impatient with the bureaucratic inefficiency of the insurance companies and angry at the impotence and instability of the government, physicians

Genocide: The Apotheosis of Behavior Control

were to be found in increasing numbers among those Germans who trans-ferred their political allegiance to the cause of the Nazis' National Social-ism. By 1933, when the Nazis came to power, unemployment was wide-spread among physicians, whose prestige had fallen far from the inspiring image of doctors as "high priests of nature in human society."

But Virchow's vision was destined to come to life again. A supremely healthy and vigorous "master race" was the ideological touchstone of the National Socialist platform, and when Hitler came to power, his party fashioned a new identity for the German physician. It was no accident that the first maxim incorporated into the Reich Physicians Ordinance of 1935 proclaimed that "the medical profession is not a trade." The Nazi physi-cian was to be restored from the role of employee to that of sacred healer —protector and guardian of the nation's racial purity.

The promise of a revolution in the status and power of physicians con-stituted a strong inducement for them to enlist in the National Socialist cause. But the ease with which the Nazi eugenics program won the sup-port of the medical community cannot be understood on this basis alone. The vision of a healthy German *Volk*, preserved and strengthened by medical knowledge and skill, was not a Nazi invention. Racial hygiene *(Rassenhygiene)* was already a well-established field in Germany, and the concept of racial purification possessed great symbolic potency within the most respected and influential social classes throughout the Weimar period. Proposals for the large-scale control of the German population through the regulation of reproductive activities were publicly discussed and had been seriously entertained in both medical and governmental circles for more than a quarter-century before the Nazis came to power.

The Third Reich was a period in which organized mass violence, on a scale unequaled in modern history, was aimed at millions deemed in the light of Nazi sociobiology to be politically, racially, ethnically, and eco-nomically inferior human beings. The most numerous and most relent-lessly pursued victims of Nazi violence were the Jews of Europe, and in a process extending over several years, they were systematically persecuted, segregated, incarcerated, and killed. Death camps and labor camps claimed the lives of almost six million Jews—a million and a half of whom were children. In eastern Europe, where the largest mass of European Jewry was concentrated, they perished alongside other uncounted millions. As a Jew who lost many relatives to the Nazis between 1933 and 1945, it has not been easy for me to grasp the reality that "the final solution of the Jewish problem" was part of a much broader racial purification process that was intended to exterminate human beings deemed to be deviant, de-generate, diseased, disordered, or otherwise "devoid of value." Yet the monstrous reality is that the Nazi extermination program was a logical extension of sociobiological ideas and eugenics doctrines which had nothing specifically to do with Jews and which flourished widely in Germany well before the era of the Third Reich.

These ideas did not arise in a vacuum. They were rooted in concepts of biological determinism and hierarchy which I have already discussed. Moreover, the episode described in the introduction—the administrative mass killing of mental patients—was a practical exercise in racial purification for which sociobiological concepts provided a supposedly scientific justification and an explicit formulation indispensable for purposes of public indoctrination. My purpose in this chapter is to argue that sociobiological ideas of a specific kind played a doubly influential role in this process. In the first place, they provided the rationale that enabled physicians and scientists to conceive, plan, and carry out the "destruction of lives devoid of value," and secondly they helped to shape and ratify the Nazi thesis that "racial quality" is the criterion for judging the worth of individuals and nations.

Eugenics was an ideal political device for implementing the objectives of National Socialism in Germany. I have already discussed how eugenics proposals tinged with genocide were considered intellectually and politically respectable in the United States and elsewhere long before Hitler rose to power, promising to save his own foundering nation by a radical biological transformation of its corrupted elements. If we want to understand why genocide became the powerfully attractive and deadly weapon it was in the service of nazification, we must examine the web of relationships between the crisis in German medicine, the popularity of sociobiological ideas, and the prevailing atmosphere of political desperation.

The circumstances were not at all the ones that Rudolf Virchow had forseen, but with the advent of National Socialism, physicians did become "the high priests of nature" in German society. In July of 1933, within four months after Hitler assumed supreme dictatorial power, a *Law for the Prevention of Genetically Diseased Progeny* was enacted. Immediately thereafter, medical science became the principal instrument of domestic biological warfare, and physicians, assuming the ultimate power of behavior control, became full and willing partners in the identification and extermination of "unworthy" human life.

The theoretical foundations upon which the practical proposals of the German eugenicists were based can be traced back to 1859, when Charles Darwin's *Origin of Species* appeared. Like Copernicus' *Revolutions of the Celestial Orbs* more than three hundred years earlier, Darwin's book, which was an instant sensation and bestseller, introduced a new way of viewing the world and its contents, exerting a powerful influence upon socially established ideas. Like Copernican astronomy, Darwinian biology carried implications that were immediately perceived as a threat to the established social order. Yet with remarkable rapidity, it generated ideological offshoots that gave a new rationale to prevailing patterns of behavior control. In order to understand why Darwinian biology evoked two seemingly contradictory responses, it is necessary to consider each of them in turn.

The most socially threatening thing about Darwinism may be summarized in a single sentence: It provided an account of the genesis of the world that left the Creator out. It was this omission that provoked one Victorian political figure, William Gladstone, to complain that Darwin had "relieved God of the labors of creation" and caused another, Benjamin Disraeli, to ask, "What is the question now placed before society with a glib assurance the most astounding? The question is this: Is man an ape or an angel? My Lord, I am on the side of the angels." Darwin himself disowned the intention of drawing theological inferences from his theory. "I see no good reason," he wrote in the conclusion to *The Origin of Species*, "why the views given in this volume should shock the religious feelings of any one."

Nevertheless, the theory of evolution did shock the feelings of many persons, and not without good reason. In Victorian England, it was still the essence of worldly wisdom to believe that the phyla, genera, and species which comprised the Great Chain of Being were essentially disparate and although they might be grouped together in various ways for purposes of taxonomic classification, the distinctions among them were fixed immutably for all time. Hence, the only thing that they had in common was that God had created them all in a single stroke. This was what literal interpretation of Scripture required one to believe, and it was this view of the natural order that Darwin denied so convincingly:

Although much remains obscure, and will long remain obscure, I can entertain no doubt, after the most deliberate study and dispassionate judgement of which I am capable, that the view ... that each species has been independently created ... is erroneous. I am fully convinced that species are not immutable; but that those belonging to what are called the same genera are lineal descendants of some other and generally extinct species. ... Furthermore, I am convinced that Natural Selection has been the most important, but not the exclusive means of modification.[3]

In other words, Darwin's theory denied the existence of invariant categories in favor of the conception of incessant change. Thus the key to understanding Darwinism is the idea of natural selection: the process by which species and varieties of species arise and become extinct under the influence of changing material circumstances. And the key to understanding the process of natural selection is the concept Darwin referred to in the subtitle of *The Origin* as "the struggle for life." "I should premise," wrote Darwin about the term *struggle for existence* or *struggle for life*, "that I use this term in a large and metaphorical sense including dependence of one being on another, and including (which is more important) not only the life of the individual, but success in leaving progeny." What Darwin did *not* mean to imply was that the struggle for existence consists solely or even mainly of a competition *within* species for scarce resources. He was emphatic in using the metaphor more broadly, to include the struggle all species and members of species must wage to flourish in the face of inclement natural circumstances. Thus "a plant on the edge of a desert is said to struggle for life against the drought, though more properly it should be said to be dependent upon the moisture."[4] All in all, however, when confronted with the basic question of why some species and members of species survived while others became extinct, the answer was "the survival of the fittest." Another naturalist, Alfred Russell Wallace, whose views on the matter will be considered in more detail, described the process of natural selection in this way when he wrote that "by the mere weeding out of those less adapted to the actual conditions, the fittest alone would continue. . . ." In other words, since "from the effects of disease the most healthy escaped; from enemies, the strongest, the swiftest or the most cunning; from famine, the best hunters or those with the best digestion; and so on."[5]

There was, as Darwin himself concluded, "grandeur in this view of life." If its careful and detailed arguments were largely responsible for the power of the *Origin of Species* to persuade, the book's conclusion gave it also the power to shock. In place of the traditional view of the Great Chain of Being, Darwin offered a new view of nature as Becoming:

Thus, from the war of nature, from famine and death, the most exalted object which we are capable of conceiving, namely, the production of the higher animals directly follows. There is grandeur in this view of life, with its several powers, having been originally breathed by the Creator into a few forms or into one; and that, whilst this planet has gone cycling on according to the fixed law of gravity, from so simple a beginning endless forms most beautiful and most wonderful have been and are being evolved.[6]

With these words, Darwin concluded his book. And upon the implied challenge to scriptural authority, the established authorities felt obliged to act.

Perhaps it is an exaggeration to say that politicians like Gladstone and Disraeli considered it a national peril that the "Darwinians" were hacking away at the theological foundations of Victorian society, but there can be no doubt that most theologians perceived in Darwinism a singularly dangerous threat. Several centuries before, the Catholic Church had tried to impose its own view of the cosmos in the face of new discoveries. The attack on Galileo succeeded in the short run; modern science was then in its infancy. Now it suddenly appeared that science was again invading the central province of theology and was threatening to take control of defining human nature as well. It plainly seemed necessary to defeat the Darwinian heresy, and the bishops therefore undertook to defend the interests of the church as an institution.

At a notable meeting of the British Association for the Advancement of Science, held at Oxford in June 1860, the defense of the Anglican Church against the heretical doctrine of Darwinism was placed in the hands of the bishop of that city, Samuel Wilberforce. While Bishop Wilberforce was scheduled to address the meeting on the inadequacies of Darwinism, it is doubtful that he ever actually read *The Origin of Species* or had given much prior thought to the substance of Darwin's theory. Indeed, it is likely that he was chosen to lecture on the subject mainly because of his acknowledged gifts as an orator. In any event, he spent the day before the lecture being tutored on the defects of Darwinism by a celebrated anti-Darwinian anatomist named Sir Richard Owen.

Charles Darwin did not attend the meeting. Since the publication of his book, he had become something of an invalid and recluse. Amid the acrimonious debate that presently swirled around his theory, he professed to be indisposed and had retired to bed at his country house, leaving a young professor of paleontology from London the task of dealing with the bishop's remarks. The standin was Thomas Henry Huxley.

Huxley was pleased to discover that despite Owen's tutoring, Bishop Wilberforce remained impenetrably ignorant of all the substantive content of Darwin's theory. He noticed, however, that Wilberforce was an able controversialist and that he was skillfully exploiting the audience's hostility toward what the bishop called "the monkey theory." At last, flushed with a sense of triumph, he paused and, turning to Huxley, asked in mock politeness the famous question whether it was "through his grandfather or his grandmother that he claimed his descent from a monkey?"[7] Huxley's reply

was as quiet and grave as the Bishop's had been loud and jovial. He said that he was there only in the interests of science, that he had heard nothing to prejudice his client's case. Mr. Darwin's theory was much more than a hypothesis. It was the best explanation of the species yet advanced. He touched on the Bishop's obvious ignorance of the sciences involved; explained clearly and briefly, Darwin's leading ideas; and then, in tones even more grave and quiet, said that he would not be ashamed to have a monkey for his ancestor; but he would be "ashamed to be connected with a man who used great gifts to obscure the truth. . . ." Huxley had committed forensic murder with wonderful artistic simplicity, grinding orthodoxy between the facts and the supreme Victorian value of truth-telling.

The story is told that when the Bishop of Worcester returned home from the Oxford meeting, distressed at the fate that had befallen poor Wilberforce, he told his wife at tea that the horrid professor Huxley had declared that human beings were descended from the apes, to which she is said to have replied, "Descended from the apes! How awful! Let us hope that it is not true; but if it is, let us pray that it will not become generally known." Questions about the truth or falsity of propositions are not the same as questions about public knowledge or understanding. The former are always questions of meaning and may be settled more or less well by individuals using rational means; the latter are often questions of power and are sometimes settled by organizations using whatever means happen to be at their disposal. The wife of a bishop presumably understood that there are certain ideas which, if "generally known," can sorely threaten the security of established hierarchies.

That the theory of evolution through natural selection was not as revolutionary as all that may be inferred from at least two facts, one trivial and the other profound. The trivial fact is that despite the theological furor raised by the appearance of his book, Darwin soon became something of an English national hero; when he died some twenty years later, he was buried in Westminister Abbey. At the time, the intensity of the theological debate had been reduced to a level where the most heated opposition was of the kind that caused one clergyman to complain that the honor thus bestowed upon the biologist was "proof that England is no longer a Christian country."[8]

The more significant fact is that the theory of evolution rapidly became the basis of social Darwinism, a social philosophy that far from threatening to undermine the foundations of Victorian society served instead to buttress them. In other words, Darwin's theory was revolutionary only to the extent that it overthrew an earlier hypothesis about the genesis of living things; its social impact was, if anything, highly conservative. One reason for the ease with which Darwin's theory was transformed into a social philosophy of elitism is that Darwin himself never questioned (indeed, he fully embraced) the traditional theological concept of species as comprising a "great chain of Being." In Darwin's terminology this was referred to as "the taxonomic ladder," but like its predecessors its real meaning lay in the implied existence of a biological hierarchy, in which the superior organisms were at the top and the others at the bottom.

Darwin's personal commitment to this idea appears to have been fundamental and was in any case repeatedly made explicit throughout *The Origin of Species*. Its main importance for social philosophy, of course, is that the concept of a taxonomic hierarchy lends itself readily to invidious comparisons of emotional, intellectual, moral, and other behavioral characteristics between different human groups. While *The Origin of Species* hardly touches upon questions of human evolution, ideas about the alleged inferiority of various human groups appeared in Darwin's writings long before the book and its sequel, *The Descent of Man*, appeared.

By his own account, the most important event in Darwin's life as a naturalist, was the voyage he took from 1831 to 1836 on the *H.M.S.*

Beagle. He was twenty-two years old when he left and, as he later described it, owed to the voyage itself "the first real training or education" of his mind. Much later, in *The Descent of Man,* he described the impression left by his first encounter with the natives when the ship landed at Tierra del Fuego:

The astonishment which I felt on first seeing a party of Fuegians on a wild and broken shore will never be forgotten by me, for the reflection at once rushed into my mind—such were our ancestors. These men were absolutely naked and bedaubed with paint, their long hair was tangled, their mouths frothed with excitement, and their expression was wild, startled and distrustful. For my own part, I would as soon be descended [from a monkey or an ape] as from a savage who delights to torture his enemies, offers up bloody sacrifices, practices infanticide without remorse, treats his wives like slaves, knows no decency, and is haunted by the grossest superstitions.[9]

It is clear that Darwin applied to the Fuegians the moral judgment that he derived from his own social background and, by the time of his departure some three years later, he had been persuaded that the Fuegians could be transformed by the civilizing influence of their white superiors into "complete and voluntary Europeans." That is to say, he was somewhat converted from the view that the natives were innately inferior to the view that their inferiority was environmentally acquired and amenable to civilization. Neither of these views was new, nor was Darwin's opinion (expressed in a pamphlet written during his return voyage) that missionaries could and should do excellent work to change the life and habits of the "savages."

Darwin's opinions on hierarchy in nature and on a number of other points stand in remarkable contrast to the ideas of another naturalist who was, in effect, the cofounder of Darwinism. This was Alfred Russell Wallace. Unlike Darwin, who was brought up in a well-to-do academic family and attended a first-rate university, Wallace was born and raised in impoverished circumstances and never received a formal scientific education. He was, however, fascinated by the world of flora and fauna and had devised a way to support his field studies by gathering specimens from around the world and selling them to museums and collectors in England. Departing in 1848, long after Darwin had completed his voyage on the *Beagle* but still more than a decade before the *Origin of Species* appeared, Wallace wandered the globe, observing and collecting samples of exotic and previously unknown forms of life. It struck him as inconceivable that that almost infinite variety of living things he encountered had been created in a single decisive stroke, and the implications of what he saw led Wallace's thinking along paths similar to Darwin's.

Wallace had already concluded that the diversity and distribution of species was the result of some kind of evolutionary process when in February of 1858 he was taken ill with a fever on a small island between New

Guinea and Borneo. It was in the course of this illness that Wallace had been struck by the idea of the survival of the fittest, which came to him as he reflected on Malthus's theory about the factors limiting human population growth. As soon as he was sufficiently recovered, he sketched out his ideas and sent a short description to Darwin, whom he knew to be interested in evolution. Darwin was astounded by the coincidence of their ideas. He had been working on the theory for more than twenty years and was only slightly more than a year from completing the *Origin of Species.* To commemorate this coincidence, it was arranged to have short papers by Darwin and Wallace presented simultaneously to a meeting of the Linnaean Society of London in the absence of both. But in the following year, when the *Origin* appeared, Wallace's name tended to drift from view.

While their evolutionary theories developed along parallel lines, their personal attitudes toward primitive peoples were diametrically opposed. Darwin tended to keep the natives at a distance and mingled very little among them. Wallace, by contrast, lived for eight years among the inhabitants of South America, and his lasting impression of them was one of surprise, delight, and respect. According to Loren Eiseley,

Wallace reveals scarcely a trace of the racial superiority so frequently manifested in nineteenth-century scientific circles.

"The more I see of uncivilized people, the better I think of human nature" he wrote a friend in 1855, "and the essential differences between civilized and savage men seem to disappear."[10]

It may safely be presumed that Darwin would have been horrified at the idea of exchanging his life as a cultured Englishman for the life of a South American Indian villager, and it seemed both reasonable and desirable to him that the natives be induced to follow more "civilized" ways. Wallace, perhaps because he felt less biologically superior, also felt less sure of the superiority of his accustomed way of life. It is plain in any case that Wallace rejected the conception of the native as a physical and mental inferior. In an article published in 1869, he argued forcefully against the prevailing presumption that a low state of moral and intellectual development existed among so-called primitive people and specifically rejected the idea that evidence concerning the relative sizes of different brains could be used to justify European ethnocentrism, since "natural selection could only have endowed the savage with a brain a little superior to an ape, whereas he actually possesses one but very little inferior to that of the average member of our learned societies."[11] Somehow Wallace managed to hold on to the liberating idea of evolution through natural selection without falling victim to the dogmatic extremism of hierarchical theory.

As it developed Wallace and Darwin had one other thing in common in spite of the divergence in their judgments of primitive peoples. According

Genocide: The Apotheosis of Behavior Control

to Darwin's *Autobiography*, it was sometime in 1838 that *he* happened to read, "for amusement," Malthus's *On Population* and was struck by the idea that the struggle for existence, by favoring some variations over others, would lead to the formation of new species. This noteworthy coincidence, however, should not obscure the important point that both Wallace and Darwin had got the key element for the theory of natural selection not from field research but from reflection upon the implications of a work in social philosophy.

As I noted previously, the immediate shock waves unleashed by Darwinism were relatively short-lived compared to the longer-term effort to apply the theory of evolution through natural selection to human society. There were only the slightest intimations of human evolution contained within *The Origin of Species,* but its message left no doubt that Darwin fully intended not only to refute the biblical account of Genesis but also to extend the struggle for existence and the concept of biological hierachy to the realm of human existence. In Victorian England, such an extension of Darwinism to human affairs was immediately offered up as an explanation for what was already being practiced industrially, economically, internationally, and domestically, namely, the growth of the factory system, the emergence of laissez-faire capitalism, the expansion of Empire, and the maintenance of a hierarchically stratified social order. To the leading biological and social theorists of the day, the perfection of human beings by the process of evolution through natural selection provided a natural foundation for the perfection of human society through industrial, economic, and social *progress.* This is the initial phase of the modern coalescence of social and biological theory, the point at which the themes of biological determinism and biological hierarchy began to assume their present form, first as social Darwinism and, more recently, as sociobiology.

Today, when the principle of natural selection is so widely accepted as *the* explanation for the origin of species, it is easy to mistake criticism of Darwinian ideas about human nature and human society for a rejection of Darwin's major thesis that human beings are descended from some earlier group of prehominid primates. My purpose is to scrutinize the concepts of biological determinism and biological hierarchy as they were derived from evolutionary theory and to show that these concepts are ideologically biased and wholly useless in explaining the facts of human social existence in modern society. Let me begin by emphasizing that it is not my intention to repudiate evolutionary theory as such but merely to point out certain flaws and consequences inherent in social Darwinist and sociobiological efforts to reduce the analysis of human society to the status of a biological problem. Human existence is a biological fact, but the nature of human behavior in human society cannot be understood in terms of a one-dimensional sociobiological analysis. That, in any case, is my contention. The following discussion is intended to defend it.

The notion of struggle among individuals in the midst of scarcity was a familiar social doctrine long before Darwin and Wallace used it as a basis for the theory of natural selection. Indeed, "struggle for existence" was already a widely used catch phrase in Victorian society and had been employed in what is now commonly called social Darwinist discourse for more than a decade before the *Origin of Species* appeared. The arguments in its favor were developed most fully, or at least with the greatest rigor, by Herbert Spencer. To Spencer is owed the grisly conception that nature as a whole is "red in tooth and claw." His book "Social Statics" presented a detailed argument intended to show that the predations of Victorian society were merely the natural and inevitable social expression of the vast and incessant struggle for existence which all living species waged in order to survive.

Typical of Spencer's sociobiological notions is the following argument against the social legislation that was being proposed in some quarters as a means of alleviating the misery of the poor:

The poverty of the incapable, the distresses that come upon the imprudent, the starvations of the idle, and those shoulderings aside of the weak by the strong, are the decrees of a large, far-seeing benevolence. We must call those philanthropists spurious who, to prevent present misery, would entail greater misery upon future generations. All defenders of the poor law must be so classified. That rigorous necessity which, when allowed to act upon them becomes so sharp a spur to the lazy, and so strong a bridle to the random, these paupers' friends would repeal. Blind to the fact that under the natural order of things society is constantly excreting its unhealthy, imbecile, slow, vacillating, faithless members, these unthinking men advocate interference that not only stops the purifying process but even increases the vitiation.[12]

The gist of Spencer's argument was that the misery of the lower classes was coupled to certain inherent defects in their moral character and that these defects were ultimately due to their innate biological inferiority. In other words, Spencer imagined that he could see "survival of the fittest" writ large in human society as the decree of nature.

Certainly this analysis was hardly out of tune with the viewpoint of men such as Mr. G. A. Lee, the owner of a large cotton mill in which numerous children were employed from 6 A.M. to 8 P.M. daily. Although he possessed few pretensions as a sociobiologist, Mr. Lee shared Spencer's moral preconceptions, and especially his convictions about the salutary effects of adversity upon productivity and his desire to foster the virtues of diligence and efficiency among the working poor. "Nothing is more favorable to morals," Mr. Lee opined, "than habits of subordination, industry and regularity."[13]

Toward that end, Mr. Lee and other industrialists used the methods of behavior control that were most readily available. These consisted, for the most part, in paying low wages (positive reinforcement), administering occasional floggings (punishment), and assessing fines for infractions of various kinds (negative reinforcement). The first two methods hardly require explanation, but in respect to the latter it is interesting to note that in a spinning mill near Manchester children and adults were required to work fourteen hours a day in temperatures exceeding eighty degrees without being allowed to send for drinking water and were subject to penalties of a shilling or more for opening a window, having dirty hands, washing their hands, and whistling. Of course, the ultimate instrument of behavior control was the constant threat of being discharged; to put it differently, unemployment was a severe form of negative reinforcement and punishment occasionally meant starvation.

Although these and other methods of behavior control can be described (as I have described them) in the language of modern psychology, they were, of course, not very subtle. No doubt a behavioral psychologist could point out ways of making the spinners and other workers adhere to their work schedules more efficiently by using less harsh and punitive methods. Nevertheless, the example makes explicit what is otherwise invariably latent in all discussions (ancient and modern) of behavior control within hierarchically organized social institutions, namely, that in the context of a hierarchical social system, behavior control moves down and conformity moves up. Thus, all such discussions are really discussions of the power of some people (those at the top) over other people (those at the bottom). This is an aspect of the problem that is frequently overlooked amid the special pleading on behalf of a morally and ethically neutral science of behavior control.

But the control of the factory workers' behavior by means of harsh employment practices was not the only behavior control measure suggested by what purported to be a concern for the moral well-being of the poor. Spencer's argument that nature's "purifying process" should not be interfered with by misguided efforts at social legislation provided sociobiological support to those who were opposed to such things as universal public education, as in this argument, advanced by the president of England's most prestigious scientific organization, the Royal Society:

Giving education to the labouring classes of the poor . . . would in effect be found to be prejudicial to their morals and happiness; it would teach them to despise their lot in life, instead of making them good servants in agriculture and other laborious employments to which their rank in society has destined them . . . it would enable them to read seditious pamphlets . . . it would render them insolent to their superiors.[14]

Spencer's sociobiological theory thus made its appearance at a time when cut-and-dried rules of hierarchical social and economic organization generally prevailed. It provided, in effect, the stamp of biological approval to the prevailing political and economic structure of Victorian society. Although he did not appear to glimpse the fact that theories of political economy are invariably based upon theories of human nature and that notions of biological hierarchy are a fundamental ingredient in classical economic theory, one of the leading political economists of the nineteenth century, John Cairnes, aptly characterized this circular feedback network and its behavior control implications in terms of his own field:

Political Economy too often makes its appearance, especially in its approaches to the working classes, in the guise of a dogmatic code . . . a system promulgating decrees, "sanctioning" one social arrangement, "condemning" another, *requiring from men not consideration but obedience.* Now, when we take into account the sort of decrees which are ordinarily given . . . —decrees which . . . in the main amount to a handsome ratification of the existing form of society as approximately perfect—I think we shall be able to understand the repugnance, and even violent opposition, manifested toward it by people who have their own reasons for not cherishing that unbounded admiration for our present industrial arrangements which is felt by some expounders of so-called economic laws.[15]

To Cairnes it seemed "not unnatural that [political economy] should come to be regarded with suspicion, as a system possibly contrived in the interests of employers, which it is the workmen's wisdom simply to repudiate and disown." It seems to me that the doctrines of sociobiology deserve to be viewed with similar suspicion and, to the extent that they are comparably biased, it is reasonable that they too should be repudiated and disowned.

The specific form of sociobiological argument varies, depending upon the state of contemporary biological theory and the nature of the social arrangements, whether real or imagined, that the argument is intended to ratify. In Spencer's case, modern evolutionary theory did not yet exist, but the notion of "survival of the fittest" enjoyed wide popular currency. It was the key with which he sought to explain the essential biological inevitability of laissez-faire political and economic arrangements. The goal of his argument, more specifically, was to prove that the predatory characteristics manifested on all sides within Victorian society were biologically determined by the inherent nature of the human species and that therefore the predations "*must* be undergone, and the sufferings *must* be endured. . . . no reforms that men ever did broach or ever will broach, can diminish them one jot."[16]

In order to make his case Spencer began, as sociobiologists commonly do, by presenting as self-evident to any rational observer those aspects of society that the argument was in fact intended to explain. It must have been obvious to anyone who lived in England around 1850 that social reality was marked by a vast struggle for existence, resulting in great disparities in wealth, power, and living conditions between the upper and the lower classes. Spencer smuggled into the description, however, a set of assertions intended to forestall the otherwise plausible idea that some forms of social inequality were due to factors inherent in the prevailing mode of social organization and might be altered by social means. In the case of poverty, for example, the claim of biological determinism was asserted in connection with a description in which no less than eight highly charged adjectives were used to characterize the poor. The result was an image of the impoverished as wholly lacking in moral virtue and therefore as responsible for their own predicament. As I will show, when the purpose of a sociobiological argument is to justify the prevailing socioeconomic hierarchy, the paradigm often consists of what William Ryan has aptly termed "blaming the victim."[17] The terms used by Spencer in this connection—idle, weak, lazy, random, unhealthy, imbecile, slow, and faithless—were obviously intended to describe qualities inherent in the members of the lower classes, which nature (barring human "interference") would surely and benevolently "excrete" from human society. The reader of Spencer's argument was thus left to draw the inescapable inference that human beings possessing the contrasting qualities of industriousness, strength, energy, purposefulness, health, intelligence, quickness, and loyalty would naturally be found among the upper classes.

Having thus defined the problem of poverty in accordance with his own social prejudices, Spencer proceeded to introduce a trick which logicians call the fallacy of equivocation. The fallacy of equivocation entails the deliberate use of a term or a phrase in more than one sense within the same argument. Spencer equivocates in his use of the term *decree* or *law* to mean, on the one hand, a law of nature (for example, "the decrees of a large, far-seeing benevolence") and, on the other hand, a juridical or man-made law (as in "the poor law"). Since a natural law is by definition inviolable, the use of *law* in this sense has the effect of removing the discussion of social issues from the realm of human purpose to the realm of biological determinism.

Another and more interesting equivocation in Spencer's argument arises in connection with the idea of the "survival of the fittest," which, although not laid out in so many words in the passages I have quoted, is obviously the law of nature Spencer had in mind when he referred to the decree by which the natural order goes about "excreting" society's worthless members. What the reader is supposed to understand, according to Spencer, is that the people in question are not only morally but also biologically unfit to survive. By now we have a pretty good idea of what Spencer means by the first of these. But what does he mean by the latter? In order to answer this question and to show where the equivocation comes in, we must recall the way in which Wallace and Darwin used the term "survivial of the fittest."

In terms of the origin of species through natural selection, "fitness" has a very special technical meaning. Perhaps the best way to distinguish between the way Spencer uses it and the way it is properly used in a biological sense is to point out that in the latter sense it may be applied equally to a human being and to a plant. This does not mean that there are "good" and "bad" plants but only that some plants manage to survive under a given set of circumstances, while others do not. Thus the only meaning of fitness, in terms of evolutionary biology, is the ability to survive and reproduce.

There is no mystery in this definition and, although Darwin's theory had not been published at the time Spencer wrote his treatise, the concept of "survival of the fittest" had long been in use, and it continued to be used as a catch phrase long after the biological definition was made plain. If an organism is alive and living and reproducing, it is not biologically unfit, whatever else it may be. It may be recalled, in this connection, that one of Darwin's criteria of fitness for survival was "success in leaving progeny." If one wanted to apply that criterion to human beings of various social classes (as many of Spencer's sociobiological successors have), it would appear that the impoverished masses whose "unbridled breeding habits" so alarmed the Reverend Malthus are more biologically fit than almost anybody else.

One additional flaw in Spencer's thesis is worth consideration before going on to examine more recent examples of sociobiological thought. Spencer conceived himself to be a great optimist. His "progressivism" (as embodied in his advocacy of laissez-faire political economy) was based upon the idea that through the inexorable law of struggle which everywhere reigns supreme in the world, humanity is evolving toward "the greatest perfection and the most complete happiness."[18] Nature, left to itself, without human interference in the form of "world-rectifying schemes," would ensure inevitable progress by benevolently weeding out the unfit, analagous to the predator-prey relationship in the animal world, in which the task of the predator is to

weed out the sickly, the malformed, and the least fleet or powerful. . . . [Thus] all vitiation of the race through the multiplication of its inferior samples is prevented; and the maintenance of a constitution completely adapted to surrounding conditions and therefore most productive of happiness is ensured.[19]

What can "happiness" mean in this context? It cannot refer to the experience of individual members of a species because, as the process of Darwinian natural selection weeds out the prey less adept at fleeing, it also produces a race of more efficient hunters. The notion of perfectability fails because the predatory life is one in which the *relative* degree of insecurity remains unchanged. Like most forms of sociobiological reasoning, Spencer's argument is based on an analogy between the animal world and human society whose premises do not justify its conclusions. But for the apostles of laissez-faire economic competition, the appeal of social Darwinism transcended questions of logic. For men like Andrew Carnegie and John D. Rockefeller, evolution was either a substitute for theology (Carnegie) or the working out of God's law in the affairs of men. Thus, for Rockefeller, the small businesses he trampled in his rise to power were succumbing not to human greed and power but to natural law and social inevitability.[20]"

During the half-century after Spencer's *Social Statics* appeared, and especially after the advent of evolutionary theory and the establishment of modern genetics, theories of biological determinism appeared in numerous new versions, although the basic theme remained essentially unchanged, and sociobiologists continued to claim conclusions on the basis of premises from which they did not follow and to invent concepts to account for contradictions that might otherwise prove fatal to their argument. Among them was Sir Francis Galton, whose concept of eugenics flourished in England and America before finding ultimate expression in Germany's Third Reich.

In Germany—as in England and the United States—there was considerable interest in eugenics before the turn of the century. Recall that German physicians and medical scientists who were becoming fed up with the bureaucratic regimentation imposed upon their activities by the large insurance trusts were looking nostalgically backward to the glories of an earlier time before the practice of medicine had become specialized and fragmented. More specifically, they wanted a return of *Ganzheitsbetrachtung*—the treatment and care of the "whole person." For the devotees of *Ganzheitsbetrachtung* within the medical profession, it was but a small and easy step to the concept that physicans ought to be deeply involved in guarding the health of the people as a whole. Eugenics, with its promise of human progress through better breeding, seemed to offer the medical community a framework for repairing its own internal fragmentation while at the same time pursuing the ideal of universal human health.[21]

An early German exponent of eugenics was a practicing physician, Dr. Alfred Ploetz, who in 1895 published a book entitled *The Excellence of Our Race and the Protection of the Weak*. It attempted to show, in a manner reminiscent of Spencer and Galton, that a misdirected humanitarianism was threatening the quality of the race by fostering the protection of its weaker members. As in the United States, the possibility of applying eugenics to questions of industrial efficiency and national destiny was quickly recognized, and in 1900 the head of Germany's largest armaments firm, Alfred Krupp, announced that the company was sponsoring an essay contest: the son and heir of the firm's founder, Friedrich Alfred

Krupp, had set aside a sum of money to be awarded to the writer who best answered the question, What does the theory of evolution teach us in regard to the internal political development and legislation of states?

While the guiding idea behind all of social Darwinism was that the theory of evolution through natural selection has important implications for human social organization, it is apparent from succeeding events that the winner of the prize was expected to go well beyond the kind of broad platitudes about "survival of the fittest" put forward by earlier theorists such as Herbert Spencer. What was required, in other words, was a social prescription, generally consistent with the teachings of evolutionary theory, and having broad applicability to problems of law and order and the conduct of civic, economic, and political affairs.

The competition drew many submissions, but for three years no award was made. Then, in 1903, it was announced that the prize had been won by Wilhelm Schallmayer, a Bavarian scholar who had been warning since 1891 of "the physical degeneration threatening civilized man," for a book with the title, *Inheritance and Selection in the Life-History of Nationalities: A Sociopolitical Study Based upon the Newer Biology*. Its appearance and reception signaled and helped to promote a shift away from the laissez-faire form of biological sociology and toward a new species of social Darwinist thought. One product of the new social biology (or sociobiology) was the idea that natural selection could not be depended upon as the basis for social progress and "perfectability." Nature, according to this view, needed to be guided and assisted by some form of *social* selection, and Schallmayer's central point was that social selection was already being promoted, in the wrong direction, by programs of social reform that aided individuals to survive who might otherwise not do so. Accordingly, Schallmayer's social prescription was for an explicit eugenics program aimed at controlling aspects of human behavior that had traditionally been excluded from official jurisdiction. His principal proposal was for the establishment of a system of premarital screening and advising (*Eheberatung*). Permission to marry was to be denied, according to one of his proposals, in cases where either member of a couple was judged by a physician to possess "undesirable" inheritable traits or diseases.

The intellectual and political climate was ripe for such proposals. In 1902, a new periodical intended to give biological shape to political questions had been founded, called the *Politisch-Anthropologische Revue* (Political Anthropological Review). Until it ceased publication in 1922, it remained a leading platform for sociobiological arguments intended to promote national consciousness on the question of racial purification. In 1904, Alfred Ploetz founded the *Archiv für Rassen und Gesellschaftsbiologie* (Archive for Racial and Social Biology), a journal that he continued to edit until 1937 and that became the chief organ of the *Rassenhygiene* (racial hygiene, or eugenics) movement in Germany. By 1905, the racial hygienists and other sociobiologists had established a eugenics organization to promote their ideas, and by 1914 they were successful in getting the Reichstag to consider the enactment of a eugenic sterilization law, although that particular attempt to gain legislative endorsement was cut short by the outbreak of World War I.

It is interesting the note that sociobiology and the eugenics movement had no wide audience in Germany before the First World War, and its supporters had apparently made no previous attempts to secure the passage of eugenic control legislation. In both respects, the contrast with the United States is startling. By 1914, not only had eugenic sterilization laws been enacted in many states, beginning with Indiana in 1907, but American eugenicists had made sufficient headway in respected academic circles to make their "science" the subject of courses at Harvard, Columbia, Cornell, Brown, Wisconsin, Northwestern, Clark, and other universities.

These developments did not go unnoticed within the German medical community. In the years since 1870, American medicine had gained considerable renown, and American physicians had achieved a reputation for applying medical skills and knowledge to the solution of social problems.

From the standpoint of sociobiologists and public officials, the defeat of Germany in World War I suggested that a biological renewal of the population would have to take place before Germany could be restored to its past glory and preeminence in domestic and international affairs. Statistical studies published after the war painted a deplorable picture of the medical and biological condition of the German people. Data on the incidence of disease, infant mortality, and disabling injuries owing to the war, coupled with severe economic conditions, created a climate favorable to the idea of moral, social, and biological renewal. From data on the differential birth rates between the upper and lower classes of the population, proponents of sociobiology and eugenics began to draw a familiar conclusion: the German *Volk* were undergoing biological degeneration.

Like their counterparts in England and America, the German eugenicists pointed with alarm to the fact that the prosperous produced fewer children than the poor, echoing Malthus, Spencer, Galton, Terman, Godddard, and Davenport in the arguments they advanced:

... the socially better off, superior parents with higher standards of living and greater cultural needs, invariably have fewer children, while the socially inferior reproduce without restraint ... In the majority of families that are allotted public support, there are six or more children. It is obvious that diseased genes can increase in this way. In other words, social inferiority is increasing due to nonself-sustaining people who increase the burden of charity upon the yet healthy minority.[22]

From this point of view, the key to restoring the health of the German people was to prevent the propagation of socially undesirable, genetically inferior "human material." Most Germans were not yet prepared to accept a program of eugenic sterilization, but the Weimar legislators, impressed by the eugenicists' arguments and acknowledging public concern for the problem of racial degeneration, responded by passing a "marriage advising law" in January 1920 under which a pamphlet was distributed through government licensing offices to all couples seeking to marry stressing the hereditary dangers of ailments like tuberculosis, venereal disease, feeble-mindedness, and mental illness. Although the law fell short of Schallmayer's earlier prescription for compulsory premarital screening, and although it dealt with seemingly noncontroversial matters of public health, it set some important precedents. It established the "health of the *Volk*" as an ideal separate from, and superior to, the health of individuals, defining the role of the practicing physician in a way that transcended the traditional concern with individual patients, as Virchow had advocated. And, on a more practical level, it placed medical science in a position to serve as an official instrument of social control, since the law stated that "*only a doctor can say* if a disease is exhibited, which, at the time, makes marriage seem inadvisable."[23]

The year 1920 also marks the opening in Germany of an explicit discussion of the intentional killing of patients deemed unworthy to live, in a book called *The Release and Destruction of Lives Devoid of Value*. Its authors, Karl Binding and Alfred Hoche, were distinguished scholars, a jurist and a psychiatrist, respectively. Almost four years before Hitler wrote *Mein Kampf*, Binding and Hoche were advocating the killing of "worthless" people under the protection of the state. Both those who are "mentally completely dead" and those who "represent a foreign body in human society" are listed as persons "who cannot be rescued and whose death is urgently necessary." Hoche, professor of psychiatry and director of the psychiatric clinic at Freiburg from 1902 to 1934, decried as "erroneous thinking" the idea of showing sympathy for "lives devoid of value." And Binding, professor of jurisprudence at Leipzig University, anticipated that although errors in judgment, diagnosis, and execution might be made, the consequences of such mistakes were bound to be inconsequential, compared to the social benefits that would eventually accrue: "Humanity loses so many members through error that one more or less really hardly makes any difference."[24]

During the early 1920s, as the financial woes of Germany increased, and as inflation destroyed personal savings and made welfare and institutional support for the diseased and dependent more problematical, the economic arguments of the eugenicists grew more insistent and more appealing. By 1923, the chief government physician for the district of

Zwickau in Saxony (southeastern Germany) had become a leading exponent of eugenic sterilization, describing as "unfit to reproduce" all individuals who were deaf and dumb, blind, insane, feebleminded and epileptic, as well as all unwed mothers and criminals eligible for parole.[25] Like Binding and Hoche before him and other eugenicists since, he advanced a seductive economic argument to the effect that Germany could no longer afford the "humanitarian luxury" of supporting "degenerates." Despite some vocal and indignant opposition, the economic line of reasoning made increasing sense to many responsible Germans. Although some critics insisted that their arguments lacked scientific foundation and others protested that "the God-given integrity of the human being" was being infringed upon, the proponents of eugenic sterilization began to make headway. A noticeable change was taking place in public opinion.

When in August 1923, the director of the health institutions in Zwickau wrote to the minister of the interior urging the enactment of a eugenic sterilization law, he tried to quell the minister's doubts concerning the possibility of a negative public reaction by pointing out that

what we racial hygienists promote is not at all new or unheard of. In a cultured nation of the first order, in the United States of America, that which we strive toward was introduced and tested long ago. It is all so clear and simple.[26]

A few months later, the minister of the interior wrote to the German Foreign Office requesting that information be gathered and provided to his office regarding eugenic control legislation in the United States.[27]

The Foreign Office immediately contacted its embassy in Washington, and requests for information were sent from there to German consulates throughout the United States. Inquiries were duly made of American mental institutions, state governments, and prisons. The replies, promptly returned to Washington and forwarded to the ministry of the interior in Berlin, were destined to have far-reaching implications for the development of German eugenics policy at a time when eugenics control legislation had already been enacted in twenty-four states.

America's example of legal eugenic control had a marked effect on politicians in Germany. Proposals for sterilization laws began to rely more and more heavily on data from the U.S. for their justification. One of these proposals devoted six full pages of text to praise for American work in biological reform, and another employed quotations from the writing of several prominent American eugenists. . . . The issue of eugenic control by the state was now seriously considered by those in the upper echelons of government and medicine.[28]

From what has already been said, it should be clear that much of the ideological groundwork for genocide was laid in Germany well before the Nazis came to power and that Nazi sociobiology did not arise out of thin air. Behind the development, under the Nazis, of compulsory sterilization programs and the massive extermination of socially undesirable human beings lay a long-established and ostensibly scientific sociobiological tradition within which scholars coolly bandied about questions of the hereditary transmission of character traits and dispassionately discussed the destruction of "lives devoid of value." More importantly, German sociobiology in general (and eugenics, in particular) appealed to many segments of the population for different reasons. To political liberals the practice of eugenics appeared to promise a happy synthesis between an enlightened welfare policy for dealing with the weakest citizens and the much more important public health problem of caring for the people as a whole. In other words, those who were optimistic about the possibilities for improving human society were able to convince themselves that in sociobiology and eugenics lay a rational and effective solution to the problem of social progress.

To political conservatives, sociobiology and eugenics held a comparable fascination. If one believes that human conduct is chiefly shaped by heredity and that basic social changes are both undesirable and useless, the selective social control of human reproductive behavior is understandably attractive as a means of managing social problems. It is probably not safe to say that the German sociobiology and racial hygiene movements were made up mainly of people holding the latter view. Across the entire political spectrum, people felt angry that the social politics of the Weimar period had failed so miserably, and many of those who were disaffected, although for different reasons, regarded eugenic control as a means of restoring law and order to what they saw as a nation nearly destroyed by social welfare programs.

Support, or at least acceptance, of sociobiological ideas among the population as a whole was one factor in the establishment of the German eugenics program in 1933. A second important factor was the support of the medical community, which had already begun to accept a redefinition of its role that placed the health of the *Volk* above the well-being of individual patients and hence placed a higher value on serving the state than upon personal loyalty and professional responsibility. But in a society predicated upon violence, where social well-being is defined as the destruction of the deviant, the diseased, and the dependent, it happened that doctors were expected to serve the state by killing their patients in the name of "curing" them.

The term *euthanasia* deserves a moment's consideration. The word is derived from the Greek words *eu* and *thanatos*, meaning "good death," and as it is generally understood refers to "mercy killing," or the act of painlessly relieving incurable or unbearable suffering. Traditional arguments about a person's right to die in peace, and about the power and responsibility of physicians to allow or encourage this, are as old as medicine itself and raise serious issues. But these traditional arguments have nothing to do with the point at issue here, because German eugenicists used the term *euthanasia* as a euphemism: in the name of racial betterment, human beings were murdered. In that context, it is pertinent to note that the earliest advocates of euthanasia in Germany (Hoche and Binding, for example) insisted that "mercy killing" should be applied to three classes of persons. First, in cases where the patient requested it; second, in cases where consent was unobtainable (as in cases of psychosis, mental subnormality, and coma); and third, in cases where the individuals in question were deemed to be a danger or burden to society. Thus arose the explicit idea that killings in the interest of the state could be termed "euthanasia."

Amid the disorder that prevailed during the final years of the Weimar Republic, it seemed that the society envisioned by the proponents of "racial science" could be brought into existence only by a resolute and strong-willed leader who wielded enormous power. Indeed, as early as 1931—two years before the Nazis came to power—the *Archives of Racial and Social Biology* carried an article by a leading sociobiologist praising Hitler as the only political figure of influence in Germany to have paid proper attention to racial science. Particularly praiseworthy, in the eyes of the author, was the National Socialist party's promise to apply sociobiological theories of racial hygiene vigorously and on the massive scale that national necessity required. In addition, Hitler's declaration that he would not be deterred by traditional bourgeois scruples in deciding significant questions for the future of the German people—that he would not, for example, confine the sterilization of inferior persons to extreme cases— were taken as promises rather than warnings.[29] When the Nazis finally came to power in 1933 and a compulsory sterilization law was enacted, one of the principal architects of that law—Ernst Rüdin, professor of psychiatry at the universities of Basel, Switzerland, and Munich—wrote a paean of praise, saying that it was thanks to Hitler that "the dream we have cherished for more than thirty years of seeing racial hygiene converted into action has become reality.[30]

The physicians of Germany were rapidly inducted into the new National Socialist reality. In 1935, the director of the University Hospital at Kiel, Dr. Hanns Löhr, published a lengthy work on the new role of medicine and medical scientists in the Third Reich.[31] His central theme was political loyalty. The new German physician, he argued, must be guided by the principle that "the health of the *Volk* stands above the health of the individual." Nazism, once in power, permitted it to be said outright: the National Socialist physician, declared Löhr, has a "holy obligation to the state." And lest there be doubt about what that obligation meant, Löhr described Nazi doctors as "biological soldiers" whose orders were to sterilize individuals harboring genetic defects and to report all such cases to the Nazi health authorities. Compulsory sterilization was the first, but not the bloodiest, battle that these biological soldiers waged on behalf of racial salvation.

In July of 1939, the fateful conference described in the introduction took place in Berlin. A number of the most illustrious members of the psychiatric profession in Germany, including the leading professors and department heads from the universities of Berlin, Heidelberg, Bonn, and Würzburg gathered to discuss a momentous project: the mass killing of German mental patients. Although no official order has been found, and no law mandating the extermination of mental patients had been passed, there is ample documentation to show that from its very inception the project was guided in all important matters by physicians. It went by many names: mercy death and euthanasia were the most common euphemisms employed, but formal and informal documents exist in which these terms are used interchangeably with such phrases as "help for the dying," "destruction of life devoid of value," "killing the incurable," and the most popular, "destruction of useless eaters." In 1939, there were an estimated 300,000 "useless eaters" in German psychiatric hospitals and clinics; by 1946, that number had been reduced to 40,000, and according to Frederic Wertham, "The most reliable estimates of the number of psychiatric patients killed are at least 275,000."[32]

For purposes of extermination, the classification of patients was reduced to a simple two-choice formula: "patients worthy to be helped" and "patients not worthy to live." By October 1939, standard report sheets had been prepared and distributed to psychiatric hospitals all over Germany, on which staff members were required to enter information regarding each patient's diagnosis, condition, and prospects for recovery (as well as sex, race, religion, and so on). Copies of each completed questionnaire were then sent to one of several panels, each composed of four psychiatrists. These panels constituted the Commission of Experts and served as the backbone of the project. Included on the commission were the psychiatrists who had originally set up the program and were responsible for its overall conduct. They made their life-and-death decisions solely on the basis of information provided by the report sheets by placing a plus or a minus on the patient's questionnaire. The entire decision process was intended to proceed rapidly, and it did. An exchange of correspondence between the central euthanasia office in Berlin and one member of the comission shows that he was able to decide the fate of 258 patients in two days.

The panel members were more than mere Nazi puppets. Most had attained international recognition as physicians and psychiatrists long before Hitler came to power; twelve were full professors at leading German universities. Several bureaucratic agencies were also involved in the project, among them the Reich Society for Mental Institutions, headed by Dr. Werner Heyde, professor of psychiatry at the University of Würzburg, and director of the mental health clinic there. After all four panel members had given their opinion, it was in his office that the final decision was pronounced on patients from the state mental hospitals. Heyde had been a key figure in the program from the start. He played a leading role in the preparatory conferences, helped to develop the questionnaires, and participated in the selection and training of other experts. When, at the outset, carbon monoxide poisoning was proposed as the best method for killing, he had evaluated and approved it, and when gas chambers had been installed in a number of mental institutions, he inspected them to ensure that they were working efficiently. An enthusiast for the project from the beginning, he lectured before high Nazi officials about its merits from time to time.

The killing of children was supervised by the Reich Commission for the Scientific Registration of Hereditary and Constitutional Severe Disorders. This special agency was set up to deal with infants and children deemed to be mentally subnormal, physically handicapped, or malformed. Children slated for death by the commission's pediatric and psychiatric experts were generally not gassed. They were transferred to special "children's divisions" (hospitals) where they were killed either by barbiturate poisoning—Luminal or phenobarbital was mixed into their food—or by starvation. In both cases, it took many days for each child to die. The starvation of children through the gradual withdrawal of food was witnessed by Ludwig Lehner, then a young student of psychology, who visited the state hospital Elgfing-Haar as part of his studies in 1939, and was conducted through a ward containing some twenty-five emaciated children by the director of the institution.[33]

No one knows or can ever know how many children were murdered by the biological soldiers of the Nazi Reich. It is known, however, that the child-killing organization was headed and staffed by doctors, that the doctors decided which children would live and which would die, and that the criteria for killing eventually included children with malformed ears, bedwetters, and those whose only designated defect consisted in being difficult to educate. Few physicians were tried specifically for the murder of children; one of the exceptions was the director of the Elgfing-Haar, who had explained the food-deprivation routine to Lehner. In 1948 he was charged at a war crimes trial with having ordered the killing of at least 120 children and with having killed some of them personally. He was convicted and sentenced to six years in prison, of which he served two.

By the middle of 1941, at least four psychiatric hospitals had become regular murder shcools where "basic training in mercy killing" meant a comprehensive course in mass extermination. By the end of 1941 many of the mental patients in Germany had been put to death. The graduates of the training schools had been equipped with the skills for killing, and now the methods that had worked so effectively for exterminating mental patients were about to be deployed on an even bigger scale to destroy still other "useless lives."

The killing of mental patients had established a precedent: lives "devoid of value" had been snuffed out on a massive scale in the name of the public order and the public health. And that having been done, the gas chambers were dismantled and moved to locations where the process was to be continued: the concentration camps to the east. There, on the basis of the same rationale, and with precisely the same methods, "the action" was repeated. The difference was that the "inferior human material" was no longer the mass of German mental patients but rather the millions of Jews, Poles, gypsies, and other ethnic, religious, or political groups who were murdered by the Nazis because they were deemed to be a threat to the survival of the master race.

The passage had been swift from the Krupp essay contest of 1900 to the extermination camps of 1940. Friedrich Alfred Krupp lived to see neither the awarding of his prize nor full flowering of the eugenics movement his sponsorship of the contest has helped to foster. He died in 1902. However, the Krupp firm itself was very much alive during the Nazi era.

Mass murder was the most horrible but not the only means by which the regime made its sociobiological doctrines of racial superiority a reality. The German war effort was supported by an enormous number of slave laborers, forcibly conscripted from all over Europe to do the heavy and dirty work that wartime production required. Slavery, as American history makes plain, is a form of behavior control for which sociobiological theory often serves as a justification. The Krupp firm became one of the principal industrial participants in, and beneficiaries of, this program of slave labor, condemning tens of thousands to work without wages in its large factories and mines. But as the principal supplier of armaments to the Nazis, the firm also established auxiliary production facilities inside various concentration camps. At one of these, located within the death camp at Auschwitz, thousands of Poles, Czechs, Jews, Italians, and others were drawn from the captive population and forced to labor at the manufacture of bomb fuses. In addition to being condemned to work for the Krupp firm as slaves, they were systematically deprived of food, rewarded for betraying each other, beaten, and exploited to exhaustion. Those who collapsed under this barbarous regime were simply transported to a nearby extermination unit. In all, during the five years of its existence, Auschwitz concentration camp and its industrial components produced tons of armaments and claimed the lives of more than four million human beings.

Throughout the Nazi period, ideas about biological determinism and biological hierarchy continued to be advanced by notable theorists whose main purpose was to promote the political interests of the regime. One such theorist was Konrad Lorenz. Perhaps those who have enjoyed his books on animal behavior or have been charmed by his image as a bearded, bemused, and kindly Germanic Mother Goose leading a gaggle of greylag goslings around the barnyard will be shocked at the undeniable link between what he wrote about animal behavior during the Nazi period and what the Nazis were doing to human beings at the same time. I recount the following in order to demonstrate the essential political dimension of sociobiology and in order to make overt the life and death issues that often lie concealed behind its scientific pretensions.

In 1940 (the year in which the Auschwitz concentration camp was opened), Lorenz held the position of lecturer in general psychology at the University of Königsberg (formerly the capital of East Prussia). Like Wilhelm Schallmayer, who had won the Krupp prize in 1903, Lorenz had devoted considerable thought to the sociopolitical aspects of evolutionary theory, with particular reference to what had come to be called (in Schallmayer's phrase) "the physical degeneration threatening civilized man." One outcome of Lorenz's preoccupation with this topic was a long article on "Disorders of Species-Specific Behavior Caused by Domestication," which was published as the lead article in a prestigious German scientific journal devoted to human psychology and "character study."

Lorenz's article was concerned with innate (or genetically determined) aspects of behavior in various wild and domesticated species of animals. Its main purpose, however, was to draw analogies about the behavior of human beings in "civilized society" from the observation and interpretation of the behavior of animals under various conditions of domestication. Leaving aside the fact that this is precisely the kind of "reasoning" that Spencer engaged in, that it is inherently prone to egregious errors, and is properly derided as wholly unsound by most serious students of animal behavior, it is pertinent to note that Lorenz's parallels between civilization and domestication were drawn specifically to make the point that the preservation and propagation of "degenerative mutations" is a common and perilous result of "unhealthy" ethical practices which (in Lorenz's view) had been prevalent for far too long in most human societies and which, if allowed to go unchecked, positively threatened to pollute the breeding stock and the genetic "value" of human populations. In short, what Lorenz tried to provide in his article was an updating of Schallmayer's degeneration thesis, augmented by the biological discoveries of the intervening forty years. The following excerpts from his article provide the gist of Lorenz's eugenic message to the German people:

The only resistance which mankind of healthy stock can offer ... against being penetrated by symptoms of degeneracy is based upon the existence of certain innate schemata. ... Our species-specific sensitivity to the beauty and ugliness of members of our species is intimately connected with the symptoms of degeneration ... which threaten our race (pp. 56-57).

The selection for toughness, heroism, social utility ... must be accomplished by some social institution if mankind, in default of selective factors, is not to be ruined by domestication-induced degeneracy. The racial idea as the basis of our state has already accomplished much in this respect (p. 71).

The most effective race-preserving measure is that which gives the greatest support to the natural defenses. ... We may—and we must—rely on the healthy instincts of the best of our people ... for the extermination of elements of the population loaded with dregs. Otherwise, these deleterious mutations will permeate the body of the people like the cells of a cancer (p. 72).[34]

Few sociobiologists today agree with Lorenz's idea that forms of life that would tend to die out due to the pressures of natural selection can be identified by aesthetic criteria, and not many would necessarily concur with his judgment that a misdirected humanitarianism is responsible for the tendency to preserve individuals from extinction who should properly be allowed to die. Yet these ideas reflect the determinist and hierarchical biases of what passes for sociobiological scholarship today, and Lorenz (who recently described himself as "by inheritance obsessed with eugenics") is not the only sociobiologist who is inclined to draw practical political inferences from his work.

When asked about his article recently, Lorenz was contrite: "I deeply regret," he said, "having employed the terminology of the time which was subsequently used as a tool for the setting of horrible objectives." Lorenz has acknowledged that he "believed that some good might come of the Nazis." The belief is unremarkable, and he has since retracted it. Perhaps one ought to let it go at that. But there is something larger at issue here than one man's apology for having embraced Nazi doctrines. Lorenz has not renounced—and he and other like-minded sociobiologists continue to maintain today—a fundamental commitment to the idea that biological defects are at the root of social troubles. You or I may look in vain in Lorenz's more recent writings for any praise of nazism as such. But if we read, for example, his book On Aggression, we will find, on almost every page, the kind of biological determinism that still characterizes sociobiology.

There is not (and never has been) any solid foundation for the spurious determinist theories that blame social turmoil on human diversity. Extrapolations from domestication to civilization are wholly unwarranted, and there is no scientific or logical reason to accept analogies drawn from the behavior of geese to the behavior of humans. Nevertheless, such theories, their appeal enhanced by the appearance of scientific objectivity, are still used by those in power to justify efforts to control the behavior of those whom they have defined as defective, disloyal, or merely different.

What lessons have been learned from this grim history? Are current forms of sociobiological scholarship fundamentally different from their predecessors in any significant respects? One thing to be noticed at the outset is that today's sociobiologists are not particularly modest or cautious in their claims. Professor Edward O. Wilson's widely heralded *Sociobiology: The New Synthesis*, sets out "to explore the biological basis of all forms of social behavior in all organisms, including man." A new science of human nature is allegedly in the process of being developed, one that will allow sociobiologists to consider human beings and their social behavior objectively

... in the free spirit of natural history, as though [we] were zoologists from another planet completing a catalog of social species on Earth. In this macroscopic view the humanities shrink to specialized branches of biology; history, biography and fiction are the research protocols of human ethology; and anthropology and sociology together constitute the sociobiology of a single primate species.[35]

Leaving for later a more detailed discussion of the reasons why the spirit of sociobiological inquiry is not and cannot be "free" in the sense intended, and ignoring the absurd pretense that sociobiologists are not part of the species they are purporting to "catalog," what is the thrust of current sociobiological discourse? Part of the answer is that it aims to "shrink" the study of human society, in all of its manifestations, to the status of a systematic biological science. The effort to do so, moreover, includes a strong emphasis upon the formless social Darwinist idea that the social behavior of organisms, including human beings, is largely determined by the insensate forces of natural selection. "In a Darwinist sense," says Professor Wilson, "the organism does not live for itself. Its primary function is not even to reproduce other organisms; it reproduces genes, and it serves as their temporary carrier."[36] In spite of the fact that the relative contribution of specific genetic factors to particular forms of complex social behavior is difficult to measure in most species of animals and impossible to evaluate in human beings, there is a strong inclination on Professor Wilson's part to think that human beings are largely predisposed to conduct themselves in certain ways because of particular genetic determinants. The fundamental presupposition is, therefore, that there are specific genes whose function it is to promote particular forms of social behavior and that the structure of society, including the behavior of its members "can be studied as ... extensions of the genes that exist because of their superior adaptive value."[37] Not suprisingly, behavior patterns with "superior adaptive value" for which genes are alleged to exist are those prevailing in that segment of society to which Professor Wilson belongs.

Speaking more generally, when sociobiologists attempt to "explain" why people behave in a certain way, they do not generally examine the structure of their own society but rather make an effort to graft selected patterns of behavior onto a biological core. In this way, the selected pattern can be made to appear as if it results not from modifiable social conditions but from fixed biological causes. The effect of such "explanations," of course, is implicitly to justify a given form of behavior by locating its origins outside the social order. By considering Wilson's arguments for the biological basis of human inequality in relation to contemporary social problems, let me try to illustrate the form and content of such explanations.

The possibility of establishing a society in which basic human equality exists is allegedly foreclosed by a rather large and varying group of sociobiological arguments, each of which is intended to show (as did Plato's lie) that in one way or another, social inequality merely reflects the natural and inherent biological inequality of different individuals, races, sexes, ethnic groups, economic classes, and so on. As Professor Wilson sees it, the age-old effort to fashion biological arguments to account for social inequality is not an exercise in social mythology but a serious scholarly effort to answer a "key question of human biology,"

... whether there exists a genetic predisposition to enter certain classes and to play certain roles. Circumstances can easily be conceived by which such genetic differences might occur. The heritability of at least some parameters of intelligence and emotive traits is sufficent to respond to a moderate amount of ... selection.[38]

While no one would question the existence of different classes and social roles, it is also a fact that in contemporary American society, class and role varies with sex and race. One way of attempting to account for both of these facts would be to analyze the socioeconomic structure of institutions and the prevailing patterns of race and sex discrimination. The way sociobiology proceeds, however, is to "explain" the first fact by asserting that all societies are naturally stratified in a hierarchical fashion and the second by asserting that individuals generally come to rest at the point in the hierarchy they inherently deserve to occupy. The tenor of such "explanations" is already familiar, but the sociobiological format is new. Here is how Wilson supports his hypothesis that social stratification is the outcome of a genetic predisposition to certain forms of behavior:

Even in the simplest societies individuals differ greatly. Within a small tribe of !Kung Bushmen can be found individuals who are acknowledged as the "best people." ... !Kung men, no less than men in advanced industrial societies, generally establish themselves by their mid-thirties or else accept a lesser status for life. There are some who never try to make it, live in run-down huts, and show little pride in themselves or their work. The ability to slip into such roles, shaping one's personality to fit, may itself be adaptive. Human societies are organized by high intelligence and each member is faced by a mixture of social challenges that taxes all of his ingenuity. . . .[39]

Thus it would appear that Plato's lie was really a premature scientific truth and that it is both necessary and natural for the "best people" to assume positions of leadership. But how does one identify the individuals who are genetically best endowed to occupy the top of the social hierarchy? By defining success as not simply an indicator of intelligence but as a form of intelligence itself, Wilson is able to contend that the possession of high status is in itself evidence of a natural right to it, an argument reminiscent of Aristotle's defense of slavery. Moreover, "if a single gene appears that is responsible for success and an upwardshift in status, it can be rapidly concentrated in the upper socioeconomic classes. . . ." Thus it is no longer merely IQ that is inherited, but success itself:

The hereditary factors of human success are strongly polygenic and form a long list, only a few of which have been measured. IQ constitutes only one subset of the components of intelligence. Less tangible but equally important equalities are creativity, entrepreneurship, drive, and mental stamina.[40]

I have already examined the evidence regarding the inheritance of IQ. I have presented Professor Wilson's case for the genetic basis of social inequality in order to show that one of the more prevalent themes in contemporary sociobiology is little more than a modern version of Plato's fiction. Despite Professor Wilson's assertions to the contrary, there is not an iota of evidence to suggest that there are genes for success or intelligence in human beings, or for the other traits he discusses, such as altruism or conformity. For that matter, there is not the slightest reason to think that human genes corresponding to these arbitrary categories of behavior will ever be found. The genes in question are genes of a mythical kind which have been invented in order to buttress certain social preconceptions about the ways in which human beings "naturally" behave.

From the very beginning of recorded political discourse, efforts to justify social inequality have been predicated on sociobiological falsehoods in which the fact of human diversity is subtly and persuasively transformed into the social fiction that superior and inferior human beings exist. Once people have been ranked in a way that permits invidious comparison along an arbitrary scale, the attributes on which individuals or groups differ become more easily amenable to measurement and control, and an atmosphere of scientific "objectivity" comes to surround discussions in which human beings are regarded as so much raw material to be manufactured, manipulated, marketed, or (if powerful interests desire it) discounted, discarded, or destroyed.

In the last analysis, it was sociobiological scholarship, claiming to be scientifically objective, morally neutral, and ethically value free, that provided the conceptual framework by which eugenic theory was transformed into genocidal practice while garnering support, or at least not rousing opposition, among the German people as a whole. Moreover, this sociobiological framework, upon which the justifications for genocide were ultimately built, was plainly not a Nazi invention. It had been erected in the name of science long before National Socialism became a reality. Without meaning for a moment to exonerate from guilt for their atrocities the individuals who conceived, planned, and carried out the murderous programs of Nazi genocide, let me insist that a true bill of indictment cannot be drawn up without including the tradition of political thought that has granted a wholly undeserved measure of respectability to the lies about human superiority and inferiority.

What this indictment necessarily suggests is that the meaning of human nature and the measurement of human diversity are themselves instruments of behavior control, which simultaneously reflect and buttress the power of established social institutions. The question to consider is whether, and to what degree, contemporary social policies are directed by sociobiological ideas comparable in content and purpose to those of the past. In order to answer this question, I will focus in the remaining chapters on efforts to control the behavior, through various forms of psychotechnology, of subgroups of people labeled as social deviants.

6   **Drug Abuse:
"Better Living
through Chemistry?"**

Before considering contemporary psychotechnology, we must come to grips with something rather more subtle and perhaps even more powerful than the material techniques that make it possible to modify, measure, regulate, or otherwise control the behavior of human beings. It is essential to bear in mind that both the basic research and technological aspects of psychology are involved in the overall effort to control human behavior in human society. It is because of the interplay between these aspects that a comprehensive analysis of behavior control must focus not only upon technological methods but also upon the form and content of scientific ideas.

There is yet another factor that must be considered. The effort to control behavior ultimately depends upon the availability of suitable methods of procedure. Accordingly, organizations sponsor scholarship and employ experts to develop both the techniques and the concepts upon which behavior control programs depend. Scholars and experts therefore participate in both the effort to understand behavior and the effort to control it. That scientific neutrality is invoked to justify both aspects of behavior control may be illustrated as follows.

The book *Control of Human Behavior* which I cited in the introduction purports to provide an objective account of scientific "concepts underlying behavior control, and their implications for human engineering." Its goal, as the editors point out in their preface, is to develop "a science and methodology for guiding, directing and engineering human behavior . . . to direct attention to the amelioration of those behaviors believed to be disruptive to individual lives and the larger social good." This effort, they note further, "can be of great individual and social significance," although they acknowledge that to some observers

the concepts may be alarming, hinting at Orwellian 1984-ism; to others there may appear to be a great promise for man's future. For all, however, it must be clear that with this increase in knowledge and technology, as with other of man's discoveries and inventions, comes the grave responsibility to use it appropriately, wisely and humanely.

The sentiments in this passage are hardly exceptionable, and similar ones may be found at the start of almost all books about behavior control. Nevertheless, warnings about the ambivalence of knowledge and exhortations regarding moral and ethical responsibility often conceal the inability or unwillingness of scientists to examine the social preconceptions inherent in the organization and conduct of their own work. In the case of behavorial engineering, for example, the ostensible concern is with the causes of human behavior, as B. F. Skinner pointed out in *Science and Human Behavior:*

We want to know why men behave as they do. Any condition or event which can be shown to have an effect upon behavior must be taken into account. By discovering and analyzing these causes we can predict behavior; to the extent that we can manipulate them we can control behavior.

But like behavior control activities more generally, the more specific aim of these investigations, according to the editors of *Control of Human Behavior*, is to guide "human behavior along those lines known to result in the achievement of *socially defined* standards of success."

Thus, the effort to control behavior, although allegedly "objective" and concerned with "causes," is actually predicated, from beginning to end, upon socially defined standards. More to the point, this means either that socially defined standards are objective or that the effort to control behavior, in this particular instance, is predicated upon standards that are not. Enough has already been said to suggest that there are no grounds for believing that socially defined standards (of success, for example) are objective; that on the contrary they are based almost exclusively upon value judgments which reflect the interests of socially dominant individuals and groups.

It is not always said so plainly, but in the case under discussion, the editors openly announce that their book "is dedicated to those agencies and organizations—psychiatric hospitals and outpatient clinics, educational and training facilities, detention homes and penal institutions, and others—whose origin and maintenance is based on society's desire to alter the behavior of its members." The implications of this dedication are worth pondering. Can psychologists, whose professional efforts are dedicated to promoting the interests of socially established organizations, legitimately claim to be engaged in a morally and ethically neutral enterprise? Or is the claim of neutrality advanced in such cases to conceal the influence of organizational interests on the course of professional life?

The fact that behavioral scientists are committed to certain social preconceptions is itself not a reasonable basis for serious criticism of their professional activities. On the contrary, all human beings, including behavioral scientists, inevitably entertain certain preconceptions, and these may be expected to bias not only their professional activities, but also their day-to-day behavior. Indeed, the universal existence of social preconceptions is simply one more indication that science is inseparable from society's value structure. As an example of the way in which a well-meaning scientist who suffers the illusion of his own neutrality can be swept up in the value-ridden interplay between meaning and power, I would like to begin by recounting a personal experience. As a graduate student in psychology in the 1950s, like the great majority of my fellow students, I rarely paused to consider the possibility that psychology might be something other than a "pure" science. Furthermore, questions about the moral and ethical dimensions of the field were rarely discussed in lectures, readings, or classroom sessions, and there seemed to be a great deal else to worry about, including a formidable amount of theoretical and technical material.

In order to qualify for my doctoral degree, I had to find a worthwhile research project to serve as the basis for my thesis, and in my second year of graduate school, I landed a research assistantship on a project concerning the effects of various drugs on learning and memory in monkeys. One of my main jobs was to help carry out experiments in which monkeys trained to perform a specific memory task were injected with a given drug and tested to see how their performance was affected. In several experiments, the same drug was administered to a given monkey on successive occasions a few days apart. The usual finding was that on the first couple of testing days disruption of performance was severe, but it became progressively smaller as the injections and tests were repeated. In other words, the monkeys tended to develop a resistance or tolerance to the effects of the drug. Previous experiments of a rather different kind had shown that the repetition of a sensory stimulus—usually a tone—produced a similar effect on behavior. For example, when a tone was initially presented to a sleeping cat, the animal woke up quickly and showed various signs of arousal, including certain brain wave or electroencephalographic (EEG) changes. However, the arousal reaction gradually became less pronounced and finally disappeared altogether when the tone was repeatedly presented to the animal under similar conditions. I was struck by the apparent similarity between this "habituation of the arousal reaction" and the tolerance to repeated drug administrations. At last I had a problem to work on, and a major focus of my doctoral research project became the combined tolerance and habituation effects.

In 1959, after my doctoral research was completed and published, I turned for a time to other kinds of problems, but the idea that similar brain mechanisms were involved in the two effects remained in the back of my mind. By 1970, when I found it possible to resume work on the tolerance and habituation phenomena, several other researchers had already gone a long way toward showing that the brain mechanisms involved in both effects are strikingly similar. Since then, my own work has been devoted, in one way or another, to analyzing the relevant brain mechanisms.

Sometime around mid-1972, I happened by chance to meet two professional acquaintances at the National Airport in Washington, D.C. We were all bound for Boston, and in the course of the conversation, I learned that they had been working together on various aspects of heroin addiction and alcohol dependence. Heroin and other opium derivatives produce strong tolerance effects, so that dosages must be progressively increased to maintain a constant level of effect. My two colleagues listened, in turn, as I described my own ideas about the brain mechanisms involved in tolerance and their relation to other aspects of habituation, and a few moments later I was accepting their invitation to participate in a discussion/workshop on the "biological and behavioral aspects of the addictive disorders." I should add that my interest in the topic was sharpened by the workshop's inclusion in an annual brain research conference held each winter at a ski resort in the Colorado Rockies.

Several weeks later, a draft of the announcement to be printed in the conference program arrived. I was listed as a discussant. I had, of course, known at the outset that two of the other four participants would be the colleagues I had met at the airport; now, with the understanding that I was expected to comment on their presentations, I was interested to learn who the other participants were and what they were likely to say. In reading further, it became apparent that all but one of the speakers were going to discuss behavioral, biochemical, and pharmacological aspects of drug addiction. The exception, who was obviously planning to take a broader view, was Dr. Jerome H. Jaffe, a well-known authority on narcotics and drug addiction. Dr. Jaffe had recently been appointed director of a White House Special Action Office for Drug Abuse Prevention (SAODAP). In that capacity, he was officially responsible for coordinating all federal government activities in the field of drug abuse prevention, including scientific research and training programs, public education and addiction treatment projects, and law-enforcement efforts. In short, it was apparent that Dr. Jaffe's approach would reflect not only his scientific expertise but also his political and administrative interests as a top-level government official.

On the basis of my previous professional experience, I knew what would be expected of me in commenting on the other three presentations, but I was not at all prepared to comment on drug abuse as a social problem.

As I have already observed in various connections, the definition of social problems reflects the interests and objectives of individuals and institutions holding political power. The way in which social problems are defined, of course, determines prospective solutions—perhaps more significantly, it determines which solutions are *not* attempted. If this is so, even the process of definition entails an exercise of power, to the extent that it effectively forecloses the possibility of alternative approaches and forces society as a whole to participate in "solutions" that may or may not serve the common interest.

I now believe that this is the case for many social problems that officially sponsored programs are mandated to solve, but I did not at first understand that it is particularly clear in the case of drug abuse. At this time, in late 1972, it was (and still is) the explicit objective of government policy to make "significant progress" in what is commonly referred to as the war against drug abuse. My wife is a psychotherapist who specializes in work with families, groups and other small social systems, and while I was preparing to attend the workshop on addiction, she was involved in training counselors to work with community-based drug rehabilitation programs. This experience had made her sensitive to the SAODAP approach, and she pointed out to me at once that phrases like "significant progress" are meaningless when considered apart from the relevant administrative context. Accordingly, she encouraged me to ask myself about the social objectives to which these terms referred and to pose a number of questions about the meaning of biological and behavioral information in the context of SAODAP's programs for drug abuse prevention. In addition, she suggested that I ask myself whether my own research on the physiological mechanisms of habituation and drug tolerance was morally and ethically neutral, as I had believed, or whether it was vulnerable to exploitation as a weapon in the Nixon administration's "war."

In order to answer these questions, I had to consider my own scientific discipline in a new and wholly unfamiliar light, and as a result came to understand that in a social context where "the war against drug abuse" is defined by political leaders as a struggle to control specific aspects of human behavior, those who conduct research on drug abuse are inevitably engaged in more than a scientific exercise, and those whose contributions engender more effective methods of behavior control cannot claim to be morally and ethically neutral. I should add that while my own opinion is that the war against drug abuse is ill conceived and irrationally carried out, it has not been my intention to cast moral and ethical aspersions on the scientists and administrators who dedicate their efforts to "winning" it. Up to this point, my argument is simply that the claim of neutrality is a myth which, when accepted uncritically, obscures the moral and ethical dimensions of the problem.

At the workshop itself, and ever since, I have been struggling to understand the process of defining and solving social problems. My opinions about the nature of behavior control and its relationship to social problems have frequently evoked opposition from professional colleagues. For the most part, I have been criticized for being biased and for tending to portray the "objective"and "neutral" activities of scientists in too unfair and unfavorable a light. I will leave it to each reader to decide the merits of these criticisms, but let me add that at least some of the more insistent objections come from those who feel science and technology have been excessively criticized and vilified as the causes of many social ills, including not only abusive behavior control programs but environmental pollution, the nuclear arms race, inflation, overpopulation, and unemployment. For my part, I reject as false and spurious the effort to blame such problems on science and technology.

My own earlier failure to consider the links between behavioral science and public policy, was not the result of political naiveté. On the contrary, I was raised in a socially conscious and politically aware family and have generally maintained an active interest in public affairs outside my scientific and professional life. But I was trained, as most scientists are, to draw a sharp dividing line between the scholarly and social aspects of my own existence, and it has not been easy to overcome this false dichotomy. The public record has been an especially good source for analyzing the political dimensions of behavioral science. One of the first items that came to my attention in 1972 was a preelection interview with Richard Nixon published in the *New York Times* on November 10. In it, drug abuse was discussed in the kind of political language that is often used to justify specific behavior control programs:

... the enormous movement toward permissiveness which led to the escalation in crime, the escalation in drugs in this country, all of this came as a result of those of us who basicallly have a responsibility of leadership not recognizing that above everything else you must not weaken a people's character.... The average American is just like the child in the family ... if you make him completely dependent and pamper him and cater to him too much, you are going to make him soft, spoiled, and eventually a very weak individual.

One of the first things that struck me when I read this interview was the assumption of moral weakness that invariably seems to accompany the call for strong behavior control programs. What remains to be shown is how behavioral scientists and technologists, laboring under the banner of moral and ethical neutrality, have helped to foster this assumption.

In contemporary American society, the term *drug abuse* denotes a problem of broad and urgent public concern. As president, Richard Nixon defined the compulsive use of drugs as "the most serious threat this nation has ever faced" and established a special White House office to take charge of the government's drug abuse prevention efforts. It is always useful to examine the way in which a problem is officially defined before attempting to say anything about efforts to solve it. The word *abuse* implies disapproval, which in current conceptions of the drug abuse problem has two sources. The first is the acceptance of a dubious but professionally fostered and legally enforced distinction between two broad classes of drugs.

The first class consists of those chemical compounds that conform to the dictionary definition of drugs and that are officially approved by medical authorities and regulatory agencies for use (with or without prescription) in the prevention or treatment of diseases, for the relief of pain or suffering, or to control certain psychological, physiological, or pathological conditions. Included in this class is a wide spectrum of drugs, ranging from agents with profound effects on the central nervous system and behavior to laxatives, headache remedies, antibiotics, patent medicines, and vitamins. The second class of compounds also conform to the definition of drugs but are either officially unrecognized or disapproved of by medical authorities or legally proscribed. Included in this class are various drugs, many of which affect the central nervous system and behavior and some of which are covered by legal restrictions which make their sale, possession, and use a crime punishable by fine, imprisonment, or other penalties. Thus, the first way in which the notion of disapproval enters into current conceptions of the drug abuse problem is through a scheme of classification, according to which the drugs themselves are officially categorized as being either licit or illicit.

The second kind of disapproval is typified by the idea that there is something inherently wrong or improper about the use of certain drugs under certain circumstances. These drugs are a set of chemical compounds, both licit and illicit, that produce changes in the behavior, thoughts, moods, feelings, and attitudes of human beings. According to Dr. Jerome H. Jaffe, whom I have already referred to in connection with the 1972 conference, "whether drugs are used for relief or for the avoidance of distress, it is the *self-administration* of drugs and the *self-induced* changes in mood that are the critical factors in the development of compulsive drug abuse."[1] Like most administrators, Dr. Jaffe defined the problem as lying primarily in the errant behavior of those individuals who use licit or illicit drugs to alter their own moods and behavior. Drug abuse refers, he writes, "to the use, usually by self-administration, of any drug in a manner that deviates from the approved medical or social patterns within a given culture."[2]

The questions of medical approval and social deviance should be kept clearly in mind, because as I intend to describe it, the drug problem is more than just a matter of individual "abuses." It includes also the problem of defining social deviance and the practice of prescribing drugs to control it. Accordingly, I will be concerned with two issues: efforts to control the behavior of individuals who engage in the self-administration of illicit drugs (particularly heroin) and efforts to use licit drugs as a means of controlling the behavior of socially deviant individuals (particularly heroin users and hyperactive children). Since the thrust of my argument depends upon a "systems approach" to the problem of drug abuse, let me begin with some general remarks on that concept as applied to questions of social conformity and deviance.

Perhaps the best way to describe what I mean by the term systems approach is to distinguish it from what sociologists commonly call the structural approach to deviance. Both approaches begin from the obvious fact that within any given social context, some types of behavior conform to, and other types of behavior deviate from, social norms or values. From the structural viewpoint, the norms and values of a culture comprise the standards against which behavior is to be compared, and the focus of inquiry becomes the factors (social, economic, biological, and so forth) that appear to be decisive in causing some individuals to conform and others to deviate.

In the systems approach, the existence of standards is also acknowledged, but instead of taking them as a fixed frame of reference against which to compare the behavior of individuals, the processes by which standards of conformity and deviance are defined (and the mechanisms with which the definitions are enforced) are also considered. This is the approach that I have taken in my discussion of the concepts of meaning and power in relation to the overall problem of behavior control in human society. I have repeatedly tried to show that the effort to define and enforce social conformity reflects the perspective of politically dominant and relatively well-organized groups, whose values and interests must be taken into account in order to make sense of the methods they employ as instruments of behavior control. Thus when I say that my analysis of the drug abuse problem is political, I am using the word *political* to refer to choices or actions involving the exercise of power, which includes both the symbolic power of science and the practical power of established institutions.

I have examined several contexts in which sociobiological theories and other ostensibly "objective" concepts drawn from the behavioral sciences have been used to reflect and reinforce the attitudes of the politically dominant groups whose interests shape the lawmaking and law-enforcement processes. A consideration of the historical development of narcotic drugs and attitudes toward them will show that the same process is at work in this case.

More than six thousand years ago, the Sumerians must have known about the subjective effects of narcotic drugs. Their ideograph for the poppy was called *hul* (joy) plus *gil* (plants). Later, in the third century B.C., Theophrastus used the term "poppy juice" to refer to what we now know as opium. Arabian and medieval physicians were well versed in the concoction of a fluid opium extract called laudanum, the drinking of which eventually gave rise to the term "opium eating." Until relatively recent times, laudanum was in widespread medical and recreational use throughout Europe, Asia, and North America. In 1803, the principal narcotic constituent of opium was isolated and identified. It was found to be about ten times stronger (by weight) than raw opium and was named *morphine*, after Morpheus, the Greek god of dreams. Around the middle of the nineteenth century, instances of opium addiction began to attract wide notice, and by 1868 it was estimated that there were between 80,000 and 100,000 "opium eaters" in the United States, or one person out of 350 in the general population. At about the same time, pure morphine became commercially available and began to replace the cruder laudanum preparations. It was occasionally proposed as a cure for opium addiction.

In 1898, chemists at the Bayer pharmaceutical company in Germany succeeded in producing a slight alteration in the morphine molecule, which resulted in a drug about three times stronger than morphine. It was named heroin, for the German word *heroisch*, meaning "great" or "strong." Bayer advertised heroin widely as a cough remedy and promoted it as a cure for morphine addiction on the grounds that it was not habit-forming. By 1910, the United States had enacted its first federal legislation to control the importation and use of opium. At that time there were an estimated 200,000 opiate addicts in the country, most of them women who had become addicted to patent medicines.

During the Second World War, when the German supply of opium was cut off by the Allied campaigns in North Africa and the Mediterranean, the pharmaceutical chemists of the Third Reich undertook to develop a substitute. By 1944, they had succeeded in synthesizing a drug that bore little physical similarity to morphine or heroin but nonetheless had essentially identical potency as a pain killer. This drug, named dolophine after Adolph Hitler, was rushed into medical service for the treatment of battlefield injuries toward the end of the war. It is presently called methadone and is being used widely as a "cure" for heroin addiction, although no one claims that it is not habit-forming.

Because their effects are very largely indistinguishable, it is possible to consider the main pharmacological actions of morphine, heroin, and methadone all at once. The opiates are most noted for their extraordinary effects on pain. As the British physician Thomas Sydenham wrote in 1680, "Among the remedies which it has pleased Almighty God to give to man to relieve his sufferings, none is so universal and so efficacious as opium." It is now generally recognized that morphine is primarily responsible for the analgesic effects of both opium and heroin (the latter is converted into morphine within the body). Narcotic drugs do more than produce indifference to pain, however. In small to moderate doses, morphine, heroin, and methadone also induce drowsiness, euphoria, and general sense of well-being. When administered intravenously ("shooting" or "mainlining"), experienced users describe the immediate aftereffects as extremely pleasurable; they speak of a "rush," a "kick," a "thrill," or a "flash" of "concentrated, indescribable joy."

It is not, of course, the purely pleasurable effects of the opiates that make them the target of public concern. Indeed, the principal pharmacological actions of heroin have less to do with the current effort to control its use than do a number of so-called side effects. These are of two main types, generally referred to as abuse liability and toxicity.

The term *abuse liability*, as used by pharmacologists, refers to any drug that people are likely to use "compulsively." The term is at best imprecise, in the sense that it attributes to a drug, as a property, something that is more properly considered as a relation between certain users of the drug and the drug itself. Because of its imprecision, the concept of abuse liability lends itself readily to the fallacy of reification, that is, the conversion of an abstraction into a tangible property. Let us grant, however, for purposes of discussion, that some substances that alter moods and relieve tensions are likely to be used by some people regularly or habitually for that purpose. Such drugs are said by leading authorities to possess a high abuse liability.

At least two effects of heroin are allegedly related to its high abuse liability. One is that individuals who habitually use heroin develop a tolerance to its narcotic effects, so that more of the drug must be taken in order to reproduce the original "kick." The second effect of habitual heroin use is the tendency to develop physical dependence. That is to say, the absence of the drug leads to symptoms of hyperexcitability and discomfort. Thus, one aspect of narcotic addiction is the tendency of an individual to use the drug consistently in order to avoid the development of such symptoms. The symptoms themselves are generally referred to as a part of an abstinence syndrome, or *withdrawal syndrome*, which in the case of heroin commonly resembles a case of influenza: fever, chills, runny nose, tearing eyes, nausea, diarrhea, and rapid breathing. The severity of these symptoms varies depending upon the physical and mental state of the user, the circumstances surrounding withdrawal, and the level of tolerance and physical dependence previously reached.

These phenomena of tolerance and physical dependence, together with a number of related effects I will not discuss here, are among the most interesting and little-understood manifestations of drug action. But they do not by themselves account for heroin's so-called abuse liability. The real issue is the idea that because the pleasurable effects it produces are so intense, heroin is exceptionally habit-forming. Although most authorities would have to agree that "too little is known about the mechanisms subserving . . . differential abuse liability of different drugs,"[3] it is commonly believed that "occasional" users of heroin are extremely rare and that someone who uses the drug even once is bound to get "hooked."

Actually, not everyone who uses heroin uses it compulsively, and all users of heroin are not regular users. It is not known what turns an occasional user into a regular user or a regular user into a compulsive (or addictive) user; nor is it known if a significant majority of those who have tried heroin once or twice have gone on to become regular users. According to one estimate, less than half of those who might be called "regular" users of heroin use the drug daily.[4] As Jaffe has pointed out, "In the case of alcohol, it seems obvious that the drug effects, while experienced as pleasurable or tension reducing . . . do not compel a normal individual to use the drug repeatedly, and we readily accept the idea that social and psychological factors play major roles in the abuse of alcohol." There is no reason to assume that narcotics are any different.[5]

But if one myth about heroin concerns its abuse liability, another—perhaps more prevalent—concerns its toxicity. "No drug is free of toxic effects," states a leading contemporary textbook of pharmacology, although these may be anything from trivial to fatal. The term *toxicity* refers, of course, to the injurious or harmful effects that any drug may produce. According to popular wisdom, the toxicity of heroin is very great, and it is often referred to as a "killer drug." This ominous reputation is owed in part to official sources of drug abuse information which commonly link heroin use with the specter of "overdose deaths."

The statistics are certainly frightening. During 1971, for example, there were more than 1,200 narcotic-related deaths recorded in New York City alone. Most of these were associated with heroin, which was implicated more often than any other drug in the deaths of males between the ages of fifteen and thirty-five. There can be no doubt, as Jaffe has pointed out, that "the average death rate among young adult heroin addicts is several times higher than that for non-addicts of similar age and ethnic backgrounds."[6] These alarming statistics fail to show, however, that heroin per se is never claimed to be the actual cause of death in any but a minute fraction of heroin-related fatalities, including so-called overdose deaths. One reason is that it takes a very large dose of heroin to kill a human being; another is that there is no pure heroin on the illicit street market.

Obviously, a sufficiently large dose of heroin will kill even the most tolerant addict, but the opiates may fairly be characterized as among the least inherently toxic drugs known to pharmacology. Unlike alcohol, which in relatively small amounts is severely toxic to the liver and other internal organs, heroin produces no apparent tissue damage, little impairment of judgment or coordination, and no inclination to engage in violent behavior, even with prolonged or habitual use. Indeed, in the case of habitual users, the toxic and lethal dose levels are altered in the direction of safety by the mechanism of tolerance itself.

Heroin is not a killer drug, but the people who use it in contemporary American society are often killed. Why? Mainly because of the clandestine and criminal circumstances that invariably surround its production, distribution, and use. The great majority of so-called overdose deaths, for example, are traceable to the unpredictable covert fluctuation in the nature of what is sold as heroin on the illicit market, to synergistic (interactive) effects of combining street heroin with other drugs (such as alcohol and barbiturates), and to the adulteration ("cutting") of street heroin with quinine and other compounds that are routinely used as a source of "bulk." Other potentially toxic and lethal factors include the unhygienic

or communal use of contaminated needles, syringes, and other imple-
ments, through which hepatitis and other infectious diseases may be transmitted, and the likelihood of being injured or killed in an altercation over
a drug sale or in a raid by the police. When deaths from the foregoing
causes occur, they are officially classified as "narcotic-related deaths," but
even if it were the case that all narcotic-related deaths were caused by
heroin per se, its status as a killer drug would hardly be outstanding. In
New York City, during 1971, another drug was implicated in more than
6,000 deaths (five times the rate of narcotic-related deaths). That drug is
alcohol.

I do not wish to be understood as advocating the casual or indiscrimi-
nate use of opiates. I have reviewed the preceding pharmacological issues
solely in order to show that there is little to warrant the selection of
heroin as the prime target for efforts at drug abuse prevention. Indeed, it
can be argued that there are many drugs, including the barbiturates,
amphetamines, and alcohol, whose potentially adverse effects upon the
human body and behavior might more properly be the main focus of concern. The reason this is not so is that the real issue involved in the war
against heroin abuse is crime. Heroin is associated with crime in at least
two ways. One of them is related only indirectly to the topic of behavior
control, but it needs to be mentioned because it helps to illuminate the
absurdity of current policies in relation to heroin.

Every year more than a million kilograms of opium is illicitly harvested
throughout the world; much of it is grown and consumed in Asia. Only
about 20 percent enters the international market. In his recent book, *The
Politics of Heroin in Southeast Asia,* Alfred McCoy states that the ranks of
the primary producers and traders include remnants of the Chinese Nation-
alist Army in Burma, the Meo tribespeople of South Vietnam, and high
officials of the governments in several Southeast Asian countries. McCoy
also says that the U.S. government is involved through the CIA and its
transport facilities, especially Air America. In any event, the secondary
processing and distribution of heroin throughout the world is reputedly
controlled by organized crime syndicates whose large profits account for
the high price of heroin on the domestic street market. The markup is
staggering. The illegality of heroin is the sole reason for its high cost in this
country; in England the pharmacy cost is $0.04 per grain compared with a
U.S. street price of from $50 to $120 per grain. (A grain is equal to 60 mg;
some addicts with "heavy" habits require more than three or four times
this amount each day.) As McCoy observes,

To the average American who witnesses the daily horror of the narcotics
traffic at the street level, it must seem inconceivable that his government
could be in any way implicated. . . . The media have tended to reinforce
this outlook by depicting the international heroin traffic as a medieval

morality play: the traffickers are portrayed as the basest criminals, continually on the run from the minions of law and order; and American diplomats and law enforcement personnel are depicted as modern-day knights-errant staunchly committed to the total, immediate eradication of heroin trafficking. Unfortunately, the characters in this drama cannot be so easily stereotyped. American diplomats and secret agents have been involved . . . at three levels: (1) coincidental complicity by allying with groups actively engaged in the drug traffic; (2) abetting the traffic by covering up for known heroin traffickers. . . ; (3) and active engagement in the transport of opium and heroin. It is ironic, to say the least, that America's heroin plague is of its own making.[7]

So much for the first part of the crime story. As we turn to the question of heroin and crime on the street level, it may be well to ponder whether the legalization of heroin, perhaps under conditions comparable to those currently governing the domestic distribution of alcohol, would not simply destroy the enormously profitable criminal market which depends solely upon the fact that the opiates (except morphine and methadone) are defined as illicit drugs. In all likelihood, legalization would affect the illicit market in precisely the same way that the suspension of Prohibition affected the bootleg traffic in alcoholic beverages. Provision of a legitimate source of supply would also abolish the enormous amount of crime motivated solely by the need for large sums of money in order to support an expensive heroin habit. According to one estimate, addicts commit half of all property crime in New York City, stealing at least half a billion dollars annually to maintain their habit.

But is it not the case that a good deal of criminal activity and deviant behavior associated with the use of opiates is directly traceable to the effects of the drugs themselves? The answer is clearly no. Two independent lines of evidence support this crucial contention. First, it is common knowledge in medical circles that relatively affluent users of narcotics, including physicians (who are able to obtain adequate supplies of high quality morphine through normal pharmaceutical channels), comprise a class whose typical member "is able to discharge his social and occupational obligations with reasonable efficiency . . . and is, in general, difficult to distinguish from other persons."[8] The second line of evidence comes from a study conducted in 1971 by the Bureau of Narcotics and Dangerous Drugs (BNDD), which found that the vast majority of urban heroin addicts arrested for violations other than heroin use began to engage in criminal activities only *after* they began to use the drug. Moreover, the types of crimes they tended to commit were either "commercialized vice" (so-called crimes without victims, such as prostitution, pimping, and drug dealing) or property crimes of a nonviolent nature (such as auto theft and shoplifting) rather than armed robbery, murder, rape, aggravated assault, or other serious crimes involving violence. Many of those in the study were arrested for offenses of the latter kind, but the majority of them had begun to commit such crimes before using heroin or other similar drugs. In short, the sequence of events revealed by the study was precisely the reverse of what might be expected if heroin itself were the cause of violent criminal behavior. Indeed, it has long been recognized that the psychotropic effects of opiates are such as to actually *reduce* aggressive behavior.

The BNDD report notes, however, there is one drug that does show a causal relationship with both serious property crime and serious crimes against the person; but that drug is not heroin, it is alcohol.

From what I have said thus far, it might be inferred that the main reason for the differences in morbidity between relatively affluent addicts and "urban junkies" is socioeconomic. But, as one might expect, sociobiology offers another interpretation, intended to justify the focus of the current drug control effort upon heroin users who live in urban ghettos rather than upon the users of morphine and other opiates who occupy a higher social rank. This interpretation is based on the idea that there are inherent and significant differences between the personalities of different classes of narcotic drug users. Thus, after acknowledging that a high incidence of morphine addiction exists among members of the medical profession, a leading textbook asserts:

The personality characteristics of physician-addicts and probably those of "medical" addicts in general are distinct from those of the urban heroin addict. . . .

Most physician-addicts state that they first took the drug to overcome fatigue or to alleviate some bodily ailment, and few indicate that they were seeking thrills.[9]

In addition to being invidious, unsubstantiated, and self-serving from a social-class point of view, such contrasts are easily pressed into service as a justification for selective attention to the urban junkie as the focus of efforts at "rehabilitation." Consider, first of all, *methadone maintenance*. Quite simply, this means that instead of obtaining an illicit narcotic (heroin) on the street and then self-administering an intravenous injection, the narcotics user presents himself regularly at an officially authorized treatment facility to receive a licit narcotic (methadone) in the form of an oral dose. Originally, each enrolled addict was supposed to participate in the program for about seven months, during which time the dose level would be gradually reduced to zero, but it has not worked out that way. Principal among the reasons is the fact that it is impossible to treat, with methadone, the conditions that induce people to use narcotic drugs in the first place. Political support for maintenance programs has been sought by promoting them as a means of reducing crime; the result has been that methadone itself has become a highly sought-after street drug, in which there is presently a brisk illicit traffic.

An effective addiction treatment program would have to deal more directly with the distresses of poverty which narcotics are most commonly used to relieve. Yet the public and public officials have begun to take a much harder and more punitive approach, despite increasing evidence of the failure of methadone programs to alleviate the problems associated with the illicit drug traffic. Aided by the pejorative image of the addict, which scientists, public officials and the media tend to promote, the political trend has been toward "solutions" such as the one proposed by Nelson Rockefeller in his State of the State message to the legislature in 1973, when he was still governor of New York. As early as 1966, Rockefeller had established the New York State Narcotic Addiction Control Commission; the state had allocated more than one billion dollars to an "all-out war on narcotics." Its manifest failure was described in these words by the governor:

We have tried every possible approach to stop addiction and to save the addict through education and treatment. . . . But let's be frank—let's "tell it like it is": We have achieved very little permanent rehabilitation—and have found no cure. . . . The crime, the muggings, the robberies, the murders associated with addiction continue to spread a reign of terror.[10]

The solution? He proposed that a "bounty" be paid to citizens who informed on other citizens who were "addicts and sellers" and that mandatory life imprisonment be meted out to pushers. The *New York Times* reflecting the general air of despair that surrounds the problem, noted that many people "who once would have been quick to label the plan outrageous, reacted cautiously. . . . Those who did comment pointed out a host of problems . . . but almost unanimously applauded the prospect of being 'tough' on drugs." Within a short time thereafter, the president of the United States advanced a similar proposal and began to call for more drastic remedies to cure the nation's "heroin epidemic."

"Epidemic" is an interesting word. It was first introduced into discussions of the heroin problem by Dr. Jerome H. Jaffe in an interview with the *New York Times* on April 12, 1972. According to the article, whose headline read "Vietnam Methods of Heroin Control Urged for U.S.,"

Dr. . . . Jaffe said today that American medical techniques, including "quarantine," now provide the means to "break the back" of what he called the heroin "epidemic" in the country, much . . . as the use of heroin by the military in Vietnam was curbed. . . . "Because we know that one drug user communicates the drug experience to another, as in a flu epidemic," he said, "the armed services isolate individuals identified as hard-drug users, keeping them away from nonusers."

Dr. Jaffe's means of identifying heroin users was to require American civilians to submit to urinanalyses of a kind capable of detecting the presence of morphine metabolites. Those whose urine was found to be tainted would then be incarcerated. The article goes on to say that while these

procedures raise civil rights problems, "Dr. Jaffe believes that with sufficient support from the media the public could be persuaded to support
tests in schools and other institutions."

Viewed from a strictly structural perspective, by a professional who has
been trained to define all problems in terms of individual deviance from
established standards of conduct, the problem of social deviance invariably
appears to be no more than a technical problem of behavior control.
Technical problems have technical solutions, and among those offered by
Dr. Jaffe was a system of identification based on footprinting, supposedly
less objectionable to the public than fingerprinting, and the use of drugs
like cyclazocine which act as narcotic antagonists.[11]

It would be a mistake to dismiss Dr. Jaffe's proposals as arrant nonsense. They were made, after all, by a person who occupied a position of
political authority in an administration strongly committed to taking a
tough line against heroin addicts. Two months after the interview with Dr.
Jaffe appeared, the *Washington Post* reported a proposal by the Bureau of
Narcotics and Dangerous Drugs to reduce drug-related crime with a
method essentially the same as the one proposed earlier by Dr. Jaffe. This
time, however, it was couched in a combination of legal and medical language. The author, Dr. William McGlothlin of UCLA, called for a combination of programs centered on the "extensive civil commitment of addicts."
By "civil commitment" is meant involuntary incarceration or imprisonment by officially authorized order.

In McGlothlin's proposal the terminology of law enforcement and
medical treatment were very tightly interwoven. He envisioned that of the
270,000 addicts to be "treated," 45,000 would be "incarcerated in chemotherapy and psychotherapy centers," while the remainder would be
handled through "a major expansion of outpatient methadone maintenance programs." Backing both of these up would be "work camps and
heroin camps for outpatient violators." He also noted with satisfaction
that New York and California had already enacted legislation providing for
the civil commitment of addicts for periods of from five to seven years but
criticized the judicial authorities in both cases for being overly "reluctant
to commit arrested addicts for long periods of time."[12] It will be noticed
that McGlothin moved from the definition of heroin use as a medical problem to the use of law enforcement terminology and procedures as a means
of controlling the behavior of heroin users. The transition, which is not at
all uncharacteristic of the structural approach to social deviance, shows
rather clearly how medical science may play a role as an instrument of
behavior control.

Matthew Dumont, the former chief drug rehabilitation officer in Massachusetts, is one of the few professionals in the narcotics field who has
called attention to the consequences of collusion between the civil and

scientific authorities in the war on drugs. While serving as assistant Commissioner of mental health for the state, he wrote,

The current national drug abuse control effort is a serious threat to freedom in America. The usual law enforcement paraphernalia are being extravagantly focused on people who are neither sick nor criminal but who are being called sick as they are treated as criminals. . . . The addict is perceived as a dangerous and unwanted representative of unpopular social groups. When a scientific perspective dominated by a short-sighted medical model in conjunction with powerful technologies of prediction, monitoring and control occupies a commanding position in public policies on drug abuse, then we need to be more than anxious.[13]

The use of methadone maintenance to control the behavior of heroin users appears from the vantage point of a systems approach as an officially authorized form of drug abuse, but it is not the only one of its kind. Similar abuses surround the use of powerful psychotropic drugs to control the behavior of children.

"Minimal brain dysfunction," states a recent text, "is probably the single most common disorder seen by child psychiatrists."[14] Yet, before the 1960s the disorder hardly seemed to exist, and the term was unfamiliar even among professionals. What then is "minimal brain dysfunction," or MBD for short? (Other terms include "hyperkinetic reaction of childhood," "hyperkinetic syndrome," and "hyperactive child syndrome.") The term "hyperkinetic reaction of childhood (or adolescence)" is defined in the 1968 edition of the *Diagnostic and Statistical Manual of Mental Disorders*, published by the American Psychiatric Association, as "characterized by hyperactivity, restlessness, distractibility, and short attention span, especially in young children; the behavior usually diminishes in adolescence."[15]

A book on the subject written for a somewhat less technical audience suggests that "recognition of [MBD] is not difficult when, by the age of 5 years, at least half of the following signs are persistently and recurrently (not occasionally) present," and goes on to provide a list that includes "ceaseless, purposeless activity"; "short attention span"; "highly excitable; labile emotions (from tears to laughter in minutes)"; "poor response to reward/punishment"; "mixed L-R dominance (ex: R-handed/L-eyed/R-legged)"; "irregular developmental milestones (ex: no crawling then sudden walking; no babbling then sudden sentences)"; "'untidy' drawing, coloring, handwriting"; "inability to cope with phase-related activity (ex: collaborative games, riding bicycle, gym, etc.)"; "sleep disturbance"; and "needs constant supervision."[16]

How did it happen that MBD escaped the attention of the medical profession for so long? Surely it is not because there were previously no children who persistently and recurrently exhibited at least some of those symptoms before 1960. Anecdotes, fairy tales, folklore, and literature are full of such children, and adults since time immemorial have been alarmed by, and often impatient with, the altogether "impossible" child.

Much of the more serious literature on the behavior and misbehavior of children during the nineteenth century stressed, as it does today, that the proper management of children entails a subtle mixture of coercion by punishment or the threat of punishment and support by encouragement, love, and education. But these techniques, applied differently in different families and with different children within the same family, have not always produced the moral, mental, and physical characteristics that parents and other adults desire. Deviant and difficult-to-manage children were frequently perceived as biologically handicapped during the nineteenth century, and the opinion was often expressed by parents, teachers, and physicians that certain unfortunate children were "not born right." According to Sarah Cooper, who pioneered the kindergarten system in California during the 1880s, many children "come into the world freighted down with evil propensities and vicious tendencies. They start out handicapped in the race of life."[17]

It is important to notice that with few exceptions, the signs by which MBD is recognized are purely behavioral (the exceptions include a number of so-called "soft neurological signs" for which there is no more than slight evidence of underlying brain pathology). Indeed, as one textbook notes, there are no "hard" neurological signs by which MBD can be recognized: *"The most compelling evidence for the existence of MBD as an entity is (1) the similarity between its symptoms and symptoms of children with proven organic brain disease and (2) the remarkable response to certain medications, a response not found in non-MBD children."*[8] Although this may sound like compelling evidence, I will argue that it is not.

While MBD lacks a firm neurological basis, "physical stigmata" or "minor physiognomic abnormalities" are frequently said to be linked to it. Thus, one text lists decreased cranial size; strabismus (squint); epicanthus (a vertical fold of skin on either side of the nose, near the eyes); malformed ears; and abnormally shaped skull; "Although the discriminative cues may be difficult to specify," says the author, "it is my impression that a small fraction of MBD children fall into an unscientific but accurately described pediatric group, that of 'FLK' or 'funny looking kid'."[19] This classification recalls Erving Goffman's point that when we stigmatize a person, we imply he or she is less than human, and on this assumption, "we exercise varieties of discrimination, through which we effectively, if often unthinkingly, reduce his life chances."[20]

As I have already noted, MBD is reported to be highly prevalent. But, according to Dr. Paul H. Wender, the author of the comment on "funny-looking kids" and an expert on the subject, "its existence is often unrecognized and its prevalance is almost always underestimated." Dr. Wender lists five assertions about MBD: (1) it constitutes a large fraction of the more seriously disturbed population of children; (2) it is frequently misdiagnosed; (3) when it is diagnosed correctly, it is often maltreated; (4) the maltreatment is expensive, and by definition ineffectual; (5) the correct treatment is often dramatically effective, and is always cheap and readily accessible.[21]

Dr. Wender's first point concerns the incidence of MBD. How prevalent is it? According to one source, "Estimates have appeared stating that there are three million hyperkinetic children in the United States; that 7% of all school children are hyperkinetic, that 4% of pediatric practice consists of hyperkinetic children."[22] All of these estimates, the source implies, are too high, yet Wender cites studies suggesting that the incidence of MBD among elementary-school-age boys is on the order of 15 to 20 percent and states that in his personal experience in a university child-psychiatry clinic, about *half* of the preadolescent children "fell into the MBD category."[23]

Wender's next three points can be considered quite briefly. The point about misdiagnosis requires hardly any comment. Obviously he believes that MBD is too infrequently recognized by his colleagues. The maltreatment points refer, of course, to such things as psychotherapy, which are likely to be expensive. But the key point in his list is the last one. By a "correct treatment," Dr. Wender means the use of stimulant drugs; principally, *d*-amphetamine, although a closely related drug, methylphenidate (Ritalin) is also commonly used.

Amphetamine, commonly called "speed," is a potent stimulant drug which, in adults, has a number of effects, including an increase in alertness, insomnia, and suppression of appetite. Somewhat paradoxically, stimulant drugs appear to have dramatic calming effects upon the behavior of children who have been diagnosed as having MBD (indeed, a positive response to the drugs is one of the ways in which physicians try to determine whether to classify a child within the MBD category). No one really understands the reasons for this, but the pertinent point is that such reversals are rather common and do not necessarily indicate the presence of a disorder. Indeed, the only real justification for using speed to calm hyperactive children is that it works.

Like all drugs, amphetamine has side effects, and Wender acknowledges that such symptoms as headaches, stomachaches, tremor, tension, nail biting, sallowness, loss of appetite, and insomnia "occur in an appreciable fraction of children and are dose-related."[24] He does not mention, although it has been reported by others, that some children receiving amphetamine medication may suffer a reduction in growth rate.

All of these points, however, are secondary to the main point, which is that when children are treated with amphetamine they become quieter, more attentive, more respectful of authority, and generally less of a nuisance to their parents and teachers. It is also claimed that they are more responsive to their schoolwork and tend to learn better. Firm evidence of this is difficult to obtain, however, because it is almost impossible to disentangle the effects of docility, tractability, and obedience from the effects upon learning per se.

With the advent of the MBD syndrome, the seemingly endless search for the biological roots of social problems seems to have reached a qualitatively new dimension. Highly potent drugs that act directly upon the brain (in ways that are just beginning to be understood) are being used on a large scale in order to bring under control the behavior of children who have no demonstrable biological disease. There are approximately 50 million school-age children in the United States. According to some estimates, upwards of 2½ million (5 percent) of them have behavior disorders, learning problems, minimal brain damage, hyperkinesis, perceptual handicaps, reading disabilities, developmental dysfunctions, or any of a score of other defects attributed to them by modern mental health professionals. More than 200,000 (but still less than 10 percent) of these "problem children" are currently being "treated" with stimulant drugs "with the number increasing rapidly as proposals for mass screening begin to appear."[25]

That the entire approach to childhood deviance via MBD is highly questionable is suggested by two things. First, the diagnosis of MBD appears to be a peculiarity of contemporary American psychiatry. Other countries doubtless have their disobedient and nervous children, but in Scandinavia and England, for example, there are few if any physicians who are sufficiently audacious or skilled to identify the underlying brain dysfunction. Second, although lip service is frequently paid to alternative approaches by advocates of the drug-management approach to MBD, the more obvious alternatives remain largely unexplored. One might begin, for example, by proposing a serious program of research into the family system or into the school environment. Of course this would involve great complexity and expense—and the most reasonable "treatment" might turn out to be more freedom or better schools rather than pills and more stringent controls. But so long as the problem is seen to be merely one of behavior control, I think the cheap and simple drug approaches will continue to gain adherents, and as time passes we will have less and less of a prospect of saving children (and ourselves) from this dehumanizing chemical warfare.

I have noted that there is no conclusive evidence of a difference in the biochemistry or physiology of the brain in the so-called MBD child. Many researchers are now working on this point, however, and are searching for a distinctive biological correlate of the behavioral hyperactivity exhibited by such children. Let us suppose that a reliable physiological or biochemical correlate of MBD were to be identified tomorrow. I think such a discovery is likely: after all, it is most unlikely that differences in characteristic behavior patterns are not accompanied by comparable differences in brain organization. To many, the mere discovery of a distinctive brain correlate of MBD would unequivocally establish it as a disease and would justify the continued use of pharmacological remedies. But is this the correct approach? Does the mere existence of a difference denote the presence of disease? I do not think so. For example, it is possible to induce changes in the anatomy, physiology, and biochemistry of the brain merely by exposing animals to different regimens of experience. When rats are separated from their littermates and raised in a radically different environment, their brains show measureable differences although many of them can be reversed or minimized by altering the relevant environmental conditions.

By itself, the discovery of a difference in the brain of a so-called MBD child means nothing. Such a finding could legitimize the psychotechnological management of children only if we knew the extent to which the observed difference was independent of environmental or experiential influences, and after it was further demonstrated that the consequences of the brain difference constituted a more serious threat to the health and wellbeing of the child than the "treatment."

It is not easy to convince people to abandon the structural approach and its attendant "law and order" concepts of control in favor of the more sophisticated and scientific systems approach in which we think of individuals not in isolation but as part of a larger context that shapes them and is shaped by them. In many families, for example, if a member exhibits unexpected or deviant behavior, other members of the family may close ranks and agree that the deviant person "is in trouble," "needs help," or "ought to be taken care of." They may even seek outside aid, and the individual who has been "acting up" may be placed in the hands of a person or agency supposedly competent to help solve the problem. But whether this brings the disturbing behavior under control is beside the point. The family presumes too much when it locates the cause of the difficulty solely within the deviant individual, ignoring the possibility that it may be deeply embedded in the family system as a whole. This may protect the immediate coherence of the group, but may lead to disaster in the long run as the identified and labeled "patient" is bound more tightly than ever to the role of social deviant.

Whether in the case of the drug problem or the problem child, deviance is not so much a property of behavior itself as a value judgment conferred upon certain relationships within the reference group. Deviance, considered in this light, is a set of relationships among group members, and not merely a symptom of individual derangement that the group considers dangerous, embarrassing, or irritating, and against which it decides to bring sanctions. This is an important point, because it establishes a basis for distinguishing between deviance and disease. While the social and cultural meanings attached to different types of diseases may vary according to historical circumstances (gout in the eighteenth century, tuberculosis and epilepsy in the nineteenth), biological disease remains an entity in itself, whereas types of deviance tend to change as society evolves. The deviant in one social context may be the witch or the heretic, in another the runaway slave, the juvenile delinquent, the homosexual, the Jew, the junkie, or the "problem child."

In both families and societies, practical and political interests may be served by attributing blame, by identifying symptoms as causes, and by controlling individuals whose behavior is defined to be dangerous or disturbing. But to contend that such practices have a scientific justification denies the insights of science itself and confuses power with meaning.

Drug Abuse: "Better Living through Chemistry?"

7 **Violence:
The Pacification
of the Brain**

In the fall of 1967, following a "long hot summer" marked by riots and urban violence in the ghettos of many cities across the United States, three Boston physicians, all of them professors at the Harvard Medical School wrote a joint letter on "the role of brain disease in riots and urban violence" to the *Journal of the American Medical Association.* Their letter began with an acknowledgment that the economic cause "of the nation's urban riots is well-known" and that "the urgent needs of the underprivileged should not be minimized." "But," the letter went on to suggest, "the obviousness of these causes may have blinded us to the more subtle role of other possible factors including brain dysfunction in the rioters who engaged in arson, sniping and physical assault." The authors called for "intensive research and clinical studies of the *individuals* committing the violence," in order "to pinpoint, diagnose and treat . . . people with low violence thresholds before they contribute to further tragedies."[1]

Two of the letter's authors are well-known neurosurgeons, the third is a well-known psychiatrist. The intent of their proposal for diagnosis and treatment was to suggest the use of psychosurgery as a means of controlling violence. The purpose of this chapter is to examine the view, implicit in the foregoing letter and explicit elsewhere in their writings and the works of other influential authors, that a significant portion of the interpersonal violence and aggression in contemporary society is traceable to behavioral "dyscontrol" due to a disease or disorder of the brain, and that the proper way to bring such behavior under control is by selectively destroying specific parts of the brain.

The question How do brains work? remains one of the great unsolved riddles of modern biological science. Important clues come from a wide variety of sources, but neural and behavioral scientists are far from understanding how the brain gives rise to the intriguing phenomena of subjective experience. Whether research into the structure and functions of the nervous system will shed light on the ancient mystery of relations between the mind and the brain is unknown, but we do know that the coherence, continuity, and complexity of our conscious experience depends upon the organization and integrity of our brains.

That behavior is largely a reflection of brain function has been known since ancient times. Hippocrates, for example, asserted that "from the brain and the brain only arise our pleasures, joys, laughter and jests, as well as our sorrows, pains, griefs and tears. Through it, in particular, we think, see, hear, and distinguish the ugly from the beautiful, the bad from the good, the pleasant from the unpleasant. . . ."[2] Equally old is the knowledge that brain injury or disease is likely to produce profound effects upon behavior. Hippocrates, who helped to establish a rational approach to medical practice, was particularly critical of the idea—stemming from the view that the disease had a supernatural cause—that epilepsy could be cured by priestly incantations or other ritualistic practices. In terms with which most modern observers would agree, he insisted that the true cause of epilepsy was an affliction of the brain and was stern in his judgment of those who clung to the mystical-religious tradition, accusing them of using superstition to shelter their ignorance.

Today, epilepsy is one of a large number of ailments that are traceable to dysfunctions of the brain, and although the cause of the dysfunction remains mostly obscure, epilepsy can be treated by various methods. There are, for example, a number of drugs that are particularly effective in controlling the frequency or severity of seizures (a term that recalls the ancient idea that epileptics were possessed). In cases where the drugs do not work or cannot be administered, brain surgery may provide a degree of relief. Many forms of brain dysfunction have profound and debilitating effects upon behavior, and some of these can be effectively treated through the use of pharmacological, medical, and surgical methods. To cite one example, the presence of a brain tumor has profound effects on how a person behaves, effects that are often systematically related to the location of the tumor. There is probably no more dramatic indication of the relationship between brain function and behavior than the relief of these symptoms following the removal of certain brain tumors by neurosurgical means. There are, in other words, neurological diseases in which disturbances in behavior are due to some dysfunction within the brain and for which the only rational and ethically justifiable treatment is the judicious use of surgery or drugs. Thus under certain circumstances there is no plausible alternative to operating on the brain in order to relieve the patient's pain and suffering and possibly save his or her life.

The psychosurgery controversy has been conducted on several levels. On what might be called the theoretical level, there is disagreement among students of brain function and behavior about the scientific rationale for psychosurgery. On a more practical level, questions arise about the efficacy or success of psychosurgical operations. My aim in this chapter will be to show that the theory behind certain forms of psychosurgery can lay no legitimate claim to being scientific but on the contrary rests on a naive and generally discredited concept of brain function. I will also argue that there is no basis in fact for the exaggerated claims of therapeutic success that have been advanced by some proponents of psychosurgery. Even if psychosurgery rested upon a plausible neurobehavioral theory and worked as well as its advocates claim, the controversy would still remain unresolved on another level, that of ethics, since like all forms of psychotechnology, psychosurgery raises profound ethical questions.

As the discussion of questions like slavery, class conflict, immigration and racial purification has shown the ways in which health and sickness may be defined make it possible to use the definitions themselves as instruments of behavior control. Psychosurgery, like many other forms of behavior control technology, is promoted for the preservation or restoration of "normal," "better-adjusted," or "more competent" behavior in patients who have been diagnosed as mentally-ill, emotionally disturbed, uncontrollable, psychotic, or afflicted with a behavior disorder. In any society, the identification and diagnosis of mental patients determine how they are treated, so an evaluation of behavior control technology must consider not only its theoretical and practical development but also the social context in which it is used.

The target populations of psychosurgery are varied and the relevant social problems are numerous and complex; I will focus on the use of psychosurgery to control various kinds of violent or aggressive behavior.

It is clear that neuroscientists as well as public officials have been increasingly concerned with violence, aggression, and social turmoil in recent years. The first thing to notice is the existence of a mutual interest within the fields of medicine and public policy. They share what might almost be described as a vested interest in locating the causes of social turmoil within the domain of individual derangement, with the result that research on brain function and violent behavior is made to appear relevant to the solution of social problems. Dr. William H. Sweet, a Boston psychosurgeon, was speaking for many of his professional colleagues when he said,

. . . Human behavior, including violent assaultive action, is an expression of the functioning brain. It follows that one way to understand and control the current colossal problem of violence is to increase our knowledge of those brain mechanisms relating to emotion in general and to dangerous aggression in particular.[3]

The logic in Dr. Sweet's statement is revealing. That there is something not quite right about it may be seen by substituting almost any other "current colossal problem" for that of violence. Consider starvation, for example. Hunger triggers eating, and eating, like all forms of human behavior, is an expression of the functioning brain. But does it follow that one way to understand and control the current colossal problem of malnutrition and starvation is to increase our knowledge of those brain mechanisms relating to hunger and food-seeking behavior? Clearly not.

Yet some psychosurgeons insist upon promoting their activities on the grounds that the possibility of controlling behavior through brain manipulation holds great promise as a means of solving social problems. For example, the letter mentioned at the start of this chapter was written by Drs. William Sweet, Vernon Mark, and Frank Ervin who were all at that time members of the staff at the Massachusetts General Hospital. According to them, ". . . if slum conditions alone determined and initiated riots, why are the vast majority of slum dwellers able to resist the temptations of unrestrained violence? Is there something peculiar about the violent slum dweller that differentiates him from his peaceful neighbor?" The writers implied that the answer was affirmative and that psychosurgery might provide a way to avert "further tragedies."

Like many pejorative labels, the word *violence* is often used to obscure rather than illuminate phenomena that deserve careful examination and analysis. Since vehement or immoderate action is often labeled as violent in the light of presuppositions about the motives of the individuals engaging in it, it is important to examine, in any given instance, the perspectives from which collective or individual actions are labeled as violent. In the last analysis, violence is controversial not because it injures persons or destroys property, but because it represents an extreme difference of opinion about the propriety or justifiability of certain acts or exercises of power.

Violence—just or unjust—is a manifestation of brain function like any form of behavior. And, like other forms of behavior, violence may be made more or less likely to occur by psychosurgery or brain manipulation. However, the use of psychosurgery as a "treatment" for violence is open to serious criticism on several grounds.

The idea that violence as a social phenomenon is a symptom of brain dysfunction and should be dealt with as such implicitly denies that such behavior can be justified or even explained on any other grounds. To make an a priori judgment that all individuals who commit certain acts are sick is to make science subservient to a social ideology that ignores the essentially social nature of deviant behavior. Moreover, it serves to distract attention from the social context and obscures the need to answer questions such as Whose behavior is labeled as violent? and Toward whom are the violent acts directed?

Throughout history, one group's doctrines have been another group's heresies, and behavior viewed as senselessly violent from one perspective may be seen as "heroic resistance" from another. Thus, when repression is organized and carried out by those who claim legitimate authority, the activity may be labeled "peacekeeping" and officially praised. As one psychiatrist has noted, the victims of official violence outweigh the victims of interpersonal violence as the elephant outweighs the rat, yet the power of labeling is so strong that official violence is frequently redefined to make it appear correct, necessary, and just.

Psychologists, psychiatrists, psychosurgeons, and other mental health professionals generally focus upon the behavior of the rat, not the elephant. They are concerned almost exclusively with the kinds of violence like the murder, rape, and riot that fill our news media. The social bias inherent in the medical approach to violence leads it to focus on the lower class, or on the desperate or demented individual who places sticks of dynamite in a briefcase and threatens to blow up an office or a lavatory, the sort of person who, having been diagnosed as "incapable of controlling his or her violent impulses," might become a candidate for psychosurgery or some other form of behavior control.

But mental health professionals rarely apply their labels and propose their treatments when the violence is committed by individuals acting in an official capacity; the high public officials who ordered the destruction of Indochina by aerial and naval bombardment escape such diagnosis and treatment. The mental health approach to violence is selective; it tends to be used by the agents of the powerful to deal with the dissident behavior of the weak.

What is one to make of the claim that brain dysfunction plays a significant role in riots and other forms of social violence? Its plausibility rests, first of all, on a body of conventional wisdom that has a long history in popular literature and folklore. There are many stories in which an otherwise reasonable and gentle individual "goes into a spell," "loses control," and "runs amok. . . ." Two familiar examples are *The Wolf-Man* and *Dr. Jekyll and Mr. Hyde,* that epitomize the fear that only a thin line separates each of us from being harmed, or harming others, as a consequence of "episodic dyscontrol." The medical literature of many decades complements this popular view. It is replete with "case studies" of individuals afflicted with a form of epilepsy (psychomotor or temporal lobe epilepsy) that allegedly compels them to commit violent acts either during or between their seizures. To cite a representative example,

Among the most serious of behavior disturbances observed in this disease is a tendency to homicidal activity. . . . Murder committed by epileptics has several typical characteristics. There is violent behavior (usually with a knife). . . .[4]

Despite the widespread acceptance of this characterization of the epileptic, one group of reviewers concluded bluntly that the prevailing opinion about the "behavioral peculiarities" of epileptic patients may be a myth, pointing out that ". . . we have not been able to find a single paper which . . . meets the most rudimentary standards of experimental design and reporting."[5] Other observations indicate that people with psychomotor epilepsy are simply incapable of making a coordinated and directed assault during a seizure. One observer with fourteen years of direct experience with such patients writes that none of them had ever hurt a member of the nursing staff or another patient as a result of a seizure.[6] In summary, if there is no solid foundation to the claim that people suffering from epilepsy are particularly predisposed to exhibit assaultive or violent behavior, there is no a priori basis for believing that episodic dyscontrol due to hidden brain disease plays a significant role in urban riots or other forms of social violence. Perhaps the most balanced conclusion that can be drawn about the relationship between brain disease and violent behavior is the one that emerged from a recent extensive review of the literature by the National Institute of Neurological Diseases and Stroke, which suggested that ". . . violence and aggressive acts do occur in patients with temporal lobe (or psychomotor) epilepsy but such are rare, perhaps no more frequent than in the general population."[7]

Such doubts notwithstanding, the three authors of the letter contended that there was "evidence from several sources, that brain dysfunction related to a focal lesion plays a significant role in the violent and assaultive behavior of thoroughly studied patients," less than three years later two of them wrote a book entitled *Violence and the Brain* which attempted to show that there is a dyscontrol syndrome caused by localized brain dysfunction and that it is both possible and desirable to "treat the dysfunction directly" by psychosurgery. Their argument, which begins with the idea that a significant amount of social violence is caused by persons with brain abnormalities, goes on to propose their detection and concludes that psychosurgery is the treatment of choice for "taming" human beings who are senselessly violent, assaultive, or otherwise out of control:

In other words, we need to develop an "early warning test" of . . . brain function to detect those humans who have a low threshold for impulsive violence, and we need better and more effective methods of treating them once we have found out who they are. Violence is a public health problem, and the major thrust of any program dealing with violence must be toward its prevention—a goal that will make a better and safer world for us all.[8]

As with eugenic sterilization and the destruction of "lives devoid of value," profound social consequences may follow when physicians purport to establish public health as an ideal, separate from and superior to, the health of individuals. Under such circumstances the term *public* health no longer represents the collective of individuals but society itself, which by implication excludes those individuals whose behavior has been defined as a "public health problem."

Psychosurgery did not spring, fully formed, out of the ancient knowledge that brain injury or disease may be accompanied by dramatic changes in behavior and mental life. Its origins are more recent. The first published account of brain operations intended specifically to alter behavior (as opposed to surgery to relieve physical malformation or injury of the brain) was by Dr. Gottlieb Burckhardt who was, in 1891, director of an insane asylum at Prefargier, Switzerland. Dr. Burckhardt believed that the agitation, excitement, and impulsiveness of his more disturbed and uncontrollable patients was the result of a physical or functional derangement within their brains. He attributed "excessive behavioral excitement" to "abnormal impulses" arising from the cerebral cortex and undertook to reduce it by destroying what he believed to be the offending brain regions. "Our psychological existence," he wrote, "is composed of single elements, which are localized in separate areas of the brain." In other words, he believed that human behavior is reducible to an enumerable set of faculties, each of which has its own territory of localization within the brain, and that both insanity and criminal behavior were caused by localized derangement in particular brain "organs."

Burckhardt reported operations on six patients; one died as a consequence of the surgery and the other five patients continued to exhibit symptoms of psychosis. Burckhardt contended, however, that they were more peaceful and easier to manage and that the problems of regulating the behavior of otherwise unmanageable individuals made the operations worthwhile, in spite of their limited success.[9]

Although Burckhardt's was the first reported case of psychosurgery itself, the theory behind it emerged from several nineteenth-century disciplines. One of these, ethnology, had as one of its guiding ideas, at least among its American practitioners, that members of primitive societies were biologically and not merely culturally inferior to members of more complex societies. It was one of the leaders of the American school of ethnology, Dr. Samuel Morton, who introduced craniology as a new quantitive method of ranking human beings on the basis of brain size or cranial capacity. However, not only were Morton's measurements imprecise—the 11 percent difference in cranial size he reported between blacks and Europeans was highly subject to statistical error—but even in terms of the science of his own day there were no grounds for believing that there was any relation between the size of the brain and intellectual capacity. Craniology was greatly in vogue in the nineteenth century, but when it came to comparing the sexes rather than racial or ethnic groups, the overall disparity in weight and height between men and women raised the additional question of whether cranial capacity should be measured absolutely or relatively.[10]

Stephen Gould, a professor of geology at Harvard University recently reported the findings of his own analysis of Morton's raw data. What he found was that the "self-styled objective empiricist," having amassed a large collection of skulls from all over the world, "measured their capacity and produced the results anticipated in an age when few Caucasians doubted their innate superiority: whites above Indians, blacks at the bottom." For Gould, Morton's conclusions "are based on a patchwork of apparently unconscious finagling. When his data are properly reinterpreted, all races have approximately equal capacities." Gould's pertinent conclusion is that such "unconscious or dimly perceived finagling is probably endemic in science, since scientists are human beings rooted in cultural contexts, not automatons directed toward external truth."[11]

Phrenology, like craniology, was concerned with the brain and its relationship to human behavior, especially social behavior. Around 1795, in an intellectual climate where interest in the relationship between the brain and behavior was already beginning to flourish, a successful practicing physician, who had also attained repute as a skilled anatomist, began to lecture in Vienna on "the powers of the mind." This was Franz Josef Gall, the founder of phrenology, or, as he preferred to call it "cranioscopy." The central dogma of phrenology was that each mental and moral faculty was controlled by a specific part of the brain and that an excess or deficiency in both a trait and its corresponding "brain organ" could be detected through a cranioscopic examination of the overlying skull surface.

By his account, Gall had been struck at an early age by differences in personality and character among his friends and fellow students. His own bad memory was particularly vexing to him; as he saw it, many of his schoolmates were endowed with memories more efficient and facile than his. He lamented the differences and complained that they were able to succeed at their schoolwork with little effort and "often took away from me the rank I had earned in the written compositions."[12]

Gall made what he later described as "careful observations" of his schoolmates and thought he had discovered the secret of their success: they all had large and protruding eyes. It was not the conclusion of Gall, the student, that the protruding eyes of his gifted friends were due to the presence of an "organ of verbal memory" located behind the eyeball, but Gall, the phrenologist, eventually came to exactly that conclusion. Indeed, he became a phrenologist, or so he said, because the brain and its relation to behavior was ignored in his courses of instruction when he was a medical student. At that time, the brain was regarded as a unitary and undifferentiated structure, and apart from some medieval conjectures—according to which various mental qualities "resided" in the hollow, fluid-filled, ventricles of the brain—no one seriously entertained the idea, advanced more than two thousand years earlier, that the various functions of the mind had diverse territories of localization in different parts of the brain.

The first person known to argue that the brain was the organ of the mind—the seat of sensation, perception, and thought, and the center of intellect, feeling, and behavior—was a Greek contemporary of Pythagoras by the name of Alcmaeon. This insight—the more remarkable because of the scanty anatomical and physiological knowledge of the ancients—stood in opposition to the belief that the viscera (the heart and other internal organs) were the principal determinants of behavior, mental activity, and physical health. According to the "humoral theory," which in one form or another has survived until relatively recent times, substances such as blood, bile, and phlegm were responsible for different behavioral types, or temperaments. (The humoral terminology still lingers in descriptive terms like sanguine, bilious, and phlegmatic.) But Alcmaeon's insight went still further. At a time when most of his contemporaries placed the sensations in the viscera (as commonsense language still places feelings in the heart, the breast, the gut, and the bowels), Alcmaeon postulated that each sensation had its own specific territory of localization within the brain.

The attempt to recapture and strengthen the concept of brain localization may be glimpsed subsequently, if only sporadically, throughout the entire course of medical—and more particularly neurological and psychological—history. But it did not emerge again in any comprehensive form until Franz Josef Gall resurrected it. It would be a gross oversimplification to say that Gall merely reinvented an idea that had lain dormant since ancient times. To be sure, Gall more than anyone else helped to establish the fact that the brain is the principal material basis of human behavior and that it is a highly differentiated organ. But he and his followers went much further. To the plausible idea of brain localization, Gall added three additional postulates. The result was an absurd but highly popular system of "faculty psychology" and brain organology. Armed with its doctrines and the technique of cranioscopy, Gall and many credulous followers professed to explain scientifically the riddles of human nature and human diversity.

Gall's first postulate, and the key to his psychology, was that mental activity is reducible to a set of independent traits or faculties. He listed twenty-seven of these, nineteen of which were shared by human beings and other ("lower") animals; the eight other faculties were said to be possessed by humans alone. These were elaborately catalogued under such titles as "self-defense and courage," "caution and forethought," "vanity, ambition, love of glory," and so on.

The second postulate was that each of these faculties, aptitudes, or propensities was localized in a distinct organ or surface region of the brain. But the final, and by far the best known, postulate of phrenology was that the development of the faculties and organs covaries with the size and shape of the cranium, so that a well-developed organ is indicated by a protuberance of the skull in the relevant region, and the presence of a protuberance betokens the presence of a well-developed faculty. In like manner, poorly developed organs and faculties were allegedly related to (and diagnosable by) indentations in the skull. Consequently, or so the phrenologists claimed, it was possible to make a comprehensive and accurate psychological analysis on the basis of the bumps and indentations on a person's head.

There can be no disputing the vital scientific importance of the phrenological assertion about the primacy of the brain as the organ of the mind and the anatomical basis of behavior. On this crucial point, Gall advanced no fewer than twelve closely reasoned proofs drawn from diverse sources such as comparative anatomy (the study of brain structure and function in various species of animals), neuropathology (the study of the effects of brain injury and malformation on behavior), and clinical neurology (medical evidence that brain injury or disease affecting different parts of the central nervous system leads to different kinds of symptoms). But with the postulation of discrete mental faculties, and the attempt to link each to a distinct, corresponding brain organ, phrenology lost contact with reality. There was no basis for thinking that human behavior could be categorized this way and no reason to accept the alleged brain organs as real. The central idea of "practical phrenology"—that meaningful inferences can be drawn from cranioscopy—is nonsense.

Despite its dubious validity, phrenology enjoyed a tremendous popular reception. It appeared to offer a key to the mysteries of human nature, a means of understanding, simply and logically, why people behave as they do. Like the popularizers of psychology and psychiatry today, the phrenologists of the nineteenth century told their contemporaries how to be happy, how to solve personal problems, how to choose a mate, how to raise children, and how to succeed in business. It would be pleasant to report that this spurious and wildly overstated diagnostic technology was stringently questioned by many responsible scientists, but unfortunately it was not. Those who studied phrenology considered it a serious science, and it was received and sponsored as such by many wealthy and reputable people whose opinions set the standards of their times. During the nineteenth century phrenological ideas permeated the fields of education, medicine, and religion and had an important cultural influence upon many aspects of American life.

Phrenologists took an interest in all forms of diversity, deviance, and departures from normal behavior. Like other forms of craniology, the science of phrenology was used to "prove" the mental inferiority of all but the white nationalities of European stock. The Scotsman George Combe, an early convert to cranioscopy and after Gall and Spurzheim, one of the most respected of phrenologists, frequently expounded the familiar theme of the Negro's natural inferiority. His "evidence" was the phrenological dogma that "intellectual capacity" was localized in the anterior (frontal) parts of the brain and was indicated not only by the facial angle but by the height and width of the forehead. According to Combe and other phrenologists, the anterior portions of the skull were somewhat narrower, on the average, in Negroes, and this was said to explain why the social status of blacks was inferior to that of whites. Even some ardent abolitionists believed it, including Horace Greeley, who felt that phrenology had proved the Negro to be "temporarily" inferior.[14]

Phrenology continued to prosper as a convenient source of support for doctrines of biological inferiority until around 1870, when it was reported that the skull shapes of Africans and Scandinavians were similar enough to require them to be categorized as belonging to the same race grouping. At that point, even phrenology's staunchest supporters knew something was wrong.[15] But for a long time before that phrenologists had been rendering stern judgments on the moral tendencies, mental abilities, and social capacities of diverse individuals and groups. Gall was convinced, for example, that he could tell a male from a female human brain by its superficial appearance.[16] His student and colleague, Spurzheim, elaborated on the notion of smaller cranial capacity by asserting that it was mainly the frontal lobes (which phrenologists generally associated with the higher mental powers) that were markedly diminished in females. For as long as phrenologists flourished and cranioscopy remained a credible means of measuring human traits, such claims continued to be one of the most popular and persuasive ways of "proving" the mental inferiority and emotional instability of women.

For obvious reasons, phrenology enjoyed an extraordinarily cordial reception among the social elite. During its heyday in the United States, around 1840, phrenology was the subject of lectures and demonstrations in which distinguished authorities thrilled their rich and respectable listeners by telling them precisely what they wanted to hear. When George Combe, who was then regarded by aficionados as the foremost phrenologist in the world, made a lecture-tour of several American cities at the invitation of a group of wealthy philanthropists, he invariably flattered his audiences. In Boston, for example, Combe was pleased to announce that his "eyes never rested on such a collection of excellent brains . . . bigheaded, moral, intellectual and energetic Pilgrims, enlightened and civilized. . . ."[17]

Such flattery sounds like empty puffery unless phrenology is understood to be what it mainly was: a social philosophy in which class and character were congenially linked to doctrines of biological hierarchy. Were it not for its ability to simultaneously reflect and reinforce the social status quo, it would be impossible to understand its meteoric rise and relatively long-lived popularity, for considered as a science, phrenology did not have the slightest reason to exist. This point was well recognized by critics at the time, whose views are worth considering briefly to show that hindsight is not required to see phrenology for what it was.

One of the main lines of criticism leveled at phrenology attacked it as a pseudoscience. This charge was most often brought by "experts" who were themselves scientists or physicians. Many were in general sympathy with empirical research about questions of brain function and behavior and admired the overall effort to classify and measure human faculties, but they strongly disagreed with the way the phrenologists went about it. Perhaps the best known among those who opposed phrenology on scientific grounds was Thomas Sewall, a professor of anatomy at the Columbian College of Washington, D.C. In 1837, he published a pamphlet entitled *An Examination of Phrenology* in which he attacked its scientific pretensions in a rational and temperate way. Sewall's critique concentrated on several points of objection: (1) the anatomical structure of the brain does not reveal, upon dissection and examination, any parts of organs corresponding to those the phrenologists claimed to exist; (2) there is no factual basis for the belief (shared by the craniologists and the phrenologists) that a bigger brain is a better brain, because except in frankly pathological cases, there is no correlation between the size or volume of the brain and the capacity for mental activity or intelligence; (3) it is impossible, because of variations in the thickness of the cranial bones, to make reliable inferences about underlying brain structure from observations (however precise) of the external skull; this point is particularly pertinent with respect to the most anterior parts of the brain (to which the phrenologists imputed many of the higher psychological functions such as intelligence and memory), because the sinus cavities and unpredictable form of the interior frontal bones are mainly responsible for the shape of the front of the skull. Thus, the shape or size of the underlying "brain organs"—even supposing that they exist—cannot be ascertained by cranioscopy; (4) when, by accident or disease, a specific area of the brain is injured or destroyed, the faculty that is supposed to "reside" in that spot, and which ought to be correspondingly affected, is generally not noticeably impaired.

These were damning criticisms at the time, and they are no less so today. There was, however, another school of criticism whose members took aim at the social orientation of phrenology and its self-styled relevance to the world of practical affairs. Scientific skeptics felt it was irrational to classify and quantify human faculties according to arbitrary or biased criteria, and philosophically and religiously inclined critics added that it was, furthermore, immoral and unethical.

There were, in short, serious efforts, based on reasonable grounds, to reject phrenological ideas at the time when they were being advanced. But the partisans of the "new psychology" gave back almost as good as they got. Most of their rejoinders were heavily tinged with vituperation and pleas against the "persecution" of those who advanced new or unorthodox ideas. In general, the advocates of phrenology stood silent as their "science" was pressed into the service of various social contempt doctrines, but like so many other professional experts before and since, they cried "foul" when their objectivity was questioned. Edward Thomson was expressing the feelings of many phrenology enthusiasts when he lamented criticism of the field as "unjust and disgraceful to the age," adding that "one might suppose that the world had learned a lesson from the opposition to Columbus and to Copernicus, and the persecutions of Galileo, and the martyrdom of Servetus."[18]

In spite of such protests it was phrenology—more than any other form of psychology—that established in the public mind a receptive attitude toward the notion that human behavior (for all its obvious complexity) was ultimately reducible to classification and measurement in terms of specific faculties, propensities, or scales. It was the phrenologists—long before Binet invented the intelligence test—who first maintained that traits like intelligence were amenable to quantitative measurement. Thus phrenology laid the essential groundwork for all subsequent attempts to assign numerical values to human behavior. As a social philosophy, phrenology was able to suggest that problems like crime, delinquency, drug addiction, and prostitution were ultimately the result of organic derangement of the brain, since if the determinants of social, economic, and intellectual success lay in the realm of "brain excellence," then it surely followed that deviance and failure must have comparable origins. And once it became credible to define social deviance as the result of an abnormality in the function of one or another brain "organ," the path from phrenology to psychosurgery was short.

The peculiar contribution of phrenology to the work of Dr. Burckhardt, the first practitioner of psychosurgery was that it provided a socially appealing alternative to earlier theories which equated insanity and criminality with demonic possession. It offered a completely consistent, seemingly rational, and ostensibly plausible conception of abnormal behavior as a reflection of localized brain dysfunction. It is not difficult to understand why its advocates believed that the selective destruction of a specific brain area would effectively abolish the behavior associated with it. However, the idea that specific faculties were localized and compartmentalized like so many little black boxes was phrenology's most grievous error. By 1845, Pierre Flourens, a French scientist, had performed an experiment that clearly refuted this notion. While studying pigeons, he demonstrated conclusively that large portions of the brain could be removed without impairing any specific functions independently; in particular, he showed that the cerebellum (a part of the brain at the back of the head where the phrenologists had claimed "amativeness" or sexuality resided) could be removed without causing deleterious effects upon reproductive behavior.

Brain scientists today understand that localization of function exists, but not in the terms used by the phrenologists. The sense of vision, for example, is localized in that there are discrete pathways and centers in the brain whose integrity is essential for seeing. But the faculty of sight (or visual perception) involves an integration of activity in these primary visual pathways or centers and in many other brain regions as well. In general, the more complex and subtle aspects of behavior arise not out of the independent activity of individual brain organs but rather out of the integrated functioning of both localized and diffuse systems.

Burckhardt's efforts at psychosurgery were based on a false concept of brain localization. Since his mistake is understandable in hindsight, it would be sufficient to leave it at that, were it not for the fact that today— when the awesome complexity and subtlety of both behavior and brain function are generally appreciated—the spurious doctrines of phrenology live on. Indeed, they flourish among the uncritical champions of psychosurgery as a rational, scientific, and objective method of treatment for various "behavior disorders." The concept of treatment, therefore, deserves careful consideration as a form of behavior control shaped even more than psychosurgery by the doctrines of nineteenth-century ethnology, craniology, and phrenology. The elaboration of ideas about the innate biological inferiority of entire human groups, such as women and blacks, stimulated additional speculation to the effect that such groups were peculiarly susceptible to diseases and afflictions from which other, allegedly superior groups were immune. Many of the ethnologists of the American school, like Morton, were physicians, and medical arguments were frequently adduced to "prove" the inherent inferiority thesis.

Definitions of normal and abnormal behavior raise recurrent issues of medical ethics. There is always the risk that what is called "normal" behavior is merely a reflection of prevailing social standards, and once these are affirmed, deviation can readily be defined as "disease" or "abnormality." Although it is possible to distinguish between them, the stipulation of behavioral norms and the diagnosis of deviations are more properly considered as two interrelated aspects of a single process of social definition. In the nineteenth century, as now, those at the bottom of the social scale were peculiarly susceptible to being the objects of behavior control under the guise of medical treatment. The slaves in the period before the Civil War are a case point, which a further look at Dr. Samuel Cartwright's 1851 report to the Louisiana Medical Association may serve to illustrate.

It will be recalled that Cartwright began his report by offering a purportedly scientific description of the mental and physical "peculiarities of the negro race." Normal black people, according to Cartwright, suffered from "defective atmospherization of the blood" and therefore had to submit to "the compulsive power of the white man" in order to properly "vitalize" their blood and thereby avoid "the debasement of mind" to which they were otherwise naturally susceptible. Having established that their physiology makes it normal and even beneficial for black people to submit to servitude (although, as in many arguments of this kind, it is never entirely clear whether this is what they naturally tend to do, or what they ought to do), Cartwright turned his attention to an obvious and disturbing form of "behavioral abnormality," the runaway slave.

"The absconding from service," he wrote, "is well known to our planters and overseers, as it was to the ancient Greeks." Moreover, said Cartwright, the Greeks had a word for it: *drapetes*, which expressed both "the fact of the absconding, and the relation that the fugitive held to the person he fled from." With this bit of etymology behind him, Cartwright went on to announce that he had discovered the root cause of drapetes to be a "disease of the mind," for which he proposed the obvious name: drapetomania. According to *Dorland's Medical Dictionary* (1957), drapetomania still means "the insane desire to wander away from home," and according to Cartwright it develops when the "true method of governing negroes" is not properly followed. Although drapetomania has been "unknown to our medical authorities" and has often been mistaken for willful disobedience, as a general rule, it is easily curable provided, of course, that "proper medical advice is strictly followed." The "true method" of controlling the behavior of slaves, says Cartwright in effect, is to administer a systematic schedule of positive and negative reinforcements, and to avoid both extreme permissiveness and extreme cruelty.

When all this is done, if any one or more of them, at any time, are inclined to raise their heads to a level with their master or overseer, humanity and their own good require that they should be punished until they fall into that submissive state which was intended for them to occupy. . . . They have only to be kept in that state, and treated like children to prevent and cure them from running away.[19]

Cartwright's investigations into "the maladies of the negro race" revealed to him another disorder, this time of frankly neurological origin, which allegedly arose even under conditions where "the true method of governing negroes" was scrupulously followed. Indeed, cases of this disorder seemed to him ubiquitous, existing almost as frequently on well-governed plantations as on poorly governed ones, and were almost universal among "free negroes, or those who are not governed at all." The key to the disorder, according to Cartwright, was that slaves who tended to "raise disturbances . . .without cause or motive" also tended to "seem insensitive to pain when being punished." What Cartwright had observed was the fact (for a fact it presumably was) that certain especially troublesome slaves (defined as "rascally" by their masters) failed to show overt signs of pain upon being whipped. Thus without needing any further arguments, Cartwright was in a position to render a diagnosis: "Partial insensibility of the skin and great hebetude of the intellectual faculties." Because the "insensibility" was only partial, Cartwright drew back from calling the disease which he had discovered *an*esthesia—he called it *dysesthesia* instead.

The cause? "Imperfect atmospherization or vitalization of the blood." The treatment? Here is Cartwright's prescription:

The liver, skin and kidneys should be stimulated to activity . . . [to] assist in decarbonizing the blood. The best means to stimulate the skin is, first, to have the patient well washed with warm water and soap; then to anoint it all over with oil, and to slap the oil in with a broad leather strap; then to put the patient to some hard kind of work in the open air and sunshine that will compel him to expand his lungs, as chopping wood, splitting rails, or sawing with the cross-cut or whip saw.[20]

If repeated daily, Cartwright added, "such treatment will, in a short time, effect a cure in all cases that are not complicated by visceral derangements." He did not elaborate further, nor did he have to.

Black slavery was not the only nineteenth-century American social institution that received the benefit of such an ideologically biased medical defense. Most of the nineteenth-century ideas about the inherent inferiority of women are traceable to a form of biological determinism according to which the female reproductive system (especially the ovaries and the uterus) was directly responsible for women's behavior. In their textbooks and medical practices, male physicians promoted the idea that uterine and ovarian factors lurked behind almost every female virtue as well as every female complaint. As one gynecologist wrote in 1870, there could be no doubt about the "gigantic power and influence of the ovaries over the whole animal economy of woman."[21] Thus, medical science, with its remorseless emphasis upon the biological determinants of behavior helped immeasurably to keep women—both rich and poor—in their "proper" places within the prevailing social hierarchy.

The idea of localizing the biological basis of women's behavior in their reproductive organs is part of the long and often bitter controversy that has raged among authorities, including psychologists and psychiatrists, on the question of whether or not genetic predispositions, "intrapsychic conflict," or "inadequate histories of reinforcement" are chiefly responsible for mental illnesses or behavior disorders. It is important to stress, however, that biologically oriented psychiatrists, psychodynamically oriented psychoanalysts, and behavioristically oriented psychologists are generally agreed upon one thing: that the individual should be the focus of diagnosis and treatment. At issue here is the question of whether the organization of the brain permits one to localize the cause of complex psychological behavior, either normal or abnormal, within a given "brain organ." The answer is plainly no, yet even if it were otherwise, it would not necessarily follow that the extirpation, destruction, or manipulation of a specific brain region would benefit a person whose behavior is deemed to be somehow out of control.

In retrospect, it hardly seems surprising that the only positive statement that the first psychosurgeon was able to make was that the patients who had been subjected to his surgery had become somewhat easier to manage, that is to say, pacified. Burckhardt was generally optimistic, however, and concluded his paper with the hope that other surgeons would soon take up his methods and "tread the path of cortical extirpation with ever better and more satisfactory results," although almost a half-century was to pass before anyone stepped forward to claim that better and more satisfactory results had been obtained through the use of psychosurgery.

At an International Congress of Neurology held in London in 1935, two American brain researchers reported the results of some experiments on monkeys and chimpanzees. The investigators were Carlyle F. Jacobsen and John F. Fulton, and their report dealt with the behavioral effects of surgical destruction of the most anterior (the so-called "prefrontal") regions of the primate brain. The prefrontal area of the human brain is especially large and accounts, in part, for the large facial angle with which theorists both ancient and modern have associated intelligence and other higher functions of the brain. The idea that the prefrontal area played a special role in complex thought processes had been shared by many ethnologists, phrenologists, and physiologists during the nineteenth century, but it lacked a factual foundation. It was this lack that Jacobsen and Fulton had set out to repair.

Their study was, in effect, the first systematic investigation of the functions of the prefrontal cortex in primates based upon the technique of selective destruction or ablation, and it remains a classic among subsequent studies aimed at understanding the functions of the brain by analyzing the behavioral effects of selective lesions. Jacobsen and Fulton trained their animals to perform a specific learned response in order to obtain a reward of food being placed under one of several cups, but a grill or other device prevents the animal from reaching for it immediately. An opaque screen is then lowered in front of the animal so that the cups cannot be seen. After a predetermined delay, the screen and the restraining grill are raised out of the way, and the animal is allowed to displace the cup of its choice. In order to obtain food at better than chance frequency, the animal must remember where it was placed. Normally, monkeys and chimpanzees can (after preliminary training) perform extremely well even at delay intervals lasting a minute or longer.

After Jacobsen and Fulton had trained their animals and initial performance levels had been established, they performed an operation in which the prefrontal regions of the brain on both the left and right sides were ·destroyed under surgical anesthesia. When the animals recovered from this bilateral frontal lobectomy, they were retested and were found to be markedly impaired. The primary finding of the experiment was, in other words, that the integrity of the prefrontal area was necessary for normal performance of the delayed-response task, but additional findings suggested that the functions of this brain area were more numerous, complex, and varied than previously supposed. In order to illustrate this point, Jacobsen and Fulton described in detail the pre- and postoperative behavior of a chimpanzee named Becky, who before the operation was "highly emotional and profoundly upset whenever she made an error," and was likely to fly into violent temper tantrums when the screen was lowered in front of the baited cups or when she made a mistake. After the operation, Becky behaved very differently and sat quietly while the cups were baited and the screen lowered. "If the animal made a mistake, it showed no evidence of emotional disturbance but quietly awaited the loading of the cups for the next trial" (notice that the experimenters stopped referring to her as "she").[22]

These postoperative changes led the investigators to conclude that Becky had been tamed by the surgery and transformed into a docile and contented animal who had joined a "happiness cult." This conclusion, together with the results of the delayed-response tests, was reported at the Neurological Congress. In the audience was a Portuguese neurologist, Egas Moniz, and after Jacobsen's presentation Dr. Moniz "asked if frontal lobe removal prevents the development of experimental neuroses in animals and eliminates frustrational behavior, why would it not be feasible to relieve anxiety states in man by surgical means?"[23] Fulton was profoundly shocked by the suggestion, but Moniz returned to Portugal convinced that a scientific basis now existed on which to justify the use of brain surgery to modify behavior and to improve "the mental life of some lunatics . . . and, in particular, of obsessed and melancholic patients." Moniz's rationale was an updated version of Burckhardt's: "Normal psychic life depends upon the good functioning of [brain] synapses," he wrote, "and mental disorders appear as a result of synaptic derangements." Being, in his words, "convinced of the importance of the prefrontal lobes in mental life" he thought that it was only necessary to alter "synaptic adjustments" by surgical means in order "to modify the corresponding ideas and force thought into different channels."[24]

Moniz's stated purpose was "to annihilate a great number of associations, . . . to attack [en masse] the cell-connecting fibers of the anterior portion of both frontal lobes." Since he was not a neurosurgeon, he prevailed upon a colleague named Almeida Lima to do the actual surgery, and the first series of operations began in Lisbon early in November 1935. At first, injections of alcohol were used to coagulate the fiber tracts running between the frontal lobes and the other parts of the brain; by the end of December a leucotome (a small knife) was being used to sever the tracts.

Moniz described the first twenty cases of "prefrontal leucotomy" in a monograph published in 1936. All patients were reported to have survived the operation; seven were described as having been "cured," and another eight (who had been, according to Moniz, especially violent and agitated) were said to have become calmer and easier to manage. On the whole, Moniz later recalled, "we obtained cures and improvements but no failures to make us draw back."[25]

These claims of success are difficult to evaluate. Moniz described his cases with a minimum of clinical detail and a large measure of promotional optimism. By doing this, he established a style that was destined to be widely adopted by other psychosurgeons. Indeed, the popularity of prefrontal lobectomy or lobotomy spread rapidly and within a short time similar operations were being performed on psychiatric patients throughout the world, although it is impossible to find an accurate figure for the total number of prefontal lobotomies performed up to the present. Moniz himself probably accounted for no more than a hundred. An assault by a lobotomized patient left him with a bullet in his spine, and he retired, an invalid, in 1944; in 1949 he shared the Nobel Prize in medicine for his "discovery of the therapeutic value of prefrontal leucotomy in certain psychoses."

In 1936, Drs. Walter Freeman and James Watts introduced prefrontal lobotomy into the United States, and by 1950 they had operated on more than a thousand patients. Freeman, when he retired in 1970, had performed or supervised more than thirty-five hundred operations.[26] In the United States alone, it has been estimated that forty to fifty thousand prefrontal lobotomies of different kinds were done between 1936 and 1955.[27]

At first, candidates for psychosurgery came mainly from among groups of chronically hospitalized mental patients, most of whom had been diagnosed as incurably violent, psychotic, or otherwise deranged. In such patients, considerable improvement was usually claimed following prefrontal lobotomy. The "improvement" often consisted, however, of an increase in docility and obedience which made the patients tamer and easier for hospital officials to control or manage. Gradually, however, lobotomies came to be performed on individuals who were much less severely disturbed prior to surgery. As Valenstein points out,

One of the main factors that contributed to the upsurge of psychosurgery in the United States . . . was the number of returning veterans at the end of World War II who were psychiatrically disabled. Faced with the demand from relatives for rapid and drastic treatment, and insufficient number of trained psychiatrists, and very little in the way of psychoactive drugs, authorities in the Veterans Administration accepted the optimistic reports on prefrontal lobotomy and encouraged its use.[28]

The optimistic reports to which Valenstein referred were mainly of two types. There were, first of all, numerous individual "case studies" produced by the psychosurgeons and generally intended, not surprisingly, to prove the effectiveness of their techniques. These case studies claimed to show that the benefits of lobotomy strongly outweighed the risks and that lobotomized persons were not only tamer but generally healthy and able to function even at a high professional and administrative level. Typical of such case reports is one by Walter Freeman, which describes a physician who had been discharged from two internships because of "aggressive paranoid behavior." After his lobotomy he finished his internship, married and had a family, and established a clinic. Freeman added that he even "flies his own planes."[29]

The second type of optimistic report (of which there were far fewer) were large-scale retrospective evaluations of the lobotomy procedures performed in a given clinic or hospital district over an extended period of time. One such study, involving a thousand lobotomized patients from mental hospitals in England and Wales, reported that in terms of social behavior 24 percent were unchanged, 30 percent were improved, 17 percent were greatly improved, 24 percent were cured and living at home, and fewer than 2 percent had become worse (the few remaining persons could not be located). However, in this and other favorable studies the claimed rate of success is difficult to interpret because the case evaluations were invariably made by the psychosurgeons themselves or by investigators professionally associated with them.

Untoward side effects of prefrontal lobotomy were rarely reported at the outset, except in those few cases where a patient died. But as time passed and more and more psychosurgical cases were drawn from the ranks of those with psychoneuroses and psychosomatic complaints, the picture began to change. It began to be apparent to even the most ardent lobotomy enthusiasts that the state of patients after psychosurgery was often worse than the conditions the operation was intended to relieve. After many thousand operations had been performed, it could no longer be denied that lobotomized people were liable to be rendered apathetic, irresponsible, and asocial, their intellects were blunted, and they were likely to suffer from a drastic impairment of memory and creativity. By that time, Freeman had become the acknowledged dean of psychosurgeons, and even he was forced to admit that lobotomy produced some devastating side effects. Toward the end of his long career he wrote, "What the investigator misses most in the more highly intelligent individuals is their ability to introspect, to speculate, to philosophize, especially in regard to one's self. . . ."[30]

In this connection it is interesting to note Freeman's opinion that "women respond better than men, Negroes better than whites and syphilitics better than nonsyphilitics," although he contended that "to limit lobotomy to syphilitic Negro women would be the height of absurdity." This classification recalls the claims advanced by nineteenth-century craniologists and phrenologists of the inherent inferiority of the brain in women and blacks, and a mid-twentieth century extension of the same idea can be found in an article by an English physician who had practiced medicine in Kenya for five years. Writing in 1950, he sought to show that the normal behavior of East African blacks resembles the postoperative behavior of leucotomized or lobotomized European whites, in that the euphoria, tactlessness, "tendency to be content with inferior performance socially and intellectually," talkativeness, and "poor judgement" typical of a lobotomized European, "are equally applicable to most East Africans." Furthermore, he concluded, "on the basis of normal African behaviour, and supported by our psychiatric findings . . . African backwardness . . . can well be linked with frontal lobe idleness."[31] He added that "it seems not without significance that at least one of the few Europeans leucotomized in Kenya has, since his operation, consorted much more happily with Africans than with Europeans, in marked distinction from his previous behavior, and to the great embarrassment of his relations."

The potential of psychosurgery to control unacceptable behavior was never far from the consciousness of its practitioners. Walter Freeman acknowledged that "indolence and tactlessness are the outstanding motifs" of social behavior after lobotomy, but on the whole, he claimed, lobotomy made troublesome people easier to manage:

As a matter of fact, lobotomized patients seldom come in conflict with the law precisely because they lack the imagination to think up new deviltries and the energy to perpetrate them. . . . Maybe it was the abnormal development of these intellectual-emotional [capacities] that got the patients into trouble originally.[32]

Perhaps enough has already been said to show that the pioneers of psychosurgery exaggerated the benefits of lobotomy and ignored both the personal costs of individual patients and the social consequences for the entire society. By the end of the 1950s, the psychiatric community had lost much of its earlier enthusiasm for lobotomy. This was owing only in part to mounting disillusion because of poor results and to growing uneasiness about the poverty of psychosurgical theory. Perhaps a more significant reason was that during the 1950s several alternative forms of treatment came into widespread use, including electroconvulsive shock treatment and the introduction of potent psychotropic drugs (tranquilizers). For about two decades, psychosurgery remained overshadowed by other treatment techniques, but it did not cease entirely. On the contrary, around 1970 there emerged a new generation of psychosurgeons who are committed, like their predecessors, to brain manipulation and surgery as a means of behavior control.

From Genesis to Genocide

By and large, today's psychosurgeons are quick to acknowledge the psychosurgical excesses of the past. Indeed, they are often critical of the old-fashioned prefrontal lobotomy and of those earlier psychosurgeons whose "excessive . . . enthusiasm for surgical attack upon the mind" brought but little relief from disabling mental illness and then only "at a cost of considerable blunting of higher sensitivities."[33] The target of this criticism, however, is not psychosurgery or the theories of brain function upon which it is based. According to many contemporary psychosurgeons, the excesses and failures of the past were due to an inadequate understanding of brain mechanisms and to a lack of technical competence. In their view, psychosurgery currently commands a new and much more sophisticated set of tools and techniques for attacking the brain.

Now it is certainly correct that there have been significant advances in knowledge of brain function since the early days of prefrontal lobotomy and that psychosurgical technology has developed to a point where it is possible to perform operations on the brain that could not have been done earlier. A consideration of these advances in knowledge and of recently invented techniques will make it possible to evaluate contemporary psychosurgery and to determine whether it rests on the firm scientific foundation that earlier forms of psychosurgery lacked.

Ever since the relation between brain function and behavior became a subject of experimental research, the relative inaccessibility of regions lying deep within the brain has posed a serious impediment to localization studies. One of the oldest and most important methods of studying the living nervous system in experimental animals entails the selective destruction of a particular brain region and the notation of consequent effects upon behavior. A great deal may be learned about the neural basis of behavior by these techniques, but in order to destroy a particular part of the brain, one must first gain access to it, and that is not easy.

The brain, encased within its protective cranial vault, is naturally impervious to surgical assault. Of course, a hole may be drilled in the skull and relatively large portions of the cranium removed. Once that has been done, the surface of the brain that lies exposed can be selectively manipulated or locally destroyed. But the cerebral cortex (the most superficial part of the hemispheres) comprises only a small part of the brain; hidden beneath it, and making up the greater portion of the brain, is a vast, highly differentiated, and enormously complex system of cells, fibers, blood vessels, and other elements. This hidden region of the brain, though somewhat amorphous in appearance and gelatinous in texture, consists of highly organized neural networks whose integrity is essential to the various behavior patterns upon which individual and species survival depend.

It is impossible to gain direct surgical access to these deep neural regions without destroying the overlying cortical areas in the process. For a long time this posed a practical barrier to research on brain structures beneath the cortex and to psychosurgical operations upon them. Around the turn of the century, however, brain researchers developed a simple and elegant solution to the problem of reaching a specified point deep within the brain with minimal disturbance to overlying regions, a technique that laid the groundwork for the many innovations in human brain surgery, although it was originally developed as an aid to brain research on experimental animals.

In 1908, a British neurosurgeon, Victor Horsley, and his associate, R. H. Clarke, invented a mechanical device— a "stereotaxic instrument"— with which it was possible to direct a needle, electrode, or other probe to any desired point within the brain with considerable accuracy. (Since then, many variations of the Horsley-Clarke instrument have been developed to permit the insertion of depth probes into the brains of human beings, and other species. The essentials of stereotaxic brain surgery are not complicated. As illustrated in the figure, the frame of the stereotaxic instrument serves to place the head in a fixed position, from which it becomes possible to define a point within the brain three-dimensionally, or front to back, top to bottom, and side to side. In practice, prominent anatomical landmarks on the surface of the skull are commonly used to establish these three reference planes (usually called the frontal, horizontal, and lateral planes), and maps (stereotaxic atlases) are prepared to show the location of various brain structures in terms of their stereotaxic coordinates. Today there are stereotaxic atlases for many species of animals, including humans.

By consulting the atlas, and fixing the head of an anesthetized subject within the stereotaxic frame, the surgeon can direct a probe, with precise mechanical control, to any desired location within the brain through a small hole drilled in the skull. As a rule, the probe consists of fine wires (electrodes), and once it has reached its intended target, the electrodes may be used for various purposes, including recording, stimulation, or destruction.

In the first instance, the ongoing activity of the brain in the vicinity of the electrode tip can be detected and recorded by connecting the other end of the probe to suitable electronic amplifiers and associated equipment. It was long ago discovered that the normal functioning of the brain is accompanied by fluctuating electric potentials or "brain waves" (the EEG, or electroencephalogram, for example) and much has since been learned about brain function by recording the brain waves and other signals from various regions under different conditions. The EEG may be used to diagnose suspected focal brain disease by pinpointing a restricted region of abnormal electrical activity, although it is often difficult to

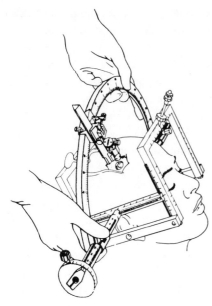

A diagram of the stereotaxic instrument attached to the head. Skin and muscle have been retracted and a "bone button" has been removed to permit the electrode holder to insert an electrode into the depth of the brain. (From Lars Leksell, *Stereotaxic and Radio Surgery. An Operative System*, 1971. Courtesy of Charles C. Thomas, Publisher, Springfield, Ill.)

determine with certainty if abnormal brain waves originate at the recording site or at a functionally related point some distance away.

In the case of stimulation, the activity of the brain can be transiently modified by passing pulses of weak electric current from an external stimulator via the electrode tip. In many experiments with laboratory animals, it has been shown that different effects are produced by stimulating different brain areas or by stimulating the same area with different kinds or amounts of current. Although great caution must be used in interpreting the effects of localized brain stimulation, the technique has been extremely useful in illuminating the functions of different brain areas. For current purposes, suffice it to say that effects produced by brain stimulation may bear only a remote relationship to the activity that is normally mediated by a given brain region and that, in most cases, the effects of stimulating a given area are likely to be varied and complex. In other words, it is rare to find that stimulation of a discrete brain area produces a single or isolated effect.

Finally, by passing a strong current through the electrode, the brain tissue in the vicinity of the tip may be destroyed. Coupled with the development of human stereotaxic techniques, this technique is of particular relevance for contemporary psychosurgery. It is now possible to destroy specific regions deep within the human brain, regions that were

Violence: The Pacification of the Brain

impervious to assault by the earlier generation of psychosurgeons, who were only capable of destroying more accessible superficial areas of the brain.

The use of stereotaxic methods and the development of electrophysiological techniques for recording, stimulation, and destruction have been accompanied by other innovations. First, it is possible to place an electrode or similar probe within the brain for an extended period of time. During the stereotaxic operation, the shaft of the electrode is fastened to the skull, the scalp is closed over the implanted electrode, and the experimental subject (or patient) is allowed to recover from the surgery.

Starting around 1920, with the studies of Walter R. Hess in Switzerland, brain researchers began to investigate the effects of stimulating various neural sites in fully awake animals who were restrained only by the connecting cables between the implanted electrodes and the external equipment. In 1949 Hess shared the Nobel prize with Moniz for his studies of the effects of stimulating deep portions of the brain in cats, and in his Nobel lecture he pointed out that stimulation of the hypothalamus (a critically important structure located deep within the brain and generally associated with a wide range of behavioral and hormonal activities upon which individual and species survival depend) leads to a dramatic and complex change in behavior, so that a formerly good-natured cat reacts when approached as if it were cornered by an attacking dog.[34]

Many psychosurgeons believed that Hess had discovered something resembling a simple phrenological "organ" of rage or aggression and subsequently have undertaken to destroy the corresponding brain regions in human beings.[35] As in the case of Moniz (whose preoccupation with "pacification" caused him to ignore the debilitating effects of prefrontal lobotomy reported by Jacobsen and Fulton), these attempts to find new forms of "sedative therapy" often ignored the association between the physiological and psychological effects of brain lesions shown by Hess's experiments.

A second innovation that deserves to be mentioned before turning to a more detailed examination of contemporary psychosurgery was an outgrowth of developments in modern electronic communications technology. As I have already noted, much of the work on the effects of brain stimulation in nonanesthetized animals entailed a degree of mechanical restraint owing to the need for interconnecting cables between the subject and the stimulating equipment. In recent years, however, miniature wireless telemetry systems have been developed with which signals may be transmitted between an electrode implanted in the brain and a remote stimulating or recording device located some distance away. Psychosurgeons may now implant electrodes in the brain, allow the subject or patient to recover from the surgery, and then connect the electrode to a portable transmitter/receiver. In this way, it is possible to monitor or manipulate the behavior and brain activity of the unrestrained (and perhaps unsuspecting) subject.

With the advent of advanced stereotaxic technology and the attendant possibility for monitoring and manipulating new targets within the brain, the major focus of psychosurgery shifted away from old-fashioned prefrontal lobotomy toward newer, more selective operations. Various approaches have been tried, though most of the favorable results claimed for psychosurgery today are based upon the effects of destroying portions of what has come to be called the brain's "limbic system." The term *limbus* denotes a border or a margin, and in the brain the limbic system is an assembly of structures that collectively form a border or margin around the deepest (and from an evolutionary point of view the phylogenetically oldest) parts of the mammalian brain. In general anatomical terms, the limbic system is comprised of a number of complex brain regions with rather forbidding names, including the hippocampus, the hippocampal gyrus, and the cingulate gyrus (all "primitive" parts of the cerebral cortex) and a number of deeper-lying structures including the amygdala, septal nuclei, anterior thalamic nuclei, and hypothalamus. The limbic system also has intimate connections with the frontal areas of the cortex, the target of the earlier psychosurgical operations.

From a more abstract standpoint, the limbic system occupies an intermediate position between the deep-lying regions (such as those explored by Hess) involved in critical life-sustaining activities of both behavioral and metabolic kinds and the more superficial regions of the cerebral cortex (to which the phrenologists attributed the various faculties of human nature, and which current theories of brain function continue to identify with various "higher cognitive functions"). Thus, the limbic system appears to be a kind of interface, situated to receive, transform, and transmit signals passing between two very different but equally important systems of the brain.

As early as 1937, James W. Papez, a student of brain function, assembled arguments and clinical evidence to support the view that, in conjunction with the hypothalamus, the parts of the limbic system and their interconnections "constitute a harmonious mechanism which may elaborate the functions of central emotion, as well as participate in emotional expression."[36] The advance over crude phrenological localization is significant. Papez, in his highly speculative theory, was not saying that emotion "resided" as a discrete faculty in a specific place within the brain but rather that the complex of functions contributing to emotional states or expressions entail interactive mechanisms in which the limbic system plays a critical part. As one longtime student of limbic structure and function has put it, "Therein lie possible mechanisms by which the brain transforms the cold light with which we see into the warm light which we feel."[37] What is known of the limbic system suggests that its "interface" functions ultimately guide behavior of a kind that is essential to self-preservation and the survival of the species. In humans, the entire range of functions—both mysterious and complex—from which we derive our sense of ourselves and our convictions about what is true and important may depend on the integrity of the limbic system.

What happens to the behavior of an organism when the structures comprising this system are injured or destroyed? In 1938, Heinrich Klüver and Paul C. Bucy described debilitating changes in social and emotional behavior in rhesus monkeys following destruction of portions of the limbic system and the overlying temporal lobes of the neocortex. The changes included a curious and compulsive "orality," during which both food and inedible objects were repeatedly placed in the mouth. There was also a form of "psychic blindness" that left the animals able to see (in the sense that they could avoid obstacles by sight and could grasp an object placed within their field of vision) but unable to recognize or remember objects on the basis of visual appearance alone. Even more striking after the operations, Klüver and Bucy's monkeys became markedly tame and hypersexual. Although rhesus monkeys are normally very wild and difficult to handle in the laboratory, the operation transformed them into animals that could easily be embraced by the experimenters and were readily fed by hand. Their sexuality was markedly altered, with a profound increase in attempts to copulate with a wide variety of both animate and inanimate objects. Finally, in what appeared to reflect a most serious threat to their survival ability, the operated animals were seemingly unable to learn from direct, even painful, experience, and as a result they repeatedly exposed themselves to dangerous or hurtful situations.[38] Klüver produced a film, for example, in which one of the operated animals was shown placing the burning end of a cigarette in its mouth. Upon being burned, the monkey quickly grabbed the cigarette and threw it down, only to pick it up and repeat the process. This occurred several times in rapid succession.

The dramatic features of the "Klüver-Bucy syndrome" quickly attracted wide attention, and subsequent experiments purported to show that the operation performed by Klüver and Bucy, as well as more restricted temporal lobe lesions (limited, for example, to a part of the limbic system called the amygdala), could transform wild, unmanageable animals into tame and tractable ones.

The discovery that many of the features of the Klüver-Bucy syndrome could be obtained following lesions restricted to the amygdala was destined to have important consequences for stereotaxic psychosurgery. From a relatively early time, however, it was clear that destruction of the amygdala produced effects well beyond mere pacification. In one study, for example, bilateral amygdalectomy (destruction of the amygdala on both sides of the brain) was performed on a number of young male rhesus monkeys, and drastic effects upon many aspects of social behavior were observed.[39] Another experiment with more far-reaching implications set out to answer the question, What are the effects of amygdalectomy on the behavior of monkeys in a free-ranging habitat? The question is important because all previous experiments had been conducted under highly restrictive laboratory conditions. Bilateral amygdalectomies were performed by Arthur Kling and several colleagues on monkeys who lived under semi-natural conditions in a large colony preserve. After recovery from the operation, and while they were still within the laboratory environment, the monkeys were tested and found to exhibit (among other things) the characteristic docility and tameness that Klüver and Bucy had described earlier; overall, the experimenters judged them to be far less aggressive and less wild than before. But later, when they were released from the laboratory and allowed to rejoin their troop, the amygdalectomized animals began to show the true costs of the pacifying surgery.

It would be an understatement to say that their behavior was inappropriate and severely disturbed. They no longer appeared to comprehend the prevailing social norms and communication signals of their peers and their responses to other members of the troop were grossly maladaptive. While they had appeared to be "tame" in the laboratory, they now appeared persistently fearful and confused, and when approached by other monkeys in a neutral or nonthreatening manner, they cowered or attempted to flee. Furthermore, they responded inappropriately to danger. When threatened, for example, by a dominant member of the troop, the amygdalectomized animals sometimes reacted provocatively rather than defensively and consequently incurred frequent severe beatings. All in all, the operation had left them unable to cope with the normal complexities of social life in their natural habitat. Because of their bizarre and disruptive behavior, they eventually became social isolates, and having withdrawn or been expelled from the troop, all of these unfortunate animals eventually died of starvation or were killed by predators.[40]

It should be clear from this experiment that discussions of "taming" can obscure the more devastating effects of bilateral amygdalectomy. But despite the ample evidence that limbic system psychosurgery leads to a drastic deterioration of emotional, sexual, and social behavior, and despite the critical involvement of complex limbic brain mechanisms in so many aspects of mental life, some psychosurgeons continue to believe that there is a "dyscontrol syndrome due to limbic brain disease" and that allegedly unmanageable human beings can be tamed or even cured by selectively destroying one or another part of their limbic systems.

Claims concerning the benefits of psychosurgery, although made and accepted by many allegedly knowledgeable authorities, are given the most detailed exposition in Vernon Mark and Frank Ervin's book, *Violence and the Brain*. Two of Mark and Ervin's more remarkable cases appear under the pseudonyms "Thomas R." and "Julia S." Both Thomas and Julia may properly be called famous; he is obviously the model for Harry Benson, the title character in Michael Crichton's best-selling 1972 novel (and movie) *The Terminal Man*. (Just as Ellis, the fictional psychosurgeon in that work, expresses—with a bit of literary license—the ideas about brain dysfunction and impulsive dyscontrol laid out in Mark and Ervin's book.) Julia achieved considerable notoriety in her own right when she was prominently featured in a *Life* magazine article in 1968 about the promise of psychosurgery as a treatment for violence.[41]

Thomas is introduced by the authors of *Violence and the Brain* in a chapter entitled "Brain Triggers for Violence":

The first time we were able to demonstrate that systems in the limbic brain both start and stop attack behavior was with patient Thomas R. He was a brilliant 34-year-old engineer with several important patents to his credit. Despite his muscular physique it was difficult to believe he was capable of an act of violence when he was not enraged, for his manner was both courteous and sympathetic.

Thomas's "history of illness" is traced back fourteen years to a time when he was in the army and underwent an operation following an acute peptic ulcer attack, after which he was in a coma for three days. After he was discharged from the army, he completed his education as an engineer, work for which he showed great talent, "but his behavior at times was unpredictable and even frankly psychotic," in spite of psychiatric treatment over a period of seven years.

Thomas's chief problem was his violent rage; this was sometimes directed at his co-workers and friends, but it was mostly expressed toward his wife and children. He was very paranoid, and harbored grudges which eventually produced an explosion of anger.... For example, during a conversation with his wife, he would seize upon some innocuous remark and interpret it as an insult. At first, he would try to ignore what she had said, but could not help brooding; and the more he thought about it, the surer he felt that his wife no longer loved him and was "carrying on with a neighbor." Eventually he would reproach his wife for these faults, and she would hotly deny them. Her denials were enough to set him off into a frenzy of violence.[42]

Thomas was referred to Mark and Ervin by a psychiatrist who, they stated, had concluded that "prolonged psychiatric treatment did not improve his behavior and ... that his spells of staring, automatisms and rage represented an unusual form of temporal lobe seizure."[43] After conducting a number of tests, they reached the same conclusion. In addition, they described him as having "periods of confusion and a number of psychotic delusions and hallucinations" while in the hospital. During a period of seven months they unsuccessfully "tried many combinations of antiseizure medicines, tranquilizers, and psychic energizers." They do not report having personally witnessed Thomas R.'s seizures, but after concluding that both temporal lobes were involved, they decided to treat his illness with stereotaxic surgery.

Arrays of electrodes were implanted bilaterally, aimed at the amygdalas, and during the next few weeks, recordings made from his brain allegedly revealed "that electrical discharges typical of epileptic seizures occurred in both the right and the left temporal lobes." In order to locate "the optimal site for destructive lesions," stimulation was delivered via the electrodes to different points in and near the amygdala on the left side of the brain. According to the authors, this produced contrasting sensations. Electric currents applied at one location, for example, produced complaints of pain and difficulty with speech and caused Thomas to say he felt he was "losing control," while at another, nearby point, stimulation repeatedly produced feelings he described as pleasant, "just like an injection of Demerol."

As one might expect, Thomas was less than enthusiastic at the prospect of amygdalectomy, given that Mark and Ervin had described him as paranoid and "highly sensitive to threats." As Mark and Ervin put it, "The suggestion that the medial portion of his temporal lobe was to be destroyed ... would provoke wild, disordered thinking." (At this point in their discussion, they insert a footnote acknowledging the physician's "extraordinary responsibility" to safeguard the rights of the patient and to secure free and informed consent for treatment.) Lateral amygdala stimulation would "relax" him to the point where he became acquiescent to the proposed surgery, but on one of these occasions, after the effect of the treatment had worn off, he "turned wild and unmanageable. The idea of anyone making a destructive lesion in his brain enraged him. He absolutely refused any further therapy, and it took many weeks of patient explanation before he accepted the idea...." Mark and Ervin did not report the substance of what transpired during those "weeks of patient explanation." Presumably they sought to persuade Thomas that his resistance to the idea of psychosurgery was just one more symptom of his illness. In any event, Thomas was induced to relent and finally submitted to having bilateral lesions made in his medial amygdala.

That is very nearly the end of Thomas's story, as far as Mark and Ervin's published accounts are concerned. Only three short sentences in their book are devoted to the surgery and its aftermath, in which they point out that in the four years since the operation, "Thomas has not had a single episode of rage. He continues, however, to have an occasional epileptic seizure with periods of disordered thinking."[44]

My first impression after reading of Mark and Ervin's account was that Thomas's preoperative behavior was inexplicable except in terms of brain dysfunction, that his was a straightforward case of a "dyscontrol syndrome" treatable by limbic system psychosurgery. Upon closer examination, however, it became apparent to me that the authors are claiming something more than this. Not only did their conclusion state that Thomas's "chief problem"—his uncontrollable rage—had been solved (although his other preoperative symptoms remained essentially unchanged), but no postoperative complications or untoward side effects of any kind are mentioned. This is nothing less than specific cure.

In the light of what is known about the effects of bilateral amygdalectomy in monkeys, the reported outcome in Thomas's case must be considered remarkable indeed. It might be argued, of course, that a man is not a monkey, and that it is impossible to predict a dire outcome for Thomas on the basis of the adverse (in fact fatal) consequences of amygdalectomy in nonhuman primates. Nonetheless, one can't help wondering about Thomas's current circumstances and future prospects. Before his operation, Thomas was "an extremely talented, inventive man," married and supporting his family through his work as an engineer. Is all this still true? One might reasonably think that the answers to these questions are relevant to an evaluation of Drs. Mark and Ervin's alleged cure, but their accounts are silent on these matters.

In past studies, it was not uncommon for psychosurgeons to minimize or ignore the frankly devastating sequelae of prefrontal lobotomy. Today's psychosurgeons take pride in their technical sophistication, but some factors remain unchanged. Fortunately, the information that Mark and Ervin neglected to provide is now available, and although incomplete and quite possibly biased, it paints a picture of Thomas's postoperative history that is very different from the one Mark and Ervin drew.

On December 3, 1973, a two-million-dollar suit was filed in Suffolk Superior Court (Massachusetts) against Dr. Vernon Mark and Dr. Frank Ervin. The plaintiff of record is Leonard A. Kille of Long Beach, California, known to us as "Thomas R." In a declaration filed by his mother, who is now his legal guardian, it is alleged that as a direct result of negligent treatment by Mark and Ervin, Thomas was "rendered of unsound and unbalanced mind and incompetent to handle his personal affairs and remains the same until today. . . , was permanently injured and incapacitated. . . , and has been permanently deprived of his earning capacity and his ability to work. . . ."; also that Mark and Ervin negligently failed to inform him fully as to the nature, risks, complications, and ramifications of the proposed procedures and/or negligently failed to obtain his informed consent to them.

The outcome of the suit is still in doubt, but some of the background to these allegations has come to light through the actions of Thomas's family. According to Peter R. Breggin, a Washington, D.C., psychiatrist and a frequent critic of psychosurgery, Thomas's mother wrote to him stating that her son had been "almost a vegetable" since the operation and requesting him to look further into the case.[45] Breggin did so, and after interviewing Thomas, his family, and other informed individuals and reviewing the hospital records, he claimed that Thomas was not overtly violent before the operation but actually became so afterward and that he has been "totally disabled, chronically hospitalized, and subject to night-marish terrors that he will be caught and operated on again...."[46] Breggin's version of the case is both lengthy and detailed; the highlights, supplemented by information I have obtained independently, may be summarized as follows:

Before 1965, Thomas had been employed as an engineer for several years. As a research and development specialist at the Polaroid Corporation, he supervised other employees and did work that earned him a number of patents on the Land camera. Although he apparently suffered from a form of epilepsy, his seizures were effectively controlled by medication, and whatever his "violent behavior" might have been, it was not of a kind or degree to attract the attention of his employers or law-enforcement officials. Breggin cites one of his hospital records, "He has never been in any trouble at work or otherwise for aggressive behavior, never been in jail or a mental hospital."

In 1965, "serious marital problems" prompted Thomas to visit his wife's psychiatrist, who according to Breggin "remembers that Thomas was depressed, but not sufficiently depressed to warrant electroshock or drugs." This is consistent with the hospital records, which report no "hallucinations, delusions, paranoid ideas or signs of difficulty with thinking." Thomas was diagnosed as suffering from nothing more than "personality pattern disturbances"—meaning he had "mild problems with no psychotic symptomatology."

His wife's psychiatrist and subsequent hospital records indicate that Thomas's preoperative violence was directed mainly at his wife and consisted of throwing objects in the heat of argument. There is little reason to doubt that she was afraid of him, but the records explicitly state that when he threw things he did so "in the room" rather than directly at her, and that these outbursts "never injured anyone." As Mark and Ervin state, the psychiatrist concluded that Thomas's fits of anger might have been related to epilepsy, and as a war veteran he was referred to a Veterans Administration Hospital where Drs. Mark, Ervin, and Sweet first saw him.

During a series of four diagnostic hospitalizations between March and September 1966, Thomas was not treated as a seriously violent person and was never restrained or confined to a locked ward. He was, however, uneasy about the "diagnostic procedures," and in a letter to his mother referred to himself as the subject of "science-fiction" studies. On at least one occasion he fled from the hospital, but family pressure apparently induced him to return. According to his mother (wrote Breggin), "he kept returning for the pre-psychosurgery workup because his wife said the marriage could not go on unless he did something about himself."

According to the plaintiff's declaration in the lawsuit, the electrodes were stereotaxically implanted in Thomas's amygdala on October 21, 1966, and remained there for nine months. Seven days later, in response to an inquiry about his condition, his mother received the following telegram: "Your son recovering well from minor surgical operation will soon be undergoing tests given by Dr. Mark and is in good condition." During January and February 1967, following a prolonged period of experimental brain stimulation, lesions were made with high frequency (microwave) current in Thomas's left amygdala in several successive stages.[47] Between February and May 1967 additional stimulation series were run on his right amygdala, and that structure was lesioned on several occasions during the month of May.

One of the signs of Thomas's alleged paranoia was that he believed his wife was unfaithful, and in this connection Breggin notes that "nowhere do Mark and Ervin tell us that during his hospitalization . . . his wife filed for divorce, served papers on him on the ward, and soon married the man that 'paranoid' Thomas had been concerned about." It is notable that the only incident of rage that Mark and Ervin reported having witnessed personally occurred when they suggested making lesions in Thomas's brain; except on this subject, according to Breggin, all the hospital records describe him as "meek and docile."

That is far from all of the story. Although Mark and Ervin claimed that after the operation Thomas no longer became enraged, they do not report that within a short time after his release from the hospital Thomas was unable to deal with the complexities of normal social life; that he had to be periodically rehospitalized; and that he became generally violent and assaultive.

Almost a month to the day after his discharge from the hospital in Boston he was admitted to a Veterans Administration hospital in California, where he had gone to live with his mother. At the time he was described as "hallucinated, delusional, and confused." It was, in effect, the first enforced psychiatric hospitalization of his life. He was placed in a locked ward under heavy sedative medication and during that period was diagnosed as psychotic and suffering from schizophrenic reaction, paranoid type." According to Breggin, the VA doctors viewed with a degree of incredulity Thomas's contention that his mind had been destroyed by psychosurgery, that "Massachusetts General Hospital was controlling him by creating lesions in his brain tissue by microwave and that they had placed electrodes in his brain tissue some time before."

Less than a year later, Thomas was hospitalized again. The intake notes read in part, "Arrested by police—involved in fight, very impulsive." By this time, Thomas had been declared totally disabled by the Veterans Administration, and during the next several years he was admitted and discharged from various hospitals, always hallucinated, delusional, and confused, always diagnosed as "schizophrenic," and always insisting that his brain had been destroyed by psychosurgery. By mid-1973, when Breggin's follow-up of Thomas ends, his most recent hospitalization showed an increasing trend toward violent and impulsive behavior. A note on his chart described him as "very aggressive, beligerent, dangerous at present." Physical restraint and intramuscular injections of a potent tranquilizing drug were used to quiet him. According to Breggin, "As in the past, throughout this hospitalization he walked about with newspapers, bags, books and other material on or around his head to protect himself from further surgery."

Since Breggin is a well-known—some would say fanatical—foe of psychosurgery, it might be argued that his follow-up is at least as biased as Mark and Ervin's original report. But Breggin is not the only source of allegations that Thomas has been anything but cured by his bilateral amygdalectomy. There is, for example, the testimony of Dr. Ernst Rodin, a Detroit neurosurgeon who visited Mark and his colleagues in Boston during the summer of 1972. At the time, Rodin was himself the coauthor of a proposal to perform psychosurgery on patients involuntarily incarcerated in the Michigan state hospital system who were allegedly subject to "severe uncontrollable aggressive outbursts." The purpose of his visit to Boston, as Rodin recounted it, was "to obtain the most up-to-date information on the results of surgery for aggressive behavior in human beings."[48] Having read *Violence and the Brain*, as well as some of Mark and Ervin's other writings, Rodin was looking forward to learning more about the Boston group's successes at first hand. However, Rodin was dismayed by the numerous disparities he discovered between the articles he had read and what he was told. "My contacts at the Boston City Hospital," he wrote, "were the ward staff of the special unit which is devoted to the study of aggressive patients . . . [including] Dr. Vernon Mark, Project Director. . . . The result of these interviews were quite disturbing. . . ."[49] For example, Rodin questioned Dr. Ira Sherwin, the project neurologist, on his experience with cases reported in the literature, especially *Violence and the Brain*, and was surprised to find inconsistencies between what Sherwin had to say about patients and what Mark had reported. Rodin noted that two patients had had unilateral amygdalectomies which were unsuccessful in controlling aggression and that one of them had suffered partial blindness as a result of the lesion; that the patient Thomas R. is "floridly paranoid and will never be able to function in society"; and that "Dr. Sherwin was not aware of any genuinely successful cases."[50]

From what has been said, it ought to be obvious that amygdalectomy may have disastrous effects upon humans (as well as monkeys) and that as a "treatment" for violence or aggression its utility is far from proved. Indeed, Thomas's fate is wholly consistent with our imperfect understanding of the brain and its complex functions. We do understand that the brain is a highly intricate and finely tuned organ whose numerous parts operate interdependently. The idea behind amygdalectomy, that the behavior of a complex and poorly understood biological system like the brain can be improved by selectively destroying it, parallels the crude phrenological notion that complex social behavior can be localized in discrete brain organs. Yet the fact is that no brain functions take place in isolation, all of them entail the integration of activity from many regions, and as the complexity of a function increases, there is a corresponding increase in the number and diversity of brain regions that appear to be involved.

It would be a mistake, however, to imagine that the only thing wrong with brain pacification is that the available methods do not work. Psychosurgeons, like all psychotechnologists, are committed to their profession and are attempting to promote it as a source of solutions for pressing social problems. From what we know of the brain and its function, it is tempting to suggest that technological barriers make such a goal impossible, or at least that the time is very far off when psychosurgery will be deployed to achieve precisely the desired effect.

In a field such as psychosurgery, where the power to control behavior is pursued as an end in itself—almost completely divorced from rational scientific theory—every new technique or gadget may be mistaken for a "breakthrough." Thus the question Does it work? takes precedence over the more important and fundamental questions of moral and ethical justification. "Julia S.," another of Mark and Ervin's patients, is a case in point.

We saw and treated Julia S. nearly two years after Thomas had been discharged from the hospital. By then, we had perfected new techniques for identifying abnormal areas of electrical discharge in the brain. In addition, we were able to use the "stimoceiver"—the same telemetered device used to send signals and receive information from orbiting astronauts. . . . In Julia's case, the relationship between brain disease and violent behavior is very clear. . . . Before the age of 2, she had a severe attack of encephalitis following mumps. When she was 10, she began having epileptic seizures. . . . Her behavior between seizures was marked by severe temper tantrums followed by extreme remorse. Four of these depressions ended in serious suicide attempts. The daughter of a professional man, she was an attractive, pleasant, cherubic blonde who looked much younger than her age of 21.[51]

According to Mark and Ervin, Julia had seriously assaulted other people on at least a dozen separate occasions. When she was eighteen, she alleg-edly injured two women in separate stabbing incidents. Although there was no necessary connection between her epilepsy and her episodic assaul-tiveness, Mark and Ervin say that "Julia's case clearly illustrates the point that violent behavior caused by brain dysfunction cannot be modified except by treating the dysfunction itself."

As with Thomas, electrodes were bilaterally implanted in Julia's amyg-dalas, and after a protracted period of stimulation and recording (via the stimoceiver telemetry device) microwave current was used to make succes-sive bilateral lesions. Writing approximately two years later, Mark and Ervin devote two sentences to her postoperative condition:

It is still too early to assess the results of the procedure, but she had only two mild rage episodes in the first postoperative year and none in the second. Since she had generalized brain disease and multiple areas of epi-leptic activity, it is not surprising that epileptic seizures have not been eliminated, or that her psychotic episodes have continued at the preopera-tive level.[52]

Mark and Ervin considered Julia's assaultive behavior aimless and attributed it directly to her brain disease. They were apparently unable or unwilling to imagine that her tantrums might have had something to do with her upbringing or environment, or that her rages might have reflected her frustration and despair at being a brain-damaged person. There has been no independent follow-up of Julia's case, to my knowledge, but in an interview with an investigator from Ralph Nader's *Center for Responsive Law*, Dr. Mark admitted that Julia continues to be in and out of mental hospitals because of her psychotic behavior: "We do not claim," he told the investigator, "that we have any surgical operation that will affect psychosis."[53]

The question arises, however, whether Julia was psychotic before the operation or if a proper diagnosis was made. A former member of the project staff who was professionally concerned with her but did not share Mark and Ervin's unswerving commitment to psychosurgery suggests that it is plausible to answer no. This person, who does not want to be identi-fied, was in daily contact with Julia and describes her as

a very narcissistic, demanding, infantile sort of a girl. When her family visited . . . they indulged her, were super-sweet and "understanding" parents. . . . If she hadn't learned in her family that acting up meant atten-tion—she certainly learned it at MGH [Massachusetts General Hospital]. It was quite apparent to me that her dish throwing, guitar smashing and fisti-cuffs were clearly appropriate responses for her in a milieu that made much of this kind of behavior. . . . Usually, the attacks appeared after another patient was getting the limelight, or one of her favorite staff mem-bers had been off a few days and returned, or a visit from parents was expected.

If this account is to be considered, we may speculate that Julia's erratic behavior was related to her life situation. Furthermore, the observer continued, no serious attempt was made to treat Julia with alternative forms of therapy during her stay at the Massachusetts General Hospital. Her epileptic seizures seemed genuine, but they had nothing to do with her "attacks." Her father was a physician and "used to send her all the latest articles on temporal lobe epilepsy"; when he visited, "they would discuss her 'unfortunate disease.'"

After the electrodes were implanted and the stimulation series began, the observer noted a profound change in Julia's behavior. She had been "a beautiful, intelligent girl" who liked to play the guitar. Now "she stopped her wonderful guitar playing. She stopped wanting to engage in long intellectual discussions. She became more and more depressed. Really depressed. Suicidal." The change in her behavior affected those who worked with her on the ward, and many of the nurses "cried for her . . . even stopped getting angry at her borderline tantrums."

The author of these remarks left the unit at about that time but later saw the article *Life* published in 1968 ("about the time of the riots") which featured Julia in photographs before, during, and after brain stimulation. Notably, the article "never mentioned her later deterioration and severe emotional suffering. . . ."

More ominous than the lack of a scientific foundation for contemporary psychosurgery and its poor medical practices is the tendency of some enthusiasts to promote it to control deviant behavior. The authors of *Violence and the Brain* have been explicit in their attempts to link interpersonal violence and other forms of deviant behavior to brain dysfunction and to suppress such behavior by destroying parts of the brain. Advocates of psychosurgery have presented increasing numbers of similar proposals and projects in recent years. Dr. M. Hunter Brown, a psychosurgeon who practices in California, is notable among those of his profession who have advocated brain operations as a means of controlling socially deviant behavior. His surgical technique involves making multiple lesions in a part of the limbic system called the cingulum which be believes to be the locus of disturbed brain function in deviant individuals. It is his view that "apprehension over modern psychiatric surgery is unwarranted and remains unsubstantiated by any scientific evidence," and that psychosurgery ought to be used extensively to deal "with the escalation of individual violence on a worldwide scale." He has made a number of specific proposals for the psychosurgical control of prisoners, and his perspective on the causes of violence has been accorded a friendly reception among some public officials and prison authorities.[54]

Prisoners are not the only group of deviants for whom psychosurgeons claim to have an effective treatment, and American psychosurgeons are not the only physicians who are committed to the use of brain manipulation as a means of deviance control. A group of German Psychosurgeons reported in 1972 that they had performed stereotaxic operations upon the hypothalamus of twenty male sexual deviants. They claimed that with fifteen of them they obtained a good result "which was in most cases excellent"; in only one case was a poor result acknowledged, and in none were serious deficits or untoward side effects reported.[55] These psychosurgeons also described an "incapacity to indulge in erotic fantasies and stimulating visions" following the operations in three cases, but curiously this obliteration of the capacity for mental imagery is not described further, nor does it qualify (in their eyes at least) as evidence that the operation does indeed have some devastating side effects.

Psychosurgery has also been promoted as a means for the effective taming of so-called hyperactive children. Allegedly unmanageable children have been subjected to stereotaxic psychosurgery in several nations, including India, Thailand, Japan, and the United States. A group of psychosurgeons in Madras, India, for example, reported in 1970 the results of operations involving the destruction of various portions of the limbic system in 115 patients, including thirty-nine children under the age of eleven. They referred to their procedures as "sedative neurosurgery" and justified relatively massive brain destruction on the grounds that it achieved effective pacification. It is clear from their account that no actual cures were accomplished, and the brief postoperative summaries invariably stress that the children become merely less troublesome afterward. In their own words, psychosurgery has "proved to be useful in the management of patients who previously could not be managed by other means," although since the emphasis in these accounts is almost always upon the behavior of the child as such, it is difficult or impossible to interpret the claim that all "other means" have been tried and failed.[56] Indeed, it is clear that many psychosurgeons are either unwilling or unable to understand that human behavior is the product of many factors in addition to intrinsic biological ones. The possible roles of parents and other important "managers" in causing or exacerbating the behavioral difficulties is virtually ignored in most psychosurgical reports.

José M. R. Delgado, the inventor of the stimoceiver, which Mark and Ervin used on both Thomas's and Julia's brains, is also a promoter of brain manipulation as a cure-all for social ills. In 1970 he told an interviewer,

The human race is at an evolutionary turning point. We're very close to having the power to construct our own mental functions . . . through a knowledge of the cerebral mechanisms which underlie our behavior. The question is what sort of humans would we like, ideally, to construct?[57]

For Professor Delgado—whose priorities are those of a practical inventor, not a moral philosopher—the answer appears to be that "we" ought to construct humans who, like well-made electrical toys, perform as "we" want them to. The question is Who are the "we"? Delgado's comments illustrate a common tendency among psychotechnologists and other social scientists to indulge in what I call the "politics of pronouns," in this way extending the interests of a narrow group to the community at large. What he is actually implying is that those who possess the necessary means —the power, the financial resources, and the hardware—will be in a position to control the behavior of those who do not. Delgado, who has conducted experiments on monkeys and chimpanzees in which computers are used to trigger brain stimulation by sending signals to animals implanted with the stimoceiver, looks forward to the time when "unwanted patterns of brain activity—for instance those correlated with assaultive or antisocial activity—could be recognized by the computer before they ever reached consciousness in order to trigger pacification of the subject."

The purposeful control of human behavior by means of electrical brain stimulation via implanted electrodes is no longer science fiction. In fact, the use of electronic telemetry systems connecting brains and computers has actually been proposed as a means of monitoring and controlling the behavior of people on parole from prisons. Delgado is correct when he says that physical control of the mind raises "theological objections because it affects free will, moral objections because it affects individual responsibility, ethical objections because it may block self-defense mechanisms, philosophical objections because it threatens personal identity." The use of brain stimulation and psychosurgery to control thoughts and behavior is surely objectionable on all of these grounds, but even more pertinent, in my view, is a political objection that Delgado fails to state, namely, that proposals to use brain technology (and other forms of psychotechnology) as an instrument of social control are predicated upon the dubious assumption that a general consensus exists within our society regarding the propriety of the thoughts and behavior patterns that it is proposed to control.

Psychosurgery is a relatively new form of behavior control technology, but this should not obscure the fact that it is also part of a broader enterprise—the psychotechnological management of socially disruptive behavior. In spite of its aura of science fiction, its basic orientation toward violence and other social problems reveals that it shares an ideology common to all contemporary forms of behavior control, a preoccupation with the deviant individual and a resolute refusal to take account of the larger social system of which all individual behavior is a part.

The Boston Hospital for Women is one of the many institutions associated with the Harvard Medical School. Its Lying-In (maternity) Division serves patients from a variety of social and ethnic groups all over the greater metropolitan area. When a pregnant woman registers in the maternity clinic or arranges for her baby to be delivered at the hospital, she receives a twenty-four-page booklet entitled *Caring for You.* A paragraph in that booklet, headed "Chromosome Test," says,

In this hospital all male infants are undergoing chromosome analysis. This new and simplified test allows the doctors to do an accurate screening examination of your baby's chromosomes and if any serious abnormalities are found, you will be so informed. It is hoped that in time this test . . . will become a universal test on all infants.

When the expectant mother goes into labor and comes to the hospital, she is asked to sign a form granting permission for a few drops of blood to be drawn from her newborn male infant for study. The mother is given to understand that in granting permission for the chromosome test, she is agreeing to a procedure that is a part of normal hospital routine; this impression is reinforced by additional written material which describes the chromosome test as one that "all male infants get . . . as part of a large National Institutes of Health grant." One paragraph refers to the test as a "service" and assures the parent that there is no charge for it.

Between 1965 and 1975 more than 16,000 male infants were screened for chromosomal characteristics by this method. However, at the time of this writing, a group of Harvard Medical School faculty members and other concerned people have succeeded in having the study stopped. The effort to do so, as one reporter described it, was "an acrimonious battle."

Chromosomes are minute bodies contained within the nuclei of living cells. They contain, in turn, the genes—double-stranded molecules of desoxyribonucleic acid (DNA)—which comprise the genetic material of a given species of plant or animal. The normal chromosomal complement of human beings consists of twenty-three pairs, or forty-six chromosomes. One of these pairs, referred to as the sex chromosomes, normally consists of two X chromosomes in females and is referred to as XX; the normal pattern for males consists of one X and one Y chromosome and is referred to as XY. The sex chromosomes are the focus of the Lying-In Hospital's study.

Humans are sometimes born with an irregular number of chromosomes, a condition called aneuploidy (from the Greek *ploid,* meaning "unit," and *aneu,* meaning "uneven"). Chromosomal aneuploidies in humans are sometimes associated with physical or mental symptoms. Down's syndrome (mongolism) is a case in point. An individual with Down's syndrome usually has short stature, stubby hands and feet, a characteristic palm print, and other unusual physical attributes. Such individuals are frequently mentally retarded as well. About one out of every 600 children born in this country is affected with Down's syndrome, and analysis of the chromosomes in their cells reveals that one of the chromosome pairs is replaced by a "triplet" (or trisonomy). Other types of aneuploidy are also known, including some that result in physical defects that may cause an infant to die shortly after birth.

Aneuploidy for the sex chromosomes has also been observed in humans. One example of this is the presence of an extra X chromosome in individuals who appear at birth to be physically (the genetic term is *phenotypically*) male. Rather than having the usual XY chromosome pattern, or karyotype, these persons have sex chromosomes of XXY. This condition is characteristically identified with slower and sometimes incomplete development of secondary sexual characteristics (such as beard and body hair) and may result also in incomplete development of the testes, enlargement of the breasts, and reproductive sterility. There may also be a moderate degree of mental retardation. Taken together, the appearance of these physical and mental characteristics in conjunction with the XXY karyotype appears to occur in about one of every 500 male births and is referred to as Klinefelter's syndrome.

Males have also been identified in whom there is an extra Y chromosome. The first such person to be described in the medical literature was a forty-four-year old man who was six feet tall, of "average intelligence," and without physical defects. His XYY karyotype was discovered in the course of a study of congenital anomalies among his children in 1961.

In 1965, the British science journal *Nature* published a report entitled "Aggressive Behavior, Mental Subnormality and the XYY Male." It described the first in a series of sex chromosome surveys conducted in a maximum-security mental and penal institution in Scotland. When the survey was completed, a total of 315 patients or inmates had been screened, and nine (2.9 percent) were reported to have the XYY karyotype. More than half of these were reported to be six feet or more in height.[1] A good deal of publicity surrounded the appearance of this report, and several other groups of researchers began to look for chromosomal anomalies among individuals incarcerated in mental or penal institutions in their countries. The results of these studies have varied. Surveys in some institutions in the United States failed to find a significant number of XYY males among patient or inmate populations, but other studies confirmed the original findings, and the idea began to catch on that the XYY karyotype was associated with "aggressive and criminal tendencies."

The idea that males with an extra Y chromosome are genetically predisposed to violent antisocial acts received great attention in 1968 when the attorneys for Richard Speck disclosed that his karyotype was XYY. Speck had been arrested for the mass murder of a group of nurses in their Chicago apartment, and the information about his genetic anomaly was introduced in support of the defense's contention that he was not guilty by reason of insanity. The subsequent discovery that Speck's karyotype was actually that of a normal XY male received much less publicity than did the initial spurious claim that he was genetically abnormal. In any event, there had already been several other cases in which the XYY karyotype was introduced as a defense in criminal trials, and a review published in a scholarly journal of medical genetics in 1968 defined individuals affected by the XYY "syndrome" as "psychopathic individuals lacking any ordinary capacity for feeling, apparently without much depth of emotion, who seemed incapable of making any rational plans for the future, and who on the whole posed behavioral problems from childhood."[2]

By the end of 1968 the XYY "syndrome" and its purported link to innate criminality had become something of a cause célèbre. In October, for example, the *New York Times Magazine* carried an article entitled "The XYY and the Criminal," and *Psychology Today* presented a review of "Chromosomes and Crime." In the latter article, Ashley Montagu, an anthropologist, speculated that the presence of a single Y chromosome is responsible for "the ordinary quantum of aggressiveness of the normal XY male" and that the presence of "a double dose of these potencies" might produce a person of almost supernatural aggressivity. "Some individuals (he wrote) seem to be driven to their aggressive behavior as if . . . possessed by a demon. The demon, it would seem, lies in the peculiar nature of the double Y chromosome complement."

With or without such overtones of demonology, it was widely believed that the extra Y chromosome causes criminal or antisocial behavior in affected individuals. Soon proposals for dealing with the problem began to appear and some observers began to look forward to the day when pre-natal genetic screening and abortion could be used routinely to "rid us of . . . sex deviants such as the XYY type."[3] By January of 1973, there had been at least one case reported in which a prospective mother chose to have an abortion after learning that she was carrying an XYY fetus.[4] This information was obtained via a procedure called amniocentesis in which a small quantity of amniotic fluid is withdrawn hypodermically from the sac surrounding a developing fetus. Cells found in the fluid can then be subjected to examination for their chromosomal makeup. In this way, information can be obtained early in pregnancy regarding the sex of the baby and other genotypic characteristics.

We have entered an era in which it is technically feasible to identify sex and other chromosomal characteristics of human beings before birth by means of relatively simple biochemical or chromosomal tests. In some ways, this will bring important health benefits to individuals with incipient genetic diseases. However, the decision to develop and deploy these techniques raises ethical and social questions that cannot be ignored. This is especially pertinent when the genetic characteristics are linked to physical or mental traits whose causes or consequences are the subject of dispute. The XYY karyotype is a case in point. In at least two states in the United States, Maryland and Massachusetts, adolescent males incarcerated in institutions for juvenile delinquents have been screened for sex-chromosome aneuploidy. In Maryland, a prolonged court battle was waged successfully to prevent this information from being used in decisions regarding questions of sentencing or parole.

Why have studies aimed at identifying XYY males engendered such controversy? The XYY karyotype is supposed to be a kind of "bad seed" which predisposes an individual to engage in antisocial or criminal behavior, but I intend to argue that there is no evidence for this and that the myth of "innate criminality" is supported only by spurious conclusions drawn from flawed research. It will not be enough, however, to show that people are mistaken in believing that a link has been scientifically established between chromosomes and crime. The controversy about XYY arises only in part from questions of logic and methodology. Its roots lie in differences of opinion regarding the causes of social behavior in general and of deviant behavior in particular.

Criminality was once thought to be caused by demonic possession, but beginning in the eighteenth century this notion was gradually replaced by the idea that criminal behavior was attributable to physical characteristics inherent within certain types of individuals. The phrenologists, for example, sought to associate bumps on the head with specific personality traits, and some physical anthropologists argued that criminal behavior reflected a degenerate form of biological organization as evidenced by physical stigmata, constitutional defects, and anthropometric "marks of inferiority." The Italian criminologist Cesare Lombroso and the American anthropologist Ernest Hooton were among those whose writings reflected a preoccupation with the biological determinants of criminality. Lombroso claimed that there were certain facial characteristics by which "criminal types" might be identified.

The criminal by nature has a feeble cranial capacity, a heavy and developed jaw, projecting (eye) ridges, an abnormal and assymetrical cranium . . . projecting ears, frequently a crooked or flat nose. Criminals are subject to [color blindness]; left-handedness is common; their muscular force is feeble. . . . Their moral degeneration corresponds with their physical, their criminal tendencies are manifested in infancy by (masturbation), cruelty, inclination to steal, excessive vanity, impulsive character. The criminal by nature is lazy, debauched, cowardly, not susceptible to remorse, without foresight, ... his handwriting is peculiar ... his slang is widely diffused ... The general ... persistence of an inferior race type. ... [5]

Lombroso and his followers attempted to establish a system whereby a predisposition to engage in antisocial behavior could be predicted on the basis of physical characteristics, and from surveys conducted in prisons, he concluded among other things that "murderers have "cold, glassy, blood-shot eyes, curly abundant hair, strong jaws, long ears and thin lips"; forgers are "pale and amiable, with small eyes and large noses; they become bald and grey-haired early"; and sex criminals have "glinting eyes, strong jaws, thick lips, lots of hair and projecting ears." Lombroso's conclusions were drawn, in all seriousness, from data collected in a manner that appeared to be scientific, and his results commanded the attention of criminologists throughout Europe and the United States. (The basic methodological flaw in Lombroso's approach to the problem of innate criminality, his failure to collect comparable observations from a representative sample of the population at large, is the kind of error that any scientist is supposed to know enough to avoid, but we will see it again when I return to the evidence allegedly establishing a link between the XYY karyotype and crime.)

The idea that criminality is traceable to bad seed was explicit in the writings of leaders of the mental testing and eugenics movements during the first decades of this century, and many prominent scientists recommended sterilization and similar eugenic measures as a means of cutting down the incidence of crime and social deviance in American society. More recently there have been claims, reminiscent of Lombroso's, that a correlation exists between delinquent or criminal behavior and bodily physique.[6] These studies, taken together, comprise the background of the reports that attempt to link sex chromosome anomalies and criminal behavior.

The first study of XYY males, the one published in *Nature* in 1965, purported to show two things: an increased incidence of XYY males in a maximum-security institution for the criminally insane and a tendency toward tallness in the affected individuals. The former claim has not been consistently borne out in subsequent studies, but I will accept it as given that the XYY karyotype occurs among incarcerated males more frequently than among the male population as a whole. Indeed, I will accept the frequency figures suggested by Ernest Hook in a recent review, which concludes that the XYY karyotype occurs in newborn males at a rate of 0.1 percent; that is, one per 1,000 live male births has an XYY karyotype. He also cites 2 percent as the rate of occurrence of XYY males in mental and penal institutions, which is about twenty times greater than one might expect on the basis of chance.

After the appearance of the first report on the XYY karyotype, several additional studies were conducted. Many of these, based upon the alleged association between XYY and tallness, were restricted to samples of prisoners preselected for height. Once again, a tendency toward enrichment (that is, increased incidence of XYY males) was found. This finding is difficult to interpret, however, because it is not clear whether the correlation is between XYY and institutionalization or between XYY and height. In any event, it was the presumed correlation with institutionalization that was used to infer the connection between the XYY karyotype and criminality. This inference presupposes that the finding of an enrichment for some biological characteristic (for example, the XYY karyotype) within a given class of prisoners establishes a link between that characteristic and criminality per se. This presupposition is crucial to the idea that the XYY karyotype is a "criminal gene" (to borrow a phrase recently used in an editorial in the journal *Science*), but it is false in at least two significant respects.

First of all, from arrest records, probation reports, and prison statistics (or from a visit to almost any penal institution in the United States), it is possible to identify beyond question at least three biological characteristics that show distinct enrichment among incarcerated offenders in general. These characteristics are age, skin color, and gender. Among those who become involved with the criminal justice system in this country today, youths, nonwhites, and males are found in exceedingly disproportionate numbers. Unless one chooses to conclude that nonwhite skin and maleness, for example, are biological characteristics that place an individual at risk for delinquent or criminal tendencies, it is obvious that the makeup of the prison population is a reflection of various forms of social discrimination.

At a time when crime has become a proverbial political football, it is well to bear in mind how it is defined for purposes of law enforcement and the administration of criminal justice. Throughout history, the kinds of behavior that have been judged to be criminal and subject to punishment have not remained constant. People, it might be said, commit crimes, but social systems create criminals by defining the norms, values, and interests whose violation constitutes criminal behavior. Each era, each society, develops its own criteria for judging behavior. In Massachusetts during the seventeenth century, for example, harsh penalties were meted out to those individuals who committed crimes against morality. By the nineteenth century, however, these crimes were punished less often. The laws proscribing intemperate language, sexual dalliance, truancy from worship, idleness, delinquency, and gambling remained on the books (and, to be sure, these forms of behavior continued to occur), but those who enforced the laws tended to ignore such acts and focused instead upon crimes against property and persons.

It is false, therefore, to imagine that "criminality" is a property inherent in certain individuals or groups rather than a quality conferred upon certain actions or behavior patterns by a process of social definition. Crime is a controversial and politically explosive issue precisely because it cannot be defined independently of social norms and values, and because fundamental disagreements exist within our society regarding the propriety and justifiability of different kinds of acts. The result is that phrases like "law and order" and "the war against crime" are little more than convenient political code words which serve to obscure the way in which crimes are defined to ensure that certain classes of people will be dealt with differently, depending upon status, class, and background. As Thomas Hobbes observed more than three hundred years ago, the most powerful instrument of political authority "is the power to give names and to enforce definitions." This comment is worth pondering in a society where betrayals of public trust go unpunished while public funds are expended to search for the genetic roots of crime. The causes of social or antisocial behavior cannot be traced to inherent attributes or genetic predispositions, and when different societies and different eras cannot even agree on a definition of antisocial behavior, the search for criminal chromosomes is as scientifically meaningless as the "disease" of drapetomania. That the search is nonetheless being pursued in the current political climate is not without significance, however. For, so long as people can be persuaded to accept spurious definitions of crime, absurd attempts to locate the root causes of social conflict within defective individuals or stigmatized groups may continue to pass unchallenged.

More important, to focus efforts and expenditures upon the bogus field of criminal defectology is to create a politically expedient diversion. If a large constituency believes that many or most crimes are committed by people who are inherently defective, public concern will be focused away from the prevailing pattern of social arrangements, a pattern in which the definers of "criminality" figure along with everyone else. The process of diversion, although not necessarily the result of intentional deception, is likely to lead to a war against crime which is really a campaign by the privileged against the disadvantaged, a campaign conducted under the camouflage of scientific objectivity by those who wish to defend and preserve a congenial status quo.

Even if there is an enrichment for the XYY karyotype within mental and penal institutions, that fact cannot be invoked as evidence for a causal connection between this karyotype and crime. Such a connection would require the additional but false assumption that incarceration is a

valid index of criminality, yet criminal acts are far more equitably distributed across society than are acts of punishment. Of the crimes punishable by imprisonment, 98.5 percent go unpunished. The 1.5 percent who
are prisoners should not be confused with the total population of criminal
offenders. When the Katzenbach Commission examined the prison population, the picture that emerged pointed overwhelmingly to background features that are socioeconomic. It was found, for example, that the most
consistently observed antecedents of incarceration are poverty, lack of
schooling, joblessness, and family instability. The portrait of the average
offender, the commission reported,

progressively highlights the disadvantaged character of his life. The offender at the end of the road in prison is likely to be a member of the
lowest social and economic groups in the country, poorly educated and
unemployed, unmarried, reared in a broken home and to have a prior
criminal record.[7]

The second problem with a direct causal relation between the XYY
karyotype and criminality is related to the fact that implicit or explicit
standards of physical attractiveness are likely to affect the ways in which
people are treated. The prevalence of such discrimination is not irrelevent
to the XYY issue, and it may help to explain the enrichment of XYY
karyotypes among incarcerated groups more plausibly than does the
theory of innate criminality.

As I have pointed out, the claim has been made that males with the
XYY karyotype may be somewhat taller than average. It has also been reported that severe skin conditions such as acne are more frequent in XYY
individuals than in XY males.[8] If it is granted for purposes of argument
that the presence of an extra Y chromosome is associated with unusual
height and blemished skin, the question to consider is whether these
factors may contribute to a self-fulfilling prophecy about the psychosocial
development of XYY individuals. As Hook points out,

Personality patterns developing in children as a reaction to large height or
"channeling" by social forces of individuals [who may appear to be more
threatening] conceivably could account for the observed frequencies of
institutionalization. It is easy to imagine why a tall deviant individual who
has difficulty with impulse control may be more likely to be placed in custody than a short individual with similar behavior, and probably several
XYY's may be in custody more because of their size than their behavior. . . .[9]

There is further evidence that physical appearance per se, even in the
absence of antisocial behavior, may be sufficient to produce such "channeling" effects. Karen Dion and Ellen Berscheid found that even nurs-
ery school children are sensitive to the physical attractiveness of their
peers. They asked several graduate student judges to rate the physical
attractiveness of children on the basis of black and white photographs and

then determined who liked whom among the children themselves. The clearest results were obtained for the males: the boys who had been judged most attractive by the graduate students were liked better than those who had been judged unattractive. Furthermore, the boys in the latter group were considered by their peers to be more aggressive than their attractive counterparts, and when the children were asked to identify the classmates who "scared" them, they named the boys who were independently judged to be less attractive.

Of course, it might have been that the less attractive boys *were* more aggressive and *did* behave in a more scary manner. From this preliminary study it is impossible to tell because the investigators did not actually observe the behavior of the children themselves. A subsequent study from the same laboratory, however, provides independent evidence that people tend to attribute more blame to physically unattractive children, regardless of actions. In this study, conducted by Karen Dion, women college students were asked to examine brief reports of classroom disturbances apparently written by a teacher. Attached to each report was a photograph of the child who had allegedly initiated the disturbance. Once again, the photographs had been previously rated independently for "attractiveness" by a separate group of judges. At the same time, different subjects received the same reports, accompanied by different photographs. Not only did the subjects tend to place more blame upon the less attractive children, but they also tended to leap to the conclusion that they were chronic troublemakers. Thus when a physically unattractive girl was pictured as the culprit in a given situation, a respondent said; "I think the child would be quite bratty and would probably be a problem to teachers. She would probably try to pick a fight with other children her own age. . . . All in all, she would be a real problem." However, when an attractive girl was pictured as the instigator in exactly the same situation, described in exactly the same words, the respondents typically excused the act as less serious and somewhat exceptional. As one subject put it: ". . . she plays well with everyone, but like anyone else, a bad day can occur. Her cruelty . . . need not be taken too seriously."[10]

These studies suggest that in social situations involving conflict or turmoil, physical appearance alone can cause a bias toward harsher or more lenient interpretations of behavior in the observer's response. And as the preliminary study shows, this bias may be detectable at a very early age.

These and similar results recall earlier instances in which biased social attitudes based upon criteria of physical appearance were shown to contain the seeds of a self-fulfilling prophecy. In other words, differential responses made toward children solely on the basis of their appearance may have consequences for how these children come to behave in the future. It is a psychological fact that the way a person is treated as a child affects his or her self image. A child who receives harsh treatment due to his or her appearance may come to think of himself or herself as bad and begin to behave accordingly. Such behavior, consistent with a self-concept originally formed on the basis of appearance, illustrates a possible basis for the "channeling" effect described earlier. The search for "criminal chromosomes" may serve further to stigmatize individuals whose only original offense was their appearance.

In his review of the XYY literature, Ernest Hook writes,

Publicity given to the first published reports of settings for deviant individuals gave rise to the unfortunate popular stereotype of XYY individuals as the most physically aggressive and violent individuals. . . . But in those mental-penal and penal settings where XYY's have been found, they do not appear to be concentrated among the most dangerous, violent and physically aggressive inmates. And, in general, their offenses are similar to or less serious than those of the XY's there.[11]

The XYY individual's behavior, a complex product of genetic, environmental, and experiential factors, seems to suggest that the effects of the XYY genotype are limited in their tendency to produce aggressive behavior. The question remains, however, whether the XYY genotype predisposes an affected individual to engage in *other* forms of antisocial behavior. A few calculations may serve to show that it does not.

Using Hook's estimate that the incidence of XYY individuals in the general population is approximately 0.1 percent (that is, one per 1,000 live male births), and assuming that there are currently about one hundred million males in the United States population, there are probably about 100,000 XYY individuals in this country. Now let us assume (data are sparse and difficult to evaluate) that one in 500 males may be confined at one time or another in a mental/penal or penal institution, and that 2 percent of those males will by XYY. In other words, of the 200,000 males who are or are likely to be incarcerated, 4,000 may be expected to be XYY. Thus, of the 100,000 presumed XYY individuals in the country, 4 percent (4,000) are "at risk" of finding themselves confined in a mental/penal or penal setting. Obviously 96 percent of all XYY males somehow manage to escape this fate. In other words, the XYY genotype is expressed in a form that predisposes the affected person to incarceration in only a minute fraction of cases. The overwhelming majority of XYY individuals may be assumed to be leading lives of a kind that do not bring them to the attention of the mental health or criminal justice systems any more frequently than their XY counterparts.

The absence of evidence suggesting a direct cause-and-effect relationship between the XYY karyotype and "criminality" leads me back to a consideration of the infant screening project described at the beginning of the chapter. The project was being conducted under a grant from the

Center for the Study of Crime and Delinquency (a division of the National Institutes of Mental Health). Its overall objective was to establish a relationship between sex chromosome patterns and human development and psychopathology. The investigators claimed that such a study was warranted because of "the frequency with which severe psychopathology of a sexual or aggressive nature is found in males with sex chromosomal aneuploidies." The study results were intended, they wrote, ultimately to "permit some determination to be made of the actual risk that patients with sex chromosomal lesions have for developing aggressive or sexual psychopathology." Toward that end, they undertook to screen all male newborns at the Boston Lying-In Hospital and planned to follow for twenty years those who were found to have sex chromosome variations.

Of the more than 16,000 male infants studied, six with the XYY karyotype were found and are still being followed by the project director, a pediatric psychiatrist, who makes visits to the childrens' homes three times a year. The parents "are informed that their children have extra chromosomal material" and the family's pediatrician is "fully informed about the child's variation."[12]

This project is susceptible to criticism on many grounds, including those of inadequately informed consent and defective experimental design. For example, the parents were not told at the outset that they were agreeing to have their prospective baby included in a long-term behavioral study, nor were they informed that the study was sponsored by a government agency concerned primarily with crime and delinquency. But that is not all. The study itself was allegedly intended to determine whether or not XYY males develop behavioral problems early in life, but the results will be uninterpretable because the parents were told that their child had a chromosomal abnormality. What was being studied (if one can call it that) was the effect upon a child's development of (a) the XYY karyotype and (b) parental knowledge of that fact. Since many parents are aware of the "bad seed" doctrine, and since most eventually made relevant inquiries, the essential prerequisites for a self-fulfilling prophecy were being met. Of course, one way to control for the possible effects of telling a child's parents that he has an extra Y chromosome would be to establish a control group of baby boys who are actually normal but whose parents are told, falsely, that they are XYY. The prospect of such an unethical proceeding can serve to point up the many harmful effects that can follow when a parent is led to expect a child to develop problems.

From Cesare Lombroso's "marks of degeneracy" and Thomas Hobbes' remarks about "innate depravity" to the currently fashionable search for "bad seed," the only real change in the myth of inborn criminality has been the growing reliance upon more scientific-sounding techniques for identifying and stigmatizing individuals. The majority of research into the causes of crime with its emphasis upon technologies of law enforcement, ignores the factors conducive to violence and criminality within the social structure as well as the inequities of the criminal justice system itself, which operates so as to reinforce existing stereotypes in the public mind. During the past few years, for example, research and development in the field of criminology has been fostered mainly from two sources: the first is the United States Department of Justice through its Law Enforcement Assistance Administration and the second is the United States Department of Health, Education, and Welfare through its Center for the Study of Crime and Delinquency. These agencies have overlapping interests, and both have been heavily committed to supporting programs based on the belief that crime and violence are mainly caused by the behavior of individuals who are inherently antisocial or defective. It is thus not surprising that the research they sponsor tends to focus on the development of more powerful instruments for behavioral screening and behavioral control.[13]

The search for criminal chromosomes is only one of many similar activities being supported by these agencies. The search for "antisocial genotypes" and "criminal minds" in young children should serve as a reminder that because a social policy is utterly lacking in intellectual respectability is no guarantee that it will not be revived when renewed social conflict creates fresh demands for repressive measures. This is particularly true in the case of those "total institutions" where behavior control is a common fact of everyday life.

The prison, wrote a Massachusetts warden in 1868, "is a moral hospital, the inmates the morally diseased. It is the duty of the prison to cure."[14] From medieval times, when imprisonment was first used as a means of penalizing transgressions, until the nineteenth century, its professed objectives were vengeance, restraint, and deterrence. But for about the last 150 years prisons in the United States and elsewhere have been built and operated on the basis of a "treatment model," according to which their purpose is not to punish but to rehabilitate, to transform the offender into a better or better-behaved person.

Modern penal institutions are ostensibly run in accordance with benevolent-sounding principles of "correction," "rehabilitation," and "treatment." Yet they have been—and are today—places of equal or greater oppression than the frankly punitive institutions they were intended to replace. In order to understand why this is the case, it is necessary to examine certain preconceptions on which the treatment philosophy of modern penology is based. Following this, a survey of some representative "treatment modalities" will serve to illustrate how modern behavior control technology, deployed under the banner of rehabilitation, is used to enforce prison discipline, to foster institutional survival, and to buttress the power of administrative personnel. Once that has been done, it may be clear why prison treatment programs do not cure, improve, or rehabilitate.

The law as a whole—and the criminal law in particular—concerns the regulation of social behavior. The criminal law itself has two distinct functions. It serves to create crimes by defining as precisely as possible the kinds of deviant or nonconforming behavior it intends to regulate. Thus, in an important sense, the amount and variety of crime and punishment in a given society greatly depends upon the number and range of behavior patterns that are defined as criminal. The criminal law also serves to define and administer treatments for individuals who commit crimes by engaging in behavior judged to fall within the purview of the law.

Given the existence of laws by which certain forms of intellectual, social, economic, sexual, or doctrinal nonconformity are defined as crimes, the administrative tasks facing the judiciary are mainly two: to assess blame for acts of criminal behavior and to mete out appropriate penalties. According to the traditional view, the offender who has been found guilty of a crime should be penalized commensurately, and toward that end, judges resort to a wide range of penalties, graded in severity from extremely mild (for example, admonishment or moral censure) to extremely harsh (capital punishment). With respect to imprisonment, the range of options might be great or small in a given case, but the general rule is that its duration ought to reflect the seriousness of the particular crime, the "degree" of conviction, and the presence or absence of mitigating circumstances.

By contrast, the treatment philosophy has its roots in a broader trend in the field of criminal law, a trend away from the assessment of individual blame and the imposition of commensurate punitive sanctions. At the heart of the treatment philosophy lies the idea, already familiar from earlier chapters, that people commit certain kinds of crimes because of inherent defects. From this it follows that if the individual is driven to act by antisocial impulses arising from a deep-seated biological derangement or behavioral disorder, personal responsibility is beside the point. And, instead of attempting to assess blame, proper diagnosis and effective treatment of the relevant defects is necessary, for the "offender's own good" as well as for the "protection of society." Thus instead of trying to make the punishment fit the crime, the proper task of the criminal justice system is seen as making the treatment fit the criminal.

The departure of the treatment model from traditional legal philosophy is profound. For example, instead of a fixed sentence in accordance with criteria pertinent to the act, the duration of imprisonment depends upon the "successful outcome" of "rehabilitation." From this follows the practice of imposing indeterminate sentences, which supposedly allows the "well-motivated" prisoner to work diligently toward rehabilitation in order to receive an earlier parole. Such a scheme, it is argued, affords society additional protection: the impenitent or "incorrigible" inmate who refuses to participate in his or her rehabilitation will remain in prison for an indefinite time.

The treatment philosophy has appealed, from the time of its inception, to many diverse groups. To liberal reformers, it appears to embody a genuine humanitarian concern for the plight of prisoners caught up in a dehumanizing, despotic, and punitive system, while to hard-line wardens, it represents an administratively efficient, powerful, and socially acceptable alternative to old-fashioned approaches.

Many states now have a form of indeterminate sentencing; the offender is given a minimum and a maximum sentence. The judicial arm of the criminial law transfers authority over the convict to the institution where he or she is to be confined. Thereafter the prisoner's fate depends on circumstances within the institution and on the actions of a parole board which reviews the prisoner's record from time to time for evidence of "progress toward rehabilitation," in order to decide whether or not to grant release from confinement.

Confinement in prison, whatever else it may be, is a form of behavior control. The environment of the prison—the architecture, the organization of space, and the activities inside—is the instrument of control. The very act of incarcerating an individual, of separating him or her involuntarily from the larger society, is but the first step in the process of behavior modification that imprisonment is intended to achieve.

For purposes of this discussion, and more generally as well, the terms behavior control and behavior modification refer to the deliberate control or to modification of behavior, the processes and procedures whereby the institution and its staff, serving as the agents of law enforcement, endeavor to regulate or modify the behavior of prisoners. In other words, an identifiable class (law enforcement agents) maintain control of another identifiable class (the subjects or prisoners). Whereas this may seem altogether too obvious to mention, the disparities of power than characterize the prison system must be spelled out to avoid confusion. One form of confusion often created by behavioral psychologists results from the claim that systems of behavior control are essentially reciprocal. As applied to the case of prison, it assumes the behavior of the prisoners controls the behavior of their guards as well as the other way around. What the prisoners do, so the argument goes, determines the institution's responses. For example, the prisoner who tries to escape creates a situation to which the pursuit behavior of the guards is a response; thus the prisoner participates in controlling the sequence of events. Using this concept, B. F. Skinner in *Beyond*

Freedom and Dignity arrives at the formulation that "in a very real sense, then, the slave controls the slave driver."[15] Suffice it to say at this point that there is a kernel of truth in this notion of reciprocal control, but also a much larger reality that is conveniently ignored.

Another confused aspect of the discussions of behavior modification and behavior control by certain behavioral psychologists is that the terms are not used to refer to the modification of behavior as such but only to those forms of control that are based upon particular psychological theories and methods. I believe that this attempt to redefine words that have a clearly understood meaning in public discourse is an exercise in professional arrogance. The restrictive definitions of behavior modification offered by some psychologists often serve to create the very confusion they are designed to dispel, as in the following example:

Before discussing legal and ethical issues in the use of behavior modification with institutionalized residents (i.e. prisoners and mental hospital patients), there are two areas of confusion that can be clarified. The first arises from the fact that behavior modification is not always distinguished from certain other forms of behavior control, especially psychosurgery and chemotherapy. Although these behavior control methodologies may indeed modify behavior, they are not techniques derived from learning theory, and hence should not be called behavior modification.[16]

The reader is left to decide whether or not to accept the psychologists's appropriation of a common sense term on the basis of its having been taken from other usage. I think that this represents an attempt to impoverish popular speech and ought to be resisted on that basis alone. When I use the terms *behavior modification* and *behavior control,* it is in the sense that most people use them. Where necessary, these terms may be qualified to indicate if the case in point is one of "psychological" behavior modification (involving the manipulation of rewards, punishments, and similar environmental stimuli), "pharmacological" behavior modification (involving the administration of drugs), "neurological" behavior modification (involving the use of psychosurgery, electrical brain stimulation, and so on), or behavior modification by other means.

My chief intent in insisting on this usage is to show that the factors critical to an understanding of behavior modification programs (in prisons and elsewhere) are common to all of these programs, regardless of variations in sources and methods of procedure; psychosurgery is one form of behavior modification and operant conditioning is another. The former entails a manipulation of the brain, the latter of environmental stimuli; the psychosurgeon destroys brain tissue, the behavioral psychologist constructs schedules of reinforcement. The features shared by psychosurgery and operant conditioning, as applied within the context of prisons and other custodial institutions are more important than the differences between them. The main reasons for this are that they exist, together with other "treatment modalities," in a common institutional context and have a common intent.

In the nineteenth-century penitentiary, the offenders who were confined to solitary cells were expected to do little more than repent in solitude. The philosophy that guided prison construction and management from the 1820s onward was that moral rehabilitation could best be achieved by punishment in the form of a stern regime of physical and social isolation. The inmate would be forced to meditate on his sins and could resolve to transgress no more.

Of all the many forms of torment imprisonment may provide, none is more feared by inmates than the suffocating confinement of total isolation. When de Tocqueville toured American prisons during his sojourn in this country and was permitted to talk with prisoners, he was impressed by their horror of isolation and their fear that it would drive them insane. Dickens wrote in 1967, after visiting the Eastern State Penitentiary in Philadelphia,

The system here is rigid, strict and hopeless *solitary confinement.* I believe it, in its effects, to be cruel and wrong. In its intentions, I am well convinced that it is kind, humane and meant for reformation; but I am persuaded that those who devised this system of Prison Discipline, and those benevolent gentlemen who carry it into execution, do not know what they are doing . . . I hold this slow and daily tampering with the mysteries of the brain, to be immeasurably worse than any torture of the body; and because its ghastly signs are not so palpable to the eye . . . and it extorts few cries that human ears can hear; therefore I the more denounce it, as a secret punishment which slumbering humanity is not roused up to stay.[17]

Recognition of failure dawns slowly upon prison administrators, but it finally became apparent that solitary confinement not only did not rehabilitate but actually caused a distressingly large number of inmates to go mad. In an attempt to prevent insanity, "cottage industries" were introduced into the prison regime, and inmates were encouraged to busy themselves in their cells with shoemaking, weaving, tailoring, and similar tasks. But the plan did not work, and its failure led to the kinds of innovations embodied in the "factory prisons" like Auburn and Sing Sing in New York State. There, prisoners spent the night in tiny solitary cells (three-and-a-half by seven feet) like so many bees in a hive, and at sunrise they were marched in silent lockstep to factories where they labored in silence until breakfast hour, marched silently to the huge mess hall where they ate in silence, marched back again to work in silence, and so on throughout the days and years. The efficiency of the factory prison system in New York impressed many observers for its complete despotism, but it was greeted enthusiastically by prison managers, who saw in its emphasis upon unremitting industry a means of subordinating the convicts.

It is hardly surprising that the industrial prison, with its capacity to generate financial profit (although seldom for the prisoners) while proclaiming to rehabilitate through forced labor, became the model for most of the United States. By the time the "new penology" was formally institutionalized with the founding of the American Prison Association in 1870, the great mass of American prisoners was laboring under the rule of "rehabilitation through industry." As the superintendent of a New York reformatory wrote, "In order to train criminals for social life they must have a strict regime and learn quick and accurate self-adjustment to a uniform requirement."[8] Industrial exploitation, however, is no longer the chosen instrument of bringing the desired "self-adjustment" about. Today the instruments are drawn from modern behavior control technology and are deployed within the context of "progressive correctional reform." The question is whether the introduction of this new terminology and technology has made any substantial difference in either the prison system or individual lives.

The state of California is instructive in this regard. Since the passage in 1917 of the indeterminate sentencing provision of its penal code, California has been a leader in the field of prison reform. Nowhere are there wider ranges between minimum and maximum sentences (robbery, for example, brings five years to life, while second-degree burglary brings one to fifteen years), and in no other state has a broader range of treatment modalities been employed. Yet the evidence indicates that the reforms have failed to fulfill their promise. One such indication is that the rate of recidivism—the tendency to return to prison after release on parole—has for many years remained virtually unchanged in California: approximately 40 percent are reimprisoned eventually.[19] Moreover, there appears to be no difference in recidivism rates between those who received psychiatric treatment in the prison and those who did not. This is an impressively poor record for a prison system that according to most observers ranks above most other correctional systems from the standpoint of emphasis on treatment.

But if statistics prove that the emphasis upon treatment does little good, other evidence suggests that it may do harm. A pertinent statistic in this respect is that since California's adoption of the rehabilitative ideal the length of prison sentences has steadily increased. From 1959 to 1969, for example, the median time served by offenders for their first conviction for a felony rose from twenty-four to thirty-six months, becoming the longest "felony first-release" time in the United States.[20]

Statistics such as these do not tell the entire story. At the heart of the rehabilitative model's failure is the arbitrary and extreme power that prison administrators and parole boards wield over every aspect of the inmate's life. Screened from public visibility and immune from the checks and balances by which other branches of government may be held accountable, the typical modern prison is a "lawless agency."[21] It may seem paradoxical to suggest that a law enforcement agency is itself lawless, but the fact is that prison officials ignore the rule of law to the extent that they exercise power over the behavior of inmates (including the power to punish and to treat) in a way that is ordinarily immune from judicial review and is not subject to due process procedures. Indeed, there is almost nothing that prison administrators cannot do, and do not do, to inmates in the name of "treatment."

The unchecked discretionary powers of prison authorities, coupled with the treatment philosophy of modern penologists, gives rise to contradictions that to be understood must be glimpsed from the prisoner's perspective. Almost anything that is done to an inmate in order to enforce conformity to the lawless discipline of prison life can be described as a form of treatment that is being provided for the inmate's good. The contradiction is implicit in prison functions like parole. Since in prison systems where the treatment philosophy prevails it is generally understood by the inmates that they must participate in a treatment program in order to become eligible for release. As the authors of *Struggle for Justice* point out, statements such as "Get a program and you'll get a parole," which are frequently heard in prison, suggest that programing is a kind of con game in which the prisoners play their part as a means of manipulating the parole process. Indeed, there are many treatment programs in prisons that require little more than a willing gesture of playing along from the inmate. But in many instances the inmate can only win the treatment game by losing his or her self-respect; thus, in order to be the winner of a parole board hearing the inmate must have a file that shows he or she has been doing "good time," placating the authorities, and "going along with the program."

There are many prisoners who are unwilling to play the game and cannot win. George Jackson was one of those men. At the time of his death at San Quentin in 1971, he had served many years in California prisons with an indeterminate sentence for a seventy-dollar armed robbery. In a letter from prison to his lawyer, Fay Stender, he wrote,

No one walks into the Board room with his head up. This just isn't done. . . . If a man gets a parole from these prisons, Fay, it means that he crawled into that room. Plus it means that he adopted the philosophical attitude toward shit in the face several times since his last board. . . . The guy who earns a parole surrendered some face in the course of his stay here. . . . He walked away from some situation to save his body—at the cost of part of his face. . . .[22]

For the prisoner who does not go along or who refuses to get a program there is an obvious disadvantage: the prison authorities may use such negative attitudes as evidence that the prisoner is not yet rehabilitated. This may result, in turn, in a change of custody classification (for example, from minimum or moderate to maximum security or from one of these to "the hole"—solitary confinement, in some prisons euphemistically called the "adjustment center"). Moreover, the prisoner who resists treatment, who insists that he or she is not mentally ill, behaviorally disordered, or biologically deranged, may find an indeterminate sentence meted out as punishment. Jessica Mitford describes one such case:

An Indian prisoner in San Quentin [was] serving an indeterminate sentence of one to fifteen years for burglary: as a first offender, he would ordinarily have been paroled after a year or so. For eight years the parole board refused to set a release date because he would not go to group therapy. In the ninth year, he escaped.[23]

According to the traditional and presumably discredited fixed-sentence model, the punishment (that is, the duration of imprisonment) was supposed to fit the crime. Under the new, and ostensibly nonpunitive, indeterminate-sentence model, the duration of punishment frequently depends upon the prisoner's willingness to submit to treatment. Moreover, the treatment is deemed effective to the extent that the behavior of the prisoner appears to undergo a set of prescribed changes. Little wonder then, that most prison programs seek to promote not only industry and cleanliness but also docility and subservience to authority. Reclassification and prolonged confinement are not the only punishments that the prison authority is empowered to mete out. As Greenberg and Stender point out, the prison's discretionary power to punish is almost boundless:

It can and does transfer [inmates] far from their families; limit and restrict their visitors; censor what they read, what they write; decide whom they may associate with inside, what medicine or other medical care they will or will not receive, what education they may or may not have, whether they will be totally locked up, for weeks, months, occasionally even years or enjoy limited personal freedom. Inmates' personal property may be misplaced and destroyed, incoming and outgoing letters sometimes not delivered, and, in the extreme, prisoners may be starved, brutalized, and killed.[24]

All of these things, it must be stressed, may be done and have been done in prisons publicly committed to the treatment philosophy. Frequently they take place during the process of inducing the prisoner to "get a program"; some are routinely done as part of a treatment program.

The programs encompass a mind-boggling array, ranging from group therapy to psychosurgery; many are drawn from the armamentarium of modern behavior control technology. Since treatment techniques are so varied, I have tried to organize the following discussion according to a roughly drawn continuum of severity. I judge the severity of the treatments in relation to several criteria, including the permanence of their effects, the degree of physical force or invasiveness used, and the extent to which it is possible for an unwilling inmate to fake participation in the treatment or otherwise avoid its intended effects.

Psychosurgery clearly stands at the more severe end of this scale. Amygdalectomy and other forms of psychosurgery have been promoted and performed in the name of "violence control," and it should come as no surprise to learn that recent waves of prison unrest have prompted some authorities to suggest extensive diagnosis and treatment of "aggressive and destructive" inmates. For example, in 1970, Dr. M. Hunter Brown, a California psychosurgeon, urged his colleagues at the Second International Congress of Psychosurgery "to initiate pilot programs for the precise [psychosurgical] rehabilitation of the prisoner-patient who is often young and intelligent, yet incapable of controlling various forms of violence."[25] He also advanced an economic argument to make his psychosurgical pacification proposal appealing to taxpayers and beleaguered prison officials alike, pointing out that "each violent young criminal incarcerated from 20 years to life costs taxpayers perhaps $100,000. For roughly $6,000, society can provide medical treatment which will transform him into a responsible, well-adjusted citizen."[26]

In September 1971 (at the time of the Attica and San Quentin massacres) the chief of the California Department of Corrections wrote a letter to his board of supervisors, the California Council on Criminal Justice, which began by noting that the probelm of treating the "aggressive, destructive inmate" has become particularly acute in recent years, although so far no satisfactory method of treatment has been developed. The letter went on to describe a plan "involving a complex neurosurgical evaluation and treatment program for the violent inmate," similar to the electrode implantation, stimulation, and destruction procedures practiced by Drs. Mark and Ervin.[27]

The letter proposed that the inmates be treated at a prison euphemistically called the California Medical Facility at Vacaville, the site of a Maximum Psychiatric Diagnostic Unit (a maxi-maxi in prison parlance). The plan to establish the MPDU at Vacaville was contained in a California Board of Corrections report on *Violence in California Prisons* which was sent to Governor Ronald Reagan in 1971. Opened soon thereafter, in February 1972, it houses up to eighty-four inmates drawn from "adjustment centers" ("solitary," or simply "the hole" in prison talk) at prisons throughout the state. According to official accounts, the MPDU is intended to offer diagnosis and treatment to the most violent among the approximately 700 inmates housed in the various adjustment centers, two-thirds of whom are black and Chicano.

With the growing availability of stereotaxic psychosurgery, brain stimulation, and other forms of "neurotechnology," and faced with growing unrest among the prison population, the prospect of behavior control via brain manipulation was obviously an appealing one for California prison administrators in 1971. (Allegations have been made about the use of psychosurgery in the California prison system before 1971, but I know of no evidence that either substantiates or refutes these claims.) However, the corrections chief's proposal ran into serious difficulty when his letter of intent fell into the hands of a group of exprisoners who released it to the public. On December 30, 1971, with opposition to the psychosurgery proposal mounting, the Department of Corrections called a press conference to announce that the project has been "temporarily abandoned for administrative reasons." The head of the Department of Corrections Research Division told reporters that financial considerations were involved in the decision to drop it, but he added, "It's quite likely that we will not proceed with this, but if we had unlimited funds, we would explore every opportunity to help anyone who wants such assistance."[28]

The psychosurgery proposal in this instance was abandoned, or at least shelved temporarily, because of public protest. But the MPDU and other maxi-maxi prisons continue to screen and treat prisoners for other types of programs and the brain manipulation proposals continue to proliferate.[29] One of the more technically sophisticated proposals of this kind is a direct extension of the automated battlefield concept that was developed during the war in Indochina. The pertinent technology is based upon "remote pulse tracking" systems developed for use in jungle warfare. In order to prevent "friendly" units from being inadvertently attacked by their own forces, they were occasionally sent into the field with one of their members wearing a wrist watch like transmitter–telemetry device. Signals from the transmitter were picked up by three distant receiving stations, and by means of triangulation the position of the transmitter could be continuously monitored. By way of "bringing it all back home," it has been proposed that parolees be required to wear these devices in order to permit continuous surveillance of their movements via a telemetry system. Ralph Schwitzgebel, for example, suggested that

a parolee thus released would probably be less likely to commit offenses if a record of his location were kept at the base station. If a two-way tone communication were included in this system, a therapeutic relationship might be established in which the parolee could be rewarded, warned or otherwise signalled in accordance with the plan for therapy.[30]

Lest the parolee be inclined to tinker mischievously with the system in order to escape surveillance, wrote Schwitzgebel, "security equipment" could prevent it.

It is not so long a step from a "two-way tone communication" system of this kind to a surveillance and control system involving a parolee, a computer, and a set of electrodes implanted in the parolee's brain. Two professors of criminology are among those who have proposed precisely such a system. They argue for remote monitoring and brain stimulation as "entirely feasible and possible as a method of control." Posing a hypothetical case in which a parolee has been wired with electrodes to record brain activity and other physiological measures, and subject only to some minor qualifications of a technical kind, they envisage the day when

a parolee with a past record of burglaries is tracked to a downtown shopping district (in fact, is exactly placed in a store known to be locked up for the night) and the physiological data reveals an increased respiration rate, a tension in the musculature and an increased flow of adrenalin. It would be a safe guess, certainly, that he was up to no good. The computer in this case, *weighing the probabilities*, would come to a decision and alert the police or parole officer so that they could hasten to the scene; or, if the subject were equipped with an implanted radiotelemeter, it could transmit an electrical signal (to the brain) which could block further action by the subject by causing him to forget or abandon his project.[31]

With respect to ensuring the "beneficial use" of the system and in order "to forestall possible ethical and legal objections," the authors of the proposal insist that the consent of the inmate should be obtained and that he should "retain the option . . . of returning to prison" if he finds the surveillance and control system "too burdensome." Moreover, they remind their readers that since the system is intended to be an aid to rehabilitation, a maximum of discretionary power in the hands of proper authorities is essential; "a law should be passed giving the users of this equipment an absolute privilege of keeping confidential all information obtained therefrom . . . and all data should be declared as inadmissible in court." In other words, the criminal justice system should remain an agency outside the law; a lawless agency capable of taking any and all control measures without due process or judicial review.

Acknowledging that some ethical objections to their correctional and therapeutic goals might still linger in the minds of some, they quote B. F. Skinner to the effect that the scientific age has arrived and Victor Hugo's "Nothing is as powerful as an idea whose time has come."

The same holds true for a technology whose time is upon us. Those countries whose social life advances to keep pace with their advancing technology will survive in the world of tomorrow; those that look backward and cling to long-outmoded values will fall . . . into . . . degradation. . . ; The nations that can so control behavior as to control the crime problem will enjoy an immense advantage over those that do not. Whether we like it or not, changes in technology require changes in political and social life and in values. . . .

They conclude that theirs is "a reasonable proposal" for dealing with "primitive humanoid traits such as intraspecific aggression, which is a disgusting trait. . . . What better place to start than with those individuals most in need of a change for the better?"[32]

Perhaps there is not yet any reason for prisoners to fear they will be subjected to behavior modification through psychosurgery, electrode implantation, remote stimulation, and other elaborate electrophysiological techniques. The reason for this is not so much that the technology does not work (the practical possibilities for technological improvements are great), but rather because these methods are neither necessary nor particularly desirable for behavior control in contemporary American society, including our prisons. The view that direct brain manipulation is not an ethically and legally acceptable method for controlling the behavior of inmates of prisons is reflected in a recent court decision barring such procedures. Among authorities other than neurosurgeons, it is believed that other methods of modification are both more effective and more acceptable.

The advocates of brain manipulation for inmates have received a legal setback recently; the case involved "John Doe," a mental patient at Michigan's Ionia State Hospital. He had been committed as a "sexual psychopath" when he was eighteen years old and was invited to participate in an experiment funded by the state whose goal was to compare the "violence control" effects of limbic system psychosurgery and the drug cyproterone acetate, an antiandrogen supposed to produce a "chemical castration" characterized by impotence, loss of sex drive, and docility. From information provided by the director, and with a promise that a successful outcome might increase the likelihood of release, Doe consented to participate in the psychosurgery treatment group; his parents also consented. The next step was to be the implantation of the electrodes, but at this point a Michigan Legal Services attorney, Gabe Kaimowitz, heard of the project and brought suit to block it.

This was an unusual step. Most litigation in the area of mental health administration has sought to implement a "right to treatment" on behalf of patients who are confined but remain untreated; Kaimowitz's suit was to block the psychosurgical treatment of Doe and other persons in similar situations. After the court appointed a lawyer to represent Doe's interests and he successfully argued that the Michigan criminal psychopath law under which Doe had been committed was unconstitutional, Doe was granted his freedom and changed his mind about participating in the project.

Although Doe was set free and the state forced by public pressure to withdraw funds for the project, the court reasoned that the case raised further issues because Kaimowitz represented the class of Michigan mental patients who might be subjects in similar projects in the future. After hearings involving a range of expert testimony about the brain and behavior, the court ruled that (1) patients involuntarily committed in state institutions are legally incapable of competent, voluntary, knowledgeable consent to psychosurgical operations which will irreversibly destroy brain tissue; (2) the First Amendment freedoms of speech and expression presuppose a right to generate ideas, a right that could be destroyed or impaired by psychosurgery; and (3) the constitutional right to privacy would be frustrated by unwarranted intrusion into a patient's brain. The court expressly refused to rule on Kaimowitz's contention that psychosurgery amounted to "cruel and unusual punishment" under the circumstances. The decision will almost certainly promote further litigation and may help to illuminate the legal and ethical aspects of proposals to use brain manipulation as a means of behavior control in prisons.

It might be argued, however, that even if psychosurgery were outlawed completely (a step that I would oppose as unnecessary, unwise, and irrelevant), it would hardly be missed by prison administrators. The reason may be inferred from the following statement by James V. McConnell, a psychologist:

... I believe that the day has come when we can combine sensory deprivation with drugs, hypnosis and astute manipulation of reward and punishment to gain almost absolute control over an individual's behavior. It should then be possible to achieve a very rapid and highly effective type of positive brainwashing that would allow us to make dramatic changes in a person's behavior and personality. . . .[33]

The term *brainwashing,* which is a translation from the Chinese, evokes the image of American prisoners of war undergoing rigorous "thought reform" and "attitude change" at the hands of their captors during the Korean War. Given its odious and sinister connotations, it might seem surprising to find brainwashing promoted by an American psychologist to reshape the behavior and attitudes of inmates in domestic prisons. Yet the idea of forcible indoctrination is not an alien concept to those who manage prisons and other institutions in this country. Indeed, more than eight years before McConnell's statement was made, a conference on the power to change behavior organized for the Federal Bureau of Prisons by the National Institutes of Mental Health heard a presentation by another psychologist in which brainwashing itself was given qualified endorsement. One purpose of the conference was to provide prison wardens and administrators with a summary of the latest developments in behavior control technology and their applications to prison management, and among the social scientists invited to address it was Dr. Edgar H. Schein, a professor of organizational psychology in the School of Management at the Massachusetts Institute of Technology. His paper was based on his studies of "the collaborative behavior of prisoners" (mostly American servicemen) who were incarcerated in North Korean and Chinese prison camps during the Korean War, and of attitude changes in civilian prisoners (also mostly Americans) "who were expelled from Communist China following periods of imprisonment of as long as five years." "I would like to have you think," he told the prison authorities, "of brainwashing not in terms of politics, ethics, and morals, but in terms of the deliberate changing of behavior and attitudes by a group of men who have relatively complete control over the environment in which the captive population lives."[34]

Schein's basic argument was that "in order to produce marked change of behavior and/or attitude, it is necessary to weaken, undermine or remove the supports to the old patterns of behavior and the old attitudes."

If one wants to produce a behavior inconsistent with the person's standards of conduct, first disorganize the group which supports these standards, then undermine his emotional supports, then put him into a new and ambiguous situation for which the standards are unclear, and then put pressure on him.[35]

Pointing out that the P.O.W.s had been subjected to isolation, physical hardships (cold, hunger, neglect), social disorganization, the withholding of mail, and other harassments to induce them to collaborate, Schein suggested to the prison officials that these techniques were not dissimilar to those used to control prisoner behavior.

Let me remind you, I am not drawing these parallels in order to condemn some of our own approaches, rather my aim is just the opposite. I am trying to show that the Chinese methods are not so mysterious, not so different and not so awful, once we separate the awfulness of the Communist ideology and look simply at the methods of influence used.[36]

Brainwashing, it might be argued, is a marginally less severe treatment than brain destruction. Its aim is to change behavior not by destroying the integrity of the brain but by depriving the individual of various social and environmental conditions up to an arbitrary point of severity. Brainwashing begins with inflicting pain and discomfort; this is followed by deprivation of such things as food and mail, and a program is specified in which these things are restored to the individual as rewards for correct behavior. It would be an exaggeration to write that Schein told the prison authorities to apply the techniques of brainwashing to the problems of managing their institutions. He did, however, invite them to draw their own conclusions from his remarks, and in his summary the chairman, who was the director of the Federal Bureau of Prisons, reminded his colleagues that the federal prison system houses some 24,000 inmates and affords "a tremendous opportunity to carry on some of the experimenting to which the various panelists have alluded." He assured his subordinates that bureau headquarters in Washington "are anxious to have you undertake some of these things: do things perhaps on your own—undertake a little experiment of what you can do with the Muslims, what you can do with some of the psychopath individuals."[37]

Schein's advice to the conference about brainwashing techniques and the director's encouragement were followed, not surprisingly, by the formal introduction of new behavior modification programs in several federal prisons. According to the director of the Federal Bureau of Prisons, the first such program was set up in 1965 at the National Training School for Boys in Washington, D.C. It was known as the CASE project, an acronym for Contingencies Applicable to Special Education. The project, as described at a congressional hearing on behavior modification programs, "was an attempt to motivate delinquent youngsters . . . to participate in education programs. Through a system of rewards [in the form of tokens] offenders were encouraged to achieve at a high level in school programs. They could then use the [tokens] to purchase a variety of items such as snacks and clothing, and participate in special recreational programs such as pool and ping pong."[38]

Behavioral psychologists take it to be a fact (and indeed it may be so) that whether one is dealing with a rat in a Skinner box or an inmate in a prison, the most efficient procedure for getting a subject to follow a prescribed course of action is systematically to reward desirable behavior. But in order to get the rat in the Skinner box to press the lever for food, it is necessary to make it hungry. The conventional method in the laboratory is to starve or limit the animal's intake of food to a point where about 20 percent of normal body weight is lost. The starvation procedure is not called punishment, but "deprivation."

Prison behavior modification programs based upon rewards may appear to be better than old-fashioned approaches smacking of punishment, retribution, and revenge. In his congressional testimony the head of the Federal Bureau of Prisons subscribed to the narrow technical definition of behavior modification as

the systematic application of the psychological principles of learning theory to the process of encouraging people to change their behavior. As such, [its] techniques can include either positive rewards or aversive techniques including a variety of punishments to promote a change in behavior. The Federal Bureau of Prisons has historically endorsed the first concept, that of positive rewards, and rejected the latter.

How does a positive reward program work in a prison? Consider START (Special Treatment and Rehabilitation Training), a program put into effect in 1972 at the medical center for federal prisoners at Springfield, Missouri. It was ostensibly intended as "an attempt to provide a more effective approach for dealing with those few, but highly aggressive and assaultive inmates who are found in any correctional instimate it was designed for as follows:

He is assaultive, and maliciously schemes to demonstrate his own physical prowess, usually pressuring the weaker, more passive element of the population. Feelings of guilt are non-existent, as he can easily rationalize maladaptive behavior, always projecting adversity onto others. He is usually verbal, to discreetly mask deceitful intent which makes him manipulative. He is egotistical to the utmost extreme, viewing himself as indestructible. He threatens the rehabilitation of a less sophisticated offender, continually indoctrinating the latter that crime does pay.[40]

In short, START was designed to be a prison-within-a-prison; a place of last resort for those inmates who were unwilling or unable to "do their own time" without causing trouble. As the assistant administrator of mental health services for the Federal Bureau of Prisons wrote, "We have to provide an alternative to merely segregating a prisoner for years and years, no matter how disruptive the guy is. It's a humanitarian obligation of ours."

Humanitarian obligation or not, the prisoner was forcibly transferred to Springfield to enter the program at Level One. Since the salient feature of the START program was to reward behavior deemed to be desirable, the only means of escaping from this isolated and degrading level was to be neat, clean, obedient, nonargumentative, and generally docile. The inmate who followed this prescription was allowed to progress to Level Two and so on; the program required at least eight months to complete.

The inmates who were referred to START were, according to the federal bureau's administrator of inmate prison services, "already in segregation because of their aggressive, destructive behavior." Some were inmates who viewed prison life as repressive and who thought that programs such as START were intended to destroy their individuality. Given that view, it might be expected that some men who were forcibly transferred into the program decided that resistance, rather than compliance, was the appropriate response. According to the administrator, "Those who resisted the program . . . remained at Level One for twelve months [and then] were removed from START and transferred back to the institution from which they had originally been referred."[41]

On February 21, 1973, in response to prisoner requests for assistance, the National Prison Project of the American Civil Liberties Union sent Arpiar G. Saunders, Jr., a staff attorney, to visit the START project. In a subsequent letter to the director of the institution, Saunders said,

In my recent visit to the Medical Center I was shocked to learn that two of the fifteen involuntary participants in the START program . . .were shackled by their arms and legs by means of leather and metal straps and chains to their steel beds. Additionally, I learned that on several occasions in the five days they had been shackled, they had been forced to eat with both hands still shackled to the bed and had experienced great difficulty in receiving staff assistance in removing the chains in order to perform necessary bodily functions. . . .

Saunders also referred to four other prisoners who had been "subjected to cruel and arbitrary treatment allegedly because of their non-cooperative attitude" by being forced to endure conditions of segregation in which they were deprived of many of their legal rights.[42]

In 1973, seven prisoners who had been forced into the START project against their will began a long hunger strike and with the aid of the National Prison Project filed a class-action legal suit against the Federal Bureau of Prisons. The court appointed three psychologists to examine the program with respect to its adherence to accepted behavior modification principles, and two of these experts concluded that the procedures were technically sound. The third expert agreed that START showed a reasonable understanding of the basic principles of behavior modification but that the prisoners' objections and their court suit suggested a failure to abide by the principle of informed consent.

While I do not dispute the evaluation of START as technically sound and agree that it cannot be disparaged for failing to meet scientific criteria, the Federal Bureau of Prisons nevertheless announced in February 1974 that it was terminating the program for economic reasons, although a more plausible explanation is resistance by prisoners and their supporters. A professional consultant to the program, disappointed at its demise, blamed it squarely on the destructive mischief of the National Prison Project:

There were existing reinforcers outside the program much stronger than any which could have been offered by the staff. Instead of encouraging more constructive behavior [they] reportedly encouraged non-participation. . . . With the promise of legal relief . . . [they] possessed a reinforcer for non-participation much greater than programmed reinforcers for participation.[43]

As the director of the Federal Bureau of Prisons said at the congressional hearing in 1974, "While mistakes were undoubtedly made in developing the START program, . . . 'behavior modification' using positive rewards is an integral part of many of our correctional programs and the Bureau of Prisons will continue to use this technique wherever appropriate."[44]

The same hearings provided an indication of what lies ahead for inmates at a new Federal Center for Correctional Research under construction at Butner, North Carolina. In testimony before the committee Dr. Martin G. Groder, the warden-designate of that institution, asserted that

none of the methods already preliminarily chosen or being considered favorably [for use at Butner] involve the methods of modern-day torture known as aversive conditioning, specifically the misuse of drugs, electric shock or psychosurgery. In fact, all these program types are basically humanistic, cooperative ventures which will stand or fall on their results or outcome though they can be seen assuredly as, at least, doing no harm.[45]

Groder told the committee that "three programs have been preliminarily identified and are moving into more advanced planning." No program was described in detail, but one of them, said Groder, "is the model called Asklepieion which I, myself, developed at the U.S. Penitentiary in Marion, Illinois."

Asklepieion is the embodiment of Schein's prescription for brainwashing, based on a "treatment philosophy" according to which most if not all offenders are "losers" ("a person who consistently does not deal with the realities of his present situation") who need to become "winners" ("Free from compulsive behavior patterns, the winner gratifies himself in ways that are socially responsible"). It all began, says Groder, when he was leading weekly therapy groups for prison inmates in 1968, discouraged and frustrated because he saw that the inmates were simply pretending to participate. He decided to introduce the prisoners to the Synanon game, a technique originally developed for drug addicts in which the individual group member was pressured to give up his defenses by making him the object of systematic ridicule and verbal abuse, directed at him by the leader as well as other group members.

After he had assembled a group of eight inmates who agreed to participate, Groder spent the first session relentlessly exposing all the trickery, lying, and stupidity he had observed in them over a period of six months. After several weeks of this ("I tell you, I was enjoying working during those weeks. I didn't have any problems with frustration"), the prisoners began to come to him one at a time to complain, "and I'd explain to them they couldn't handle me because they were dishonest . . . weak, pusillanimous punks who really had no principles." About half of the participants chose to get out and, as new groups were started, various attempts were made by "malcontents" to dismantle the program ("I had to learn how to disrupt them"). "But for those who decided they were going to learn how to handle this kind of situation, it was the most constructive thing that ever happened to them."[46]

Another answer is provided by some of the "weak, pusillanimous punks" who chose to get out. In July 1972, a group of inmates at Marion smuggled out a report addressed to the United Nations Economic and Social Council charging that Asklepieion was "an experimental program . . . to determine at first hand how effective a weapon brainwashing might be for the United States Department of Justice's future use." According to the report, "winners" are rewarded by being allowed into a pleasant living area provided with stereo sets, typewriters, books, and other amenities; he is now expected to indoctrinate newcomers into the group, "and like a good attack dog, he is graded and evaluated on his demonstrated capacity to go for the vulnerable points of any victim put before him." The report claims that the program is self-perpetuating and costs little to run because the prisoners serve as guards and informants.[47]

It should be pointed out that in his congressional testimony Groder branded as false many of the things stated in the foregoing report, and in a letter dated January 24, 1974, to former Senator Sam Ervin of North Carolina said the "horror stories" had been circulated by "a small number of self-interested politically motivated people who wish to see the prison system of this country destroyed."[48] Senator Ervin, for his part, had earlier expressed his own concern that prisoners' constitutional rights to privacy and freedom of individual thought were being eroded by certain federally funded programs, including those involving "operant conditioning (reward/punishment theory)." He urged Congress to maintain strict oversight of all such programs.[49]

The form of behavior control known as aversion therapy and referred to by Groder as "modern-day torture" may at first sight seem less enduring in its effects than psychosurgery or protracted "therapy" programs. In technical terms, aversion therapy is an outgrowth of Pavlovian and Skinnerian conditioning. Its object is to establish a connection between behavior and pain. Aversion therapy was illustrated in the film *A Clockwork Orange*, in which the hero Alex, after brutally assaulting others was forced to watch films depicting violence, either under the influence of a nauseating drug or subjected to painful shocks if he viewed the violence with pleasure.

A program of this type was established at the Connecticut State Prison at Somers in August 1973. Said to be voluntary, it was set up initially to deal with sexual deviants or pedophiles. The aversive treatment involves the flashing of certain erotically stimulating pictures on a screen (including, in this case, pictures of nude children). The presentation of the latter is accompanied by a delivery of a "painful electric shock to the groin area." Hypnosis was also used to "create a phobia about children as sexual objects."[50]

Adults who are sexually inclined toward children are the object of almost unanimous fear and loathing in our society ("child molesters"). It should be borne in mind, however, that sexual inclinations do not necessarily lead to assaultive behavior and are not invariably acted out. Not everyone who has ever harbored a sexual interest in children is a threat to society. The more general point, however, is that the prevailing contempt for deviants of this or any kind serves to establish a correspondingly broad indifference toward how they are treated. Quite apart from the fact that this aversion therapy project is being conducted in a prison (with all of the attendant coercion that "voluntary" participation is likely to entail), treating pedophiles by these methods, it might well be suggested, creates a predisposition to deal similarly with other forms of sexual or social deviance. Lacking the rule of law—and in the light of past history—there is simply no basis for believing that prison authorities will show restraint in applying techniques of behavior control to other classes of inmates, after their use upon any single class of inmates has become socially acceptable. Once the wedge of behavior control technology has been allowed to enter the prison system and to split off the most extreme class of deviants there is ample evidence to suggest that the next step will be to drive it further in.

Aversive conditioning techniques have been used in other contexts as well. Anectine is the trade name for the drug succinylcholine, a neuromuscular blocking agent closely related to the South American arrow-tip poison known as curare. Its principal medical use is as a muscle relaxant in surgical operations, orthopedic manipulations, and other procedures in which a reduction in skeletal muscle tone is required; in sufficient doses, it produces a paralysis of the muscles which control breathing. A report by the organizers of an anectine treatment program set up in the California Medical Facility at Vacaville in 1968 have described its operation:

Our technique is simply to administer 20 to 40 mg. of Succinylcholine intravenously with oxygen and an airway available and to counsel the patient while he is under the influence of the drug that his behavior is dangerous to others or to himself, that it is desirable that he stop the behavior in question, and that subsequent behavior of a nature which may be dangerous to others or to himself will be treated with similar aversive treatments. . . . Together with admonishments about the harmfulness of the behavior, the description of the specific act responsible for the patient's frightening experience is repeated over and over for the approximately 1½ to 2 minutes he is paralyzed.[51]

Like most accounts of prison behavior modification experiments, this one says relatively little about those selected to undergo this treatment, except that "nearly all could be characterized as angry young men." Since the program itself was conducted in secret and was apparently not subject to any prior external oversight, it is impossible to say how many inmates at Vacaville received the Anectine treatment, why they were chosen, or what the behavioral effects were. The report states that there were sixty-four inmates in the program, and the chief psychiatrist at Vacaville, Dr. Arthur Nugent, subsequently told the press that they were "treated" for a wide variety of offenses, including "frequent fights, verbal threatening, deviant sexual behavior, stealing, unresponsiveness to the group therapy program."

The Anectine treatment induces frightening and loathesome sensations of suffocation and drowning. As Nugent put it, the subject experiences feeling of deep terror, "as though he were on the brink of death. . . . Even the toughest inmates have come to fear and hate the drug. I don't blame them. I wouldn't have one treatment myself for the world." Nonetheless, Nugent professed to be dismayed at the adverse public reaction that greeted the news of the project's existence, and he insisted that it ought to be continued: "I'm at a loss as to why everybody's upset over this," he said.

There is apparently no contradiction, from Nugent's point of view, in subjecting prison inmates to something that no "ordinary" human being should be expected to endure. Just as it was first of all necessary for slave-holders to perceive slaves as less than human in order to justify their subjugation, it is necessary for prison authorities to believe that inmates are inherently defective in order to do to them what they would not "for the world" have done to themselves.

In the last analysis, it is the attitude of social contempt underlying the "treatment philosophy" (and not the behavior control technology itself) that allows torture to parade as therapy. Nugent and his colleagues at Vacaville—like prison officials everywhere—can justify what they do to prisoners only by first of all defining prisoners as sick, incomplete, or infantile creatures. The report of the Anectine project states that "the use of the oxygen mask during the treatment was theorized to contribute to certain deep symbolic aspects related to the small child's feelings toward what he views as the omnipotent, beneficent parent figure who holds the power of life and death."

When Willie Holder, a leader of the Prisoners' Union and a "graduate" of nineteen years in the Oklahoma State Penitentiary and California's Soledad and Folsom prisons, was asked recently about whether inmates changed for the better or for the worse during imprisonment, he answered, "I have seen them change for the worse about ninety-five percent of the time . . . . As for the five percent who were changed for the better, the prison had nothing to do with it."[52]

Prisons came into existence as places of punishment. They remain places of punishment, ruled by punitive laws (or arbitrary decree), operated by agencies organized to carry out punishment, and functioning to reinforce punitive attitudes. To punish means to inflict pain, loss, con-finement—perhaps even death—and from what we know of behavior, people are in no way improved by such injuries.

Prisons, so long as they exist, will remain and must remain forever places of punishment. The American prison system is a manifest failure. And an integral part of that failure is the system's demonstrated capacity to cloak itself in the rhetoric of reform, to absorb techniques of "treat-ment" and turn them to essentially punitive ends.

What is to be done? As a first step, I would insist that the sole purpose of prisons is to punish and that the punishment ought to fit the crime. The immediate consequence would be the abandonment of the false veneer of benevolent despotism already described as the "treatment philosophy" and a rejection of the idea that prisons exist to make the offender fit to rejoin society.

Second, I would propose that the rule of law be extended to require the maintenance of due process procedures within the environment of total institutions. I advocate a severe restriction of the discretionary power of prison authorities and parole boards.

Third, I would advocate the abolition of cash bail and parole in favor of unsupervised release and restitution of civil and legal rights.

Fourth, I would abolish the indeterminate sentence in favor of a uniform code of punishment and drastically reduce the duration of sentences for most crimes. (Indeterminate sentencing was recognized as a failure by the California correctional authorities in 1976 and has been abolished in that state.)

Finally, I would support provision of educational, recreational, medical, psychiatric, vocational, and other services on a voluntary basis; a prisoner's decision whether to participate in any of these should have no effect on time served. At the same time I would abolish all furlough programs contingent on "good behavior" and substitute regularly scheduled conjugal and family visits within the prison.

These are small steps toward meaningful prison reform, and yet I know that their practical implementation is unlikely in the foreseeable future. One reason for this—perhaps the main reason—is that the creation of a just system of criminal justice in an unjust society is a contradiction in terms. The injustice within lawless prisons is a reflection of a more general system of inequities in the promulgation of laws and of bias in enforcement. Prisons may stay as they are or change, but so long as those who make and enforce the laws are more concerned with maintaining order in the streets than with controlling crime in the suites, prisons will house a disproportionately large population of inmates with blue collars and nonwhite skins.

Penal philosophies and "treatment modalities" will come and go, but prisons will continue to reflect the contradictions inherent in the larger society of which they are a part. This means that American prisons may be expected to remain what they have always been until we have a society in which the benefits of the law, together with other social and economical amenities, are more equitably distributed. In such a society, law enforcement agencies would spend more time monitoring the mischief of CIA flunkies and less time busting ghetto junkies; they would bear down harder on excess profiteers than on people who have had too many beers; they would imprison the industrialists who manufacture unsafe automobiles and not just the individuals who steal them; they would not hesitate to penalize those who poison America's air and water at the same time as they punish those who refused to kill Indochinese women and children.

My intent in this book has been to show that the meaning of human nature and the power of behavior control are not comprehensible when considered as two different, essentially independent, aspects of human existence. I have argued that such a partial and oversimplified view tends to overlook their common embeddedness in a larger conceptual, material, and social context. Their interconnections are complex, but in order to provide a coherent theoretical framework for a wide variety of ideas and practices that are more often regarded as disparate, I have been obliged to emphasize the existence of a few basic notions that tend to recur as transformations of each other in different historical and social contexts. The argument has also obliged me to be polemical; I make no apology for that. Theories of human nature and programs of behavior control are inherently controversial because they are socially constructed. No amount of special pleading on behalf of the alleged moral and ethical neutrality of "behavioral science" should be allowed to obscure the fact that the conceptual and material products of scholarship are not value-free. To the contrary, they have long been used (and still are being used) as social weapons.

Far from aspiring to exhaustiveness, my survey of theories of human nature and behavior control practices is intended merely to illustrate the interplay between meaning and power that necessarily pervades many areas of contemporary social life. One of the things that each of us has to do in our lives is to discover, as far as possible, the grounds for believing what we are asked to believe. It is not at all clear how one may best go about doing this, but in any event it is to the largely private and poorly understood domain of feeling or "affect" to which we ultimately turn in order to make these decisions. Thus, in the last analysis, it is evidently within our value-laden, socially interconnected selves that each of us must form our individual convictions about the meaning of human nature.

The story of psychotechnology, from genesis to genocide, is a tale of manifold superstitions and cruelties, of meanings invented, fostered, and propagated for their ability to excuse the exercise of power in ways that would otherwise be plainly inexcusable. But as I reviewed the pages of my book, the belief increasingly grew upon me that no reader ought to be asked to traverse so long and uncheerful a narrative merely to arrive at a melancholy conclusion. I have been arguing all along that the solubility of our problems depends upon how they are defined. Throughout history and up until the present time, the human effort to understand the world and its contents has taken place amid violent conflicts between contending social forces. And much of the violence has tended to reinforce disagreements over the propriety of efforts to define the meaning of human nature and to exercise the power of behavior control. Often what induces human individuals and groups to fear and destroy one another is the prevalence of false and fantastic ideas about what it means to be a specifically human being. The future, however, is uncertain, and does not necessarily have to resemble the past. Our present predicament—including the prospect of nuclear annihilation—is itself a striking example of circumstances that have never before existed and in previous ages could not even have been conceived. Should we not feel free, therefore, to search for new ways to create a more meaningful, more abundant, more peaceful mode of human existence?

There is an atmosphere of pessimism surrounding many socially organized efforts to deal effectively with the whole host of urgent global problems. Different organizations and "experts" concern themselves with trying to solve such things as "the energy problem," "the pollution problem," "the starvation problem," "the international balance of payments problem," "the nuclear power problem," "the arms control problem," and so on. Some observers have been inclined to conclude that they have not been solved because they are essentially insoluble. I think they appear insoluble because they have not been properly defined. Let me illustrate this by an exercise in human imagination. Pretend that, putting this book aside, you have journeyed at mindspeed to a point from which you can see the world in its entirety. What would you see? Those who have been in that position report that our planet, viewed from nearby outer space, appears as a glistening creation, seemingly alive, a composite spherical living system that exhibits a constant and constantly changing interplay of form and motion. The swirling masses of clouds coalesce and separate, the appearance of the masses of land and water changes constantly with the time, the tides, and the seasons. Over time the continents have formed and drifted apart, cleaving the seas into great oceans. But throughout time, throughout all of the changes, the earth remains a coherent, interdependent, synchronized unity.

To return from such an imaginary journey and to consider the earth as a geopolitical entity, is to confront a tremendous contradiction. Contrast, if you will, the planet as it appears from space with the world as we habitually view it. While the biosphere is an interdependently unified system, the world of human affairs is little more than a collection of fragmented and independently organized political entities whose size and shape and boundaries rarely reflect the delicate ecological balance of nature. I cite the fragmented state of the geopolitical world in order to suggest that the picture of psychotechnology that I have drawn in this book is part of a larger scheme of fragmentation that is now very widespread. Indeed, fragmentation exists today not only between nations but also within societies and individuals. It has been suggested that it is necessary to divide things up and break them down into pieces of manageable proportion in order to deal with them effectively, but this supposed wisdom has plainly failed to yield anything like a successful solution to any of our problems and there is a very real danger that the fragmentation process makes it very difficult or impossible to understand the world and its contents in proper perspective.

What we must soon discover is that the fragmented life is a life devoid of the power to solve our problems, a life devoid of meaning. All human thoughts and feelings and actions arise in a particular social context from which they derive both their power and their meaning. Perhaps the most challenging task we face is to bring our social arrangements into accord with the arrangement of the biosphere we inhabit, to comprehend the global nature of the problems that confront us. If we are to do this—and our survival as a species demands that we do—we must begin to reverse the worldwide trend toward human social fragmentation and learn to think and feel and act in an overall pattern of human interconnectedness. Perhaps when we have a greater appreciation of our individual and collective location within the biosphere, we will have less need to develop and deploy methods of regulating human conduct and less need for theories of human nature to excuse the inexcusable. Perhaps in the more abundant, more peaceful, and more humane world we will have begun to create, we will better understand the meaning of human nature and the power of behavior control.

Notes

Notes to Chapter 1

1. R. Ulrich, T. Stachnik, and J. Mabry, *Control of Human Behavior* (Glenview, Ill.: Scott-Foresman, 1966), 1:i.

2. Walter Lippmann, "The Government of Posterity," *Atlantic Monthly* 158 (July 1936): 550.

Notes to Chapter 2

1. This injunction issued to Galileo by Cardinal Bellarmine in 1616, is quoted in Andrew D. White, *A History of the Warfare of Science with Theology* (New York: Braziller, 1955), p. 137.

2. Ibid., p. 142.

3. Calvin and Luther quoted in ibid., p. 126.

4. Ibid., p. 134.

5. Ibid., p. 139.

6. Ibid., p. 14.

7. Augustine, *The City of God*, abridged (New York: Image Books, 1958), pp. 278–279.

8. *Pro Libero Arbitrio* [On behalf of free will], in *Documents of the Christian Church*, trans. Henry Bettenson (Oxford: Oxford University Press, 1949), p. 75.

9. Plato, *The Republic*, Modern Library ed. (New York: Random House, n.d.) pp. 124–125. I have taken the liberty of recasting this passage in dialogue form.

10. Thomas Hobbes, *Leviathan*, ed. C. B. Macpherson (Baltimore: Penguin Books, 1968), pp. 161, 186.

11. B. F. Skinner, *Walden Two* (New York: Macmillan, 1948), p. 85.

Notes to Chapter 3

1. The Educational Testing Service, for example, is a $25-million operation employing some 3,000 people and occupying a three-acre site in Princeton, New Jersey.

2. Francis Galton, *Inquiries into the Human Faculty and Its Development* (London: Dent, 1907).

3. All quotations from Camper may be found in J. S. Slotkin, "Racial Classifications of the 17th and 18th Centuries," *Transactions of the Wisconsin Academy of Sciences* 36 (1944), p. 465.

4. Galton, *The Human Faculty*, pp. 20–21.

5. Alfred Binet, *Les idées sur les enfants modernes* (Paris: Flammarion, 1913), pp. 140–141.

6. Carl C. Brigham, *A Study of American Intelligence* (Princeton: Princeton University Press, 1923), p. 100.

7. Ellwood P. Cubberly, *Public School Administration* (Boston: Houghton Mifflin, 1916), p. 338.

8. Robert M. Yerkes and Josephine C. Foster, *A Point Scale for Measuring Mental Ability* (Baltimore: Warwick & York, 1923), p. 25.

9. Cited in John Lankford, *Congress and the Foundations of the Twentieth Century* (River Falls: Wisconsin State University Press, 1964), p. 31.

10. Cited by Everett Flood, "Notes on the Castration of Idiot Children," *American Journal of Psychology* 10 (1898): 299.

11. Harry H. Laughlin, *Eugenical Sterilization in the United States* (Chicago: Psychopathic Laboratory of the Municipal Court of Chicago, 1922), pp. 35–36.

12. The figure is from Clarence J. Karier, "Testing for Order and Control in the Corporate Liberal State," *Educational Theory* 22, no. 2 (1972): 154–180.

13. Quoted in M. H. Haller, *Eugenics* (New Brunswick, N.J.: Rutgers University Press, 1963), p. 133.

14. See "The Great Pellagra Cover-Up," *Psychology Today*, February 1975, pp. 83–86, and Allen Chase, *The Legacy of Malthus: The Social Costs of the New Scientific Racism* (New York: Knopf, 1977).

15. Henry H. Goddard, "How Shall We Educate Mental Defectives?," *The Training School Bulletin* 9 (1912): 43.

16. Richard J. Herrnstein, "IQ," *Atlantic Monthly*, September 1971, p. 63.

17. Lewis M. Terman, *The Measurement of Intelligence* (Boston: Houghton Mifflin, 1916), pp. 11, 6–7.

18. Lewis M. Terman, "Feeble-minded Children in the Public Schools of California," *School and Society* 5 (1917): 165.

19. Terman, *Measurement of Intelligence*, pp. 91–92.

20. See Margaret O'Brien Steinfels, "Involuntary Sterilization: The Latest Case," *Psychology Today*, February 1978, p. 124.

21. Race Betterment Foundation, *Proceedings of the First National Conference on Race Betterment*, Battle Creek, Michigan, January 8–12, 1914, p. 479.

22. Edward L. Thorndike, "How May We Improve the Selection, Training and Lifework of Leaders?," address delivered before the Fifth Congress on Educational Policies, Teachers College (New York: Columbia University Press, 1939), p. 32.

23. Henry H. Goddard, *Human Efficiency and Levels of Intelligence* (Princeton: Princeton University Press, 1920), p. 97.

24. Henry E. Garrett, *General Psychology* (New York: American Book Company, 1955), p. 65.

25. Henry E. Garrett, *Breeding Down* (Richmond, Va.: Patrick Henry Press, n.d.), p. 10.

26. William Shockley, "Dysgenics—A Social Problem Reality Evaded by Illusion of Infinite Plasticity of Human Intelligence?," *Phi Delta Kappan* 1 (March 1972): 291–295.

27. Leon Kamin, "Heredity, Intelligence, Politics, and Psychology," in *The IQ Controversy*, ed. N. J. Block and G. Dworkin (New York: Pantheon, 1976), p. 250.

28. Ibid., p. 249.

29. "Crucial Data Was Faked by Eminent Psychologist," *Sunday Times*, Oct. 24, 1976, pp. 1–2.

30. H. J. Eysenck, *Know Your Own IQ* (Baltimore: Penguin, 1962), p. 8.

31. Quoted by Richard J. Herrnstein in *IQ in the Meritocracy* (Boston: Little, Brown, 1973), p. 107 (emphasis added).

32. Arthur Jensen, *Genetics and Education* (New York: Harper & Row, 1972), pp. 75–76.

33. Ibid., p. 72 (emphasis added).

Notes to Chapter 4

1. E. H. Mullen, "Mental Examination of Immigrants: Administration and Line Inspection at Ellis Island," in *The Ordeal of Assimilation*, ed. S. Feldstein (Garden City, N.Y.: Anchor Press, 1974), pp. 51–52.

2. "Steerage Conditions," *Reports of United States Immigration Service Commission* 37 (1911): 33.

3. Mullen, "Mental Examination of Immigrants," p. 52–53.

4. Charles White, *An Account of the Regular Gradation in Man, and in Different Animals and Vegetables* (London: n.p., 1799), p. iii.

5. Samuel A. Cartwright, "Report on the Diseases and Physical Peculiarities of the Negro Race," *New Orleans Medical and Surgical Journal*, May 1851, pp. 691–715.

6. Henry H. Goddard, "The Binet Tests in Relation to Immigration," *Journal of Psycho-Asthenics* 18 (1913): 105–107.

7. Henry H. Goddard, "Mental Tests and the Immigrant," *Journal of Delinquency* 2 (1917): 271.

8. Clarence J. Karier, "Testing for Order and Control in the Corporate Liberal State," *Educational Theory* 22, no. 2 (1972): 164.

9. Robert M. Yerkes, ed., *Psychological Examining in the United States Army* (Washington, D.C.: National Academy of Sciences, 1921), p. 699.

10. Herbert Croly, as quoted in James Weinstein, *The Corporate Ideal in the Liberal State* (Boston: Beacon Press, 1968), p. xi.

11. Quoted in Robert De C. Ward, "Our New Immigration Policy," *Foreign Affairs* 3 (September 1924): 104.

12. See, for example, Norman Pollack, *The Populist Response to Industrial America* (New York: W. W. Norton, 1962), and William Appleman Williams, *The Roots of the Modern American Empire* (New York: Random House, 1969).

13. Leon J. Kamin, "The Science and Politics of IQ," *Social Research* 41 (1974): 408–409.

14. Ibid., p. 410.

15. Carl C. Brigham, *A Study of American Intelligence* (Princeton: Princeton University Press, 1923), p. 210.

16. Kamin, "Science and Politics of IQ," p. 412.

17. Cited in ibid., p. 414.

18. U.S., Congress, Senate, Committee on Immigration, *Hearings*, February 20, 1923, p. 80.

19. Lewis M. Terman, "The Conservation of Talent," *School and Society* 19 (1924): 363.

20. Brigham, *American Intelligence*, pp. 189–190.

21. U.S., Congress, House, Committee on Immigration and Naturalization, *Hearings*, January 5, 1924, p. 580.

22. Madison Grant to Henry F. Osborn, March 9, 1918. Davenport Mss. American

Philosophical Society, Philadelphia. The society's first meeting was held in Professor Osborn's house.

23. House, Committee on Immigration, *Hearings*, p. 837.

24. House, Committee on Immigration, *Europe as an Emigrant-Exporting Continent and the United States as an Immigrant-Receiving Nation: Hearings*, March 8, 1924, p. 1311.

Notes to Chapter 5

1. Friedrich Lilge, *The Abuse of Learning* (New York: Macmillan, 1948), p. 146.

2. S. Pinson Koppel, *Modern Germany: Its History and Civilization*, 2d ed. (New York: Macmillan, 1966), p. 245.

3. Charles Darwin, *The Origin of Species by Means of Natural Selection; or the Preservation of Favored Races in the Struggle for Life*, 6th ed. (New York: Appleton, 1897), 1:6.

4. Ibid., p. 78.

5. Quoted in Jacob Bronowski, *The Ascent of Man* (Boston: Little, Brown, 1973), p. 308.

6. Darwin, *Origin of Species*, 2:305–306.

7. The description of the meeting is drawn from William Irvine, *Apes, Angels, and Victorians* (New York: Time-Life Books, 1963), pp. 5–6.

8. Quoted by Andrew Dickinson White in *A History of the Warfare of Science with Theology* (New York: Braziller, 1955), p. 83.

9. Charles Darwin, *The Descent of Man* 2d ed. (New York: A. L. Burt, n.d.), p. 707.

10. Loren Eiseley, *Darwin's Century* (Garden City, N.Y.: Doubleday Anchor Books, 1961), p. 303.

11. Alfred Russell Wallace, "Geological Climates and the Origin of Species," *Quarterly Review* 126 (1869): 359–394.

12. Herbert Spencer, *Social Statics* (New York: Appleton, 1888), p. 353.

13. Quoted in J. L. Hammond and B. Hammond, *The Town Labourer, 1760–1832* (London: Longmans, Green, 1932), p. 65.

14. Quoted in ibid., p. 57.

15. John Eliot Cairnes, *Essays on Political Economy* (London: Macmillan, 1873), pp. 260–261.

16. Spencer, *Social Statics*, pp. 355–356 (emphasis in original).

17. William F. Ryan, *Blaming the Victim* (New York: Pantheon, 1971).

18. Herbert Spencer, *First Principles* (1862), cited in John Passmore, *The Perfectability of Man* (New York: Scribner's, 1970), p. 241.

19. Spencer, *Social Statics*, p. 353.

20. See Richard Hofstadter, *Social Darwinism in American Thought* (Boston: Beacon Press, 1955), p. 45.

21. The ideal of *Ganzheitsbetrachtung* is discussed by Oswald Bumke in *Eine Krisis der Medizin* (Munich: Max Hueber Verlag, 1929), p. 19.

22. Adolph Thiele, *Soziale Hygiene für Jedermann* (Dresden: Verlag von L. Ehler-

mann, 1931), pt. 1, pp. 14–15, cited by Robert J. Waldinger, "The High Priests of Nature: Medicine in Germany, 1883–1933" (B.A. thesis, Harvard University, 1973), p. 64.

23. Cited by Thiele, *Soziale Hygiene*, p. 16 (emphasis added).

24. See F. Wertham, *A Sign for Cain* (New York: Warner Paperback Library, 1969), pp. 157–158.

25. Cited by Waldinger, *High Priests of Nature*, p. 69.

26. Cited in ibid, p. 75.

27. This letter, and the remarkable sequence of communications and events that followed are cited by Waldinger in *High Priests of Nature*. He provides bibliographic references to the original documents, which he reviewed at the Bundesarchiv in Koblenz, Germany during the summer of 1972.

28. Ibid., p. 75.

29. F. Lenz, "Die Stellung des Nationalsozialismus zur Rassenhygiene," *Archiv. f. Rassen- u. Gesellschaftsbiologie* 25 (1931): 300 ff.

30. Ernst Rüdin, "Aufgaben und Zeile der Deutschen Gesellschaft für Rassenhygiene," *Archiv. f. Rassen- u. Gesellschaftsbiologie* 28 (1934): 228.

31. Hanns Löhr, *Über die Stellung und Bedeutung der Heilkunde im nationalsozialistischen Staate* (Berlin: Nornen-Verlag, 1935); English excerpts in George L. Mosse, *Nazi Culture* (New York: Grosset & Dunlap, 1966).

32. Wertham, *A Sign for Cain*, p. 155.

33. See ibid., p. 176.

34. Konrad Lorenz, "Durch Domestikation verursachte Störungen arteigenen Verhaltens," *Zeitschrift für Angewandte Psychologie und Charakterkunde* 59 (1940): 2–79. (Translations are mine.)

35. Edward O. Wilson, *Sociobiology: The New Synthesis* (Cambridge, Mass.: Harvard University Press, 1975), p. 547.

36. Ibid., p. 3.

37. Ibid., p. 22.

38. Ibid., p. 554.

39. Ibid., p. 549.

40. Ibid., pp. 554–555.

Notes to Chapter 6

1. Jerome H. Jaffe, "Drug Addiction and Drug Abuse," in *The Pharmacological Basis of Therapeutics*, 4th ed., ed. Louis S. Goodman and Alfred Gilman (New York: Macmillan, 1970), p. 310.

2. Ibid., p. 276.

3. Ibid., p. 279.

4. Matthew P. Dumont, "The Politics of Drugs," *Social Policy*, July–August 1972, pp. 32–35.

5. Jaffe, "Drug Addiction and Drug Abuse," p. 277.

6. Ibid., p. 286.

7. Alfred W. McCoy, *The Politics of Heroin in Southeast Asia* (New York: Harper & Row, 1973), p. 14.

8. Jaffe, "Drug Addiction and Drug Abuse," p. 286.

9. Ibid., pp. 285–186.

10. Cited in "Lifelong 'Cure' by Rockefeller," *New York Times,* January 7, 1973, sec. 4, p. 2.

11. Although Jaffe himself has pointed out that all such drugs possess comparable "abuse liability" to morphine, heroin, and the other narcotics whose actions they block. See "Drug Addiction and Drug Abuse."

12. "Threat of Confinement Urged in Heroin Treatment," *Washington Post,* June 11, 1972.

13. Dumont, "The Politics of Drugs," p. 35.

14. Paul H. Wender, *Minimal Brain Dysfunction in Children* (New York: Wiley-Interscience, 1971), p. 1.

15. Cited in Domeena C. Renshaw, *The Hyperactive Child* (Chicago: Nelson-Hall, 1974), p. 79.

16. Ibid., pp. 82–83.

17. Quoted in Anthony M. Platt, *The Child Savers* (Chicago: University of Chicago Press, 1969), p. 27.

18. Mortimer D. Gross and William C. Wilson, *Minimal Brain Dysfunction* (New York: Brunner-Mazel, 1974), p. 6.

19. Wender, *Minimal Brain Dysfunction in Children,* p. 29.

20. Erving Goffman, *Stigma: Notes on the Management of Spoiled Identity* (Englewood-Cliffs, N.J.: Prentice-Hall, 1965), p. 5.

21. Wender, *Minimal Brain Dysfunction in Children,* p. 1.

22. Renshaw, *Hyperactive Child,* p. 3.

23. Wender, *Minimal Brain Dysfunction in Children,* pp. 60–61.

24. Ibid., p. 102.

25. L. A. Sroufe and M. A. Steward, "Treating Problem Children with Stimulant Drugs," *New England Journal of Medicine* 289, no. 8 (1973): 407–412.

Notes to Chapter 7

1. V. H. Mark, W. H. Sweet, and F. R. Ervin, Letter to the editor, *Journal of the American Medical Association* 201 (1967): 895.

2. Hippocrates, *Selected Works,* trans. and ed. W. Jones (London: Heinemann, 1923), 2: 175.

3. William H. Sweet, Foreword to Vernon H. Mark and Frank R. Ervin, *Violence and the Brain,* (New York: Harper & Row, 1970), p. vii.

4. D. Podolsky, "The Epileptic Murderer," *Medico-Legal Journal* 30 (1962): 176–179.

5. J. Guerrant, *Personality in Epilepsy* (Springfield, Ill.: Charles C. Thomas, 1962), p. 12.

6. Ernst Rodin, "Psychomotor Epilepsy and Aggressive Behavior," *Archives of General Psychiatry* 28 (1973): 210-223.

7. M. Goldstein, "Brain Research and Violent Behavior," *Archives of Neurology* 30 (1974): 26-35.

8. Vernon Mark and Frank R. Ervin, *Violence and the Brain* (New York: Harper & Row, 1970), p. 160.

9. For a discussion of Burckhardt's work, see Elliot Valenstein, *Brain Control* (New York: John Wiley & Sons, 1973), pp. 266-268.

10. Stephanie A. Shields, "Functionalism, Darwinism, and the Psychology of Women," *American Psychologist* 30 (1975): 741.

11. Stephen Jay Gould, "Morton's Ranking of Races by Cranial Capacity," *Science* 200 (1978): 503.

12. Franz Josef Gall and Johann Gaspar Spurzheim, *Anatomie et physiologie du système nerveux en générale et du cerveau en particulier* 1 (Paris, 1810): ii.

13. See John D. Davies, *Phrenology: Fad and Science* (New Haven: Yale University Press, 1955), pp. 79-160.

14. Ibid., p. 145.

15. See "Anthropology," in *American Naturalist* 7 (February 1870): 117-118; also, Robert S. Woodworth, "Racial Differences in Mental Traits," *Science* 31 (February 1910): 171-186.

16. See A. Walker, *Woman Physiologically Considered* (New York: J. & H. G. Langley, 1850), p. 317.

17. See Davies, *Phrenology*, pp. 20-23.

18. Cited in ibid., p. 65.

19. Samuel A. Cartwright, "Report on the Diseases and Physical Peculiarities of the Negro Race," *New Orleans Medical and Surgical Journal*, May 1851, p. 709.

20. Ibid., pp. 711-712.

21. Quoted in Barbara Ehrenreich and Dierdre English, *Complaints and Disorders: The Sexual Politics of Sickness* (Old Westbury, N.Y.: Feminist Press, 1973), pp. 11-12.

22. C. F. Jacobsen, J. B. Wolfe, and T. A. Jackson, "An Experimental Analysis of the Functions of the Frontal Association Areas in Primates," *Journal of Nervous and Mental Diseases* 82 (1935): 9-10.

23. See Valenstein, *Brain Control*, p. 53.

24. Egas Moniz, "How I Came to Perform Prefrontal Leucotomy," *Congress of Psychosurgery* (Lisbon, 1948), pp. 7-18, excerpted in *The Age of Madness*, ed. Thomas Szasz (Garden City, N.Y.: Doubleday Anchor Books, 1973), pp. 157-160. Curiously, Jacobsen and Fulton are nowhere mentioned in his retrospective account.

25. Ibid., p. 158.

26. The higher number is given by Peter Breggin in an article entitled "The Return of Lobotomy and Psychosurgery," *Congressional Record*, February 24, 1972, p. E1602; the lower number is given by Valenstein, *Brain Control*, p. 55.

27. Walter Freeman, "Frontal Lobotomy in Early Schizophrenia: Long Follow-up in 415 Cases," *British Journal of Psychiatry* 119 (1971): 621-624.

28. Valenstein, *Brain Control*, p. 55.

29. Cited in ibid., p. 306.

30. Walter Freeman, "Psychosurgery," in *American Handbook of Psychiatry*, ed. Silvano Arieti (New York: Basic Books, 1959), 2: 1521–1540.

31. J. C. Carothers, "Frontal Lobe Function in the African," *British Journal of Mental Science* (1950): 38.

32. Freeman, "Psychosurgery."

33. William B. Scoville, "Surgical Locations for Psychiatric Surgery," presidential address to the Third International Congress of Psychosurgery, Cambridge, England, August 14–18, 1972.

34. W. R. Hess, "The Central Control of the Activity of the Internal Organs," in *Nobel Lectures: Physiology or Medicine, 1942-1962* (New York: Elsenier, 1964).

35. See, for example, V. Balasubramaniam and T. S. Kanaka, "Hypothalamotomy in the Management of Aggressive Behavior," in *Current Controversies in Neurosurgery*, ed. T. P. Morley (Philadelphia: Saunders, 1976), pp. 768–777.

36. James W. Papez, "A Proposed Mechanism of Emotion," *Archives of Neurology and Psychiatry* 38 (1937): 725–743.

37. Paul D. McLean, "The Triune Brain: Emotion and Scientific Bias," in *The Neurosciences: Second Study Program*, ed. G. Quarton et al. (New York: Rockefeller University Press, 1970), pp. 339–344.

38. Heinrich Klüver and Paul C. Bucy, "Preliminary Analysis of Functions of the Temporal Lobes in Monkeys," *Archives of Neurology and Psychiatry* 42 (1939): 979–100; "An Analysis of Certain Effects of Bilateral Temporal Lobectomy in the Rhesus Monkey with Special Reference to 'Psychic Blindness,'" *Journal of Psychology* 5 (1938): 33–54; "'Psychic Blindness' and Other Symptoms Following Bilateral Temporal Lobectomy in Rhesus Monkeys," *American Journal of Physiology* 119 (1937): 352–353.

39. H. Enger Rosvold, Allan F. Mirsky, and Karl Pribram, "Influence of Amygdalectomy on Social Behavior in Monkeys," *Journal of Comparative and Physiological Psychology* 47 (1954): 173–178.

40. Arthur Kling, "Effects of Amygdalectomy on Serial-Affective Behavior in Non-Human Primates," *The Neurobiology of the Amygdala*, ed. B. E. Eleftheriou (New York: Plenum Press, 1972), pp. 511–536.

41. It is interesting to note that by the time the paperback edition of *The Terminal Man* appeared in 1973 (New York: Bantam Books), Crichton apparently had some second thoughts about psychomotor epilepsy, its alleged implication in social violence, and the use of psychosurgery as a cure-all. In a postscript he wrote, "In the face of considerable controversy among clinical neuroscientists, I am persuaded that the understanding of the relationship between organic brain damage and violent behavior is not so clear as I thought at the time I wrote the book" (p. 282). On Julia, see *Life*, June 21, 1968.

42. This passage and the preceding one can be found on pp. 92–93 of *Violence and the Brain*.

43. Vernon H. Mark and Frank R. Ervin, "Is There a Need to Evaluate the Individuals Producing Human Violence?," *Psychiatric Opinion*, August 1968, pp. 32–33.

44. Description of Thomas's treatment can be found on pp. 94–97 of *Violence and the Brain*.

45. Helen J. Geis, quoted in the *Boston Globe*, December 10, 1973.

46. Peter R. Breggin, "An Independent Follow-up of a Person Operated upon for Violence and Epilepsy by Drs. Vernon Mark, Frank Ervin and William Sweet of the Neuro-Research Foundation of Boston," excerpted in *Rough Times* (publication of the Radical Therapist Collective), November–December, 1973. p. 8.

47. Compare Mark and Ervin, *Violence and the Brain*, pp. 96–97.

48. Dr. Ernst Rodin to Dr. J. S. Gottlieb, memorandum, August 9, 1972. This revealing document became part of the public record when it figured in a civil court action brought by the Medical Committee for Human Rights on behalf of the first proposed candidate for psychosurgery in Rodin and Gottlieb's project. The project was ultimately blocked by the court's decision in *Kaimowitz v. Department of Mental Health*, Civil no. 73-19434-AW (Cir. Ct., Wayne County, Mich., July 10, 1973); the Rodin memorandum was submitted in evidence in Exhibit AC-4 in that case. See also "Comment [on] *Kaimowitz v. Department of Mental Health*: A Right To Be Free from Experimental Psychosurgery?," *Boston University Law Review* 54 (1974): 301–339. See also page 198 in this book.

49. The project had been shifted in 1969 from the Massachusetts General Hospital to Boston City Hospital, where Mark is currently director of neurosurgery. Boston City Hospital is a large, beleaguered urban hospital located in the predominantly poor and black Roxbury section of Boston and serving mainly as a community institution.

50. Rodin, memorandum, pp. 3–4.

51. Mark and Ervin, *Violence and the Brain*, pp. 97–98.

52. Ibid., pp. 107–108.

53. Sharland Trotter, "Violent Brains," mimeo (Washington, D.C.: Center for Responsive Law, 1975), p. 12.

54. M. Hunter Brown, "Multiple Limbic Targets for Schizophrenia and Aggression," paper presented at the American Psychiatric Association's annual meeting, May 10, 1973. See also M. Hunter Brown, "The Captive Patient, a Forgotten Man," mimeo, and Ian Calder, "Noted Surgeon Claims . . . Brain Surgery Could Transform the Most Violent Murderer into a Normal Citizen," *National Enquirer*, July 9, 1972.

55. D. Muller, F. Roeder, and H. Orthner, "Further Results of Stereotaxis in Sexual Deviations," *Neurochirurgica* 16 (1973): 113–126.

56. V. Balasubramaniam, T. S. Kanaka, and B. Ramamúrthy, "Surgical Treatment of Hyperkinetic and Behavior Disorders," *International Surgery* 54 (1970): 18–23.

57. Maggie Scarf, "Brain Researcher José Delgado," *New York Times Magazine*, November 15, 1970.

Notes to Chapter 8

1. The original report by P. A. Jacobs et al. (*Nature* 208 [1965]: 1351–2) was followed three years later by another: P. A. Jacobs et al., "Chromosome Studies on Men in a Maximum Security Hospital," *Annals of Human Genetics* 31 (1968): 339–358.

2. W. M. Court-Brown, "Males with an XYY Sex-Chromosome Complement," *Journal of Medical Genetics* 5 (1968): 341.

3. Bentley Glass, "Science: Endless Horizons or Golden Age?," *Science* 171 (1971): 28.

4. The case is cited by Ernest Hook, "Behavioral Implications of the Human XYY Genotype," *Science* 179 (1973): 138–151.

5. Quoted by Anthony Platt, *The Child Savers* (Chicago: University of Chicago Press, 1969), pp. 21-22.

6. See, for example, W. H. Sheldon, *Varieties of Delinquent Youth* (New York: Harper & Row, 1949); S. Glueck and E. Glueck, *Physique and Delinquency* (New York: Harper & Row, 1956).

7. *The Challenge of Crime in a Free Society: A Report by the President's Commission on Law Enforcement and Administration of Justice* (New York: Avon Books, 1968).

8. See, for example, Hook, "Behavioral Implications of XYY Genotype."

9. Ibid., p. 144.

10. The preliminary study by Dion and Berscheid has not been published, but it is described by Eliot Aronson in *The Social Animal* (San Francisco: W. H. Freeman, 1972), pp. 216-217. The subsequent study, by Karen K. Dion, is entitled "Physical Attractiveness and Evaluation of Children's Transgressions," *Journal of Personality and Social Psychology* 24, no. 2 (1973): 207-213.

11. Hook, "Behavioral Implications of XYY Genotype," p. 145.

12. Stanley Walzer, "Chromosome Abnormality and Behavioral Variations," mimeo (application for Research Grant 2R01-MH17960-06, January 1, 1974), p. 12.

13. During the Nixon administration, Dr. Arnold Hutschnecker, a physician with personal connections to the White House, submitted to the president a five-page memorandum entitled "A Plan for Prevention of Violent Crime," in which he claimed that existing studies indicate a "drive to violence and crime can be discovered as early as the age of six." Hutschnecker proposed that all six-to-eight-year-old children, especially slum children, should be screened; those children shown to have criminal tendencies should be subjected to immediate "corrective treatment," including "Pavlovian methods which I have used effectively in the Soviet Union." Hutschnecker's attitude is typical, in that he gives lip service to the social causes of crime but focuses on the character of the delinquent individual, which he obviously considers the real source of the problem.

14. Cited by R. V. Denenberg, *New York Times*, February 17, 1974.

15. B. F. Skinner, *Beyond Freedom and Dignity* (New York: Knopf, 1971), p. 169.

16. Jil Diane Bottrell, "Behavior Modification Programs: Analogies from Prisons to Mental Institutions," paper presented at a symposium on Legal and Ethical Issues of Behavior Modification Programs in Prisons, American Psychological Association, New Orleans, September 2, 1974.

17. Charles Dickens, *Pictures from Italy and American Notes* (London, 1867), p. 283.

18. Zebulon Brockway, quoted by Kenneth Lamott in "Is Prison Obsolete?," *Horizon* 17, no. 3 (Summer 1975): 45.

19. Jessica Mitford, "Prisons: The Menace of Liberal Reform," *New York Review*, March 9, 1972, pp. 12-15.

20. Cited in American Friends Service Committee, *Struggle for Justice: A Report on Crime and Punishment in America* (New York: Hill and Wang, 1971) p. 91.

21. David F. Greenberg and Fay Stender, "The Prison as a Lawless Agency," *Buffalo Law Review* 21 (1972): 799-838.

22. Ibid., p. 807.

23. Mitford, "Prisons," p. 12.

24. Greenberg and Stender, "Lawless Agency," p. 803.

25. Cited in Elliot Valenstein, *Brain Control* (New York: John Wiley & Sons, 1973), p. 255.

26. Quoted by Ian Calder, "Noted Surgeon Claims . . . Brain Surgery Could Transform the Most Violent Murderer into a Normal Citizen," *National Enquirer*, July 9, 1972, p. 3.

27. Raymond K. Procunier to California Council on Criminal Justice, September 1971.

28. See Peter Gann et al., "Psychosurgery and California Prisons," in *Synapse* (University of California at San Francisco campus newspaper), April 7, 1972, and Jessica Mitford, "The Torture Cure," *Harpers*, August 1973, p. 26.

29. In a three-hour NBC special program on "Violence in America," televised in January 1977, Dr. M. Hunter Brown discussed psychosurgery and advocated it for inmates at Vacaville. An actual surgical procedure was shown and its "benefits" in treating violence promoted. Clearly psychosurgery in prisons is not a dead issue.

30. Ralph Schwitzgebel, "Electronic Innovation in the Behavioral Sciences: A Call to Responsibility," *American Psychologist* 22 (1967): 364.

31. Barton L. Ingraham and Gerald W. Smith, "The Use of Electronics in the Observation and Control of Human Behavior," *Issues in Criminology* 7 (1972): 42.

32. Ibid., p. 52.

33. James V. McConnell, "Criminals Can Be Brainwashed—Now," *Psychology Today*, April 1970, p. 14.

34. Edgar H. Schein, "Man against Man: Brainwashing," *Corrective Psychiatry and Journal of Social Change* 8 (1962): 92.

35. Ibid., p. 94.

36. Ibid., p. 97.

37. Discussion, in ibid., p. 99.

38. U.S., Congress, House, Committee on the Judiciary, *Behavior Modification Programs in the Federal Bureau of Prisons: Hearing*, February 27, 1974, p. 66.

39. Ibid., p. 67.

40. As quoted in Clay Steinman, "The Case of the Frightened Convict," *The Nation*, December 3, 1973, p. 590.

41. Robert B. Levinson, "Behavior Modification Programs in the Federal Bureau of Prisons," paper presented at the Annual Convention of the American Psychological Association, New Orleans, September 2, 1974, p. 8.

42. Arpiar G. Saunders, Jr., to Dr. Pasquale J. Ciccone, February 26, 1973, in "Behavior Therapy in Prisons: *Walden II* or *Clockwork Orange?*," paper presented to the Eighth Annual Convention of the Association for Advancement of Behavior Therapy, Chicago, November 1-3, 1974.

43. Albert F. Scheckenbach, "Behavior Modification and Adult Offenders," paper presented to the American Correctional Association Convention, Houston, Texas, August 1974, quoted by Levinson, "Behavior Modification Programs," pp. 12-13.

44. House, *Behavior Modification Programs: Hearing*, February 27, 1974, p. 68.

45. Ibid., p. 73.

46. Jim Elliot, "The Asklepieion Method," *Group Leader's Workshop* 18 (1973): 3–34.

47. Quoted by Mitford, "The Torture Cure," pp. 18, 24.

48. See U.S., Congress, Senate, Committee on the Judiciary, *Individual Rights and the Federal Role in Behavior Modification*, 1974, pp. 229–232.

49. See the *Congressional Record*, May 8, 1973; cited in Senator Ervin's Preface to ibid., p. v.

50. From a prospectus prepared by the program managers, as cited by Saunders, "Behavior Therapy in Prisons," p. 30.

51. Arthur L. Mattocks and Charles Law, "Anectine Therapy Program," cited by Mitford, "The Torture Cure," p. 21.

52. Quoted by Lamott, "Is Prison Obsolete?," pp. 45–46.

Index